14-130-125

The Mirage of Safety

Food Additives and Federal Policy:

THE MIRAGE OF SAFETY

by Beatrice Trum Hunter

CHARLES SCRIBNER'S SONS
NEW YORK

Copyright © 1975 Beatrice Trum Hunter

Library of Congress Cataloging in Publication Data

Hunter, Beatrice Trum.
   The mirage of safety.

   Bibliography
   Includes index.
      1. Food additives.   2.   Food adulteration and inspec-
   tion—United States.   3.   United States.   Food and Drug
   Administration.   I.   Title.
   TX553.A3H87   614.3'1   75-20299
   ISBN 0-684-14426-3

Portions of this book are based on articles which appeared in *Consumer Bulletin* and
in *Consumers' Research Magazine* and are used here with the kind permission of
Consumers' Research, Inc., Washington, New Jersey 07882.

1 3 5 7 9 11 13 15 17 19 C/C 20 18 16 14 12 10 8 6 4 2

Printed in the United States of America

To F. J. Schlink,
with homage

Contents

Abbreviations Defined

APHIS: Animal and Plant Health Protection Service (USDA)

BHA: butylated hydroxyanisole

BHT: butylated hydroxytoluene

BVO: brominated vegetable oils

CMC: Consumer Marketing Service (USDA)

CRS: Chinese Restaurant Syndrome

DEP: diethyl pyrocarbonate

DES: diethylstilbestrol

DNA: deoxyribonucleic acid

EDTA: ethylenediamine tetraacetic acid

EPA: Environmental Protection Agency

ETU: ethylene thiourea

FAO/WHO: Food and Agricultural Organization of the World Health Organization (United Nations)

FASEB: Federation of American Societies for Experimental Biology

FDA: Food and Drug Administration (HEW)

FD&C: Food, Drugs, and Cosmetics

FEMA: Flavoring Extract Manufacturers Association

GRAS: Generally Recognized as Safe

HEW: Department of Health, Education and Welfare

LD_{50}:   lethal dose

MCA: Manufacturing Chemists' Association, Inc.

MSG: monosodium glutamate

NADA: new animal drug application

NAS–NRC: National Academy of Sciences–National Research Council

NCI: National Cancer Institute (HEW)

NDGA: nordihydroguaiaretic acid

NIH: National Institutes of Health (HEW)

PCBs: polychlorinated biphenyls

ppb: parts per billion

ppm: parts per million

PVC: polyvinyl chloride

RNA: ribonucleic acid

SAPP: sodium acid pyrophosphate

USDA: United States Department of Agriculture

USPHS: United States Public Health Service (HEW)

1

Consumer Be Damned!

• It is a common saying that we are what we eat. If this is true, then Americans are becoming a nation of processed, packaged, and preserved people. Last year [1971], Americans bought more processed than fresh foods for the first time in our history. We spend more than $60 billion for these convenience foods including such items as TV dinners, snack foods of all kinds, and frozen foods. With these foods we each consume every year more than four pounds of chemical preservatives, stabilizers, colorings, flavorings, and other additives. And the amount of these artificial substances is increasing every year. Their use has doubled in the past 15 years, from 400 million pounds to more than 800 million pounds. Today, more than 3,000 chemicals are deliberately added to our foods. These developments raise three basic questions: *(1)* How much do we know about the hazards to human health from these chemicals? *(2)* How much assurance of chemical safety should we require? *(3)* What must the federal government do to assure that the chemicals we absorb are safe?

Senator Abraham S. Ribicoff

• Chemical companies have many compelling reasons for assiduously courting the food industry.

Chemical and Engineering News

• Use of food additives in the United States in 1970 was about $485 million, according to Richard L. Hughes of Arthur D. Little, Inc. Use of food additives in 1980 will rise to about $756 million.

Chemical and Engineering News

• Food additives are big business. The chemical and drug industries have joined the food industry in a food–industrial complex that the FDA is supposed to regulate. The result is a proliferation of food chemicals that are unnecessary, an unknown number that are unsafe, many of them untested, and most of them poorly monitored, at best.

Senator Gaylord Nelson

• The use of direct food additives in food manufacture will have approximately doubled by 1974 from the level of use prior to the passage of the Food Additives Amendment [1958] of the Food, Drug, and Cosmetic Act [1938]. Over one million pounds of 2,500 food additives will be consumed. Both the methodology for their detection and their long-term toxicological significance require an expansion of research activities by the FDA. Unknown alterations of products further complicate attaining the necessary security in the safety of the food supply. The primary need at present is for the development of multi-additive detection methods to facilitate surveillance and measurement of actual additive intake levels.

Food and Drug Administration

• I am not going to tell you that FDA has devised the perfect system for keeping hazardous chemicals out of our foods . . . you'll simply have to live with it.

Herbert L. Ley, Jr., Commissioner of FDA

• . . . The line that "the additive is O.K. if it helps sales and does not make the consumer notably ill" is clearly not good enough.

The Lancet

"People are finally waking up to the fact that the average American daily diet is substantially adulterated with unnecessary and poisonous chemicals and frequently filled with neutral, nonnutritious substances. We are being chemically medicated against our will and cheated of food value by low nutrition foods. It is time to take a careful look at the prolific use of additives permeating our foods." Senator Gaylord Nelson made that statement on the floor of the United States Senate in 1972 when introducing legislation to eliminate the use of unsafe, untested, and unnecessary chemical additives in the food supply.

Congress had already considered the problem of chemical additives in the food supply. In 1950, the House of Representatives had held hearings on Chemicals in Food Products. Popularly called the Delaney Hearings, after Chairman James J. Delaney, the hearings continued until 1958. Dozens of expert witnesses testified, expressing concern about specific chemical additives. They repeatedly cautioned against the introduction and use of substances that were inadequately tested, sometimes hazardous, and frequently unnecessary.

The Delaney Hearings culminating in 1958 with an amendment to the original Food, Drug, and Cosmetic Act of 1938, required the pretesting of additives. But the new legislation was weakened by serious loopholes. Within two years after passage of the 1958 amendment, the FDA had received 391 petitions for additional regulations, concerning over 1,900 uses of chemicals in food production, processing, or handling.

The 1960s were marked by an enormous rise in the production and consumption of convenience foods, which in turn created a sharp increase in the use of food additives. Higher temperatures, greater pressures, and more agitation are required to prepare these high-profit convenience foods than conventionally prepared foods. Because of this, the convenience foods require many additives to make up for the flavor, color, texture, and other properties lost during the processing. And since convenience foods are not necessarily eaten immediately after they are packaged, an array of preservatives, antioxidants, and other additives is needed to extend their shelf life and keep them marketable for long periods of time.

Between the mid-1950s and the mid-1960s, the use of food additives more than doubled. By the late 1960s another food trend further increased the use of additives: formulas being developed for simulated or fabricated foods—such as imitation fruit juices and textured vegetable proteins—depended heavily on food additives.

The 1960s brought more congressional hearings on problems created by these food trends. Various congressional committees held investigations concerning the problems of food dyes, candy additives, and pesticide residues on foods.

By 1970, the number of food additives covered by formal regulations, including new uses for additives previously regulated, had swelled to 2,703. In addition, there were an unknown number of nonregulated additives. Finally, Pandora's box burst open. Hearings were held on cyclamates and diethylstilbestrol (DES). Although both were banned, their ultimate fates were not put to rest. Hearings were held on sodium nitrate and sodium nitrite and on antibiotics in animal feed. Reports on the adverse effects of many food additives were publicized: monosodium glutamate (MSG), brominated vegetable oils (BVO), diethyl pyrocarbonate (DEP). Two officially approved food dyes long in use (FD&C Red No. 2 and FD&C Violet No. 1), as well as other, long-used additives (saccharin and carrageenan) were also included. Under close scrutiny, congressional members were shocked to learn that the "Generally Recognized as Safe" (GRAS) list was actually a loose, ill-defined group. Several highly critical reports, issued by the Committee on Government Operations, charged the Food and Drug Administration (FDA) with inadequate regulations; indecisive, contradictory and illegal actions; and excessive delays in making regulatory decisions. One witness charged that the United States Department of Agriculture (USDA), through various administrations, was consistently careless, negligent, and indifferent to the well-being of the American people. Congressional hearings demonstrated that the USDA's testing program was utterly inadequate for effective public health protection. The continuous and repeated flow of adverse findings on food additives, coupled with congressional criticisms, forced both the FDA and the USDA to seek more effective techniques for testing and regulating additives and to develop satisfactory methods for evaluating the data on the safety of many food additives.

The current United States consumption of intentional food additives per capita is usually quoted as about five pounds per year. But this estimate is misleading; it excludes sugar, salt, and starch. These three additives are not innocuous in the excessive quantities in which they often are consumed, and they should be included in the total figure. A more accurate estimate of the 1972 per capita adult consumption of intentional additives in the United States is sugar, 102.4 pounds; table salt, 15 pounds; corn syrup, 8.4 pounds; dextrose, 4.2 pounds; and other chemical additives (1,800 or more), 1 pound. Thus, *the annual per capita adult consumption of intentional additives in the United States is currently about 140 pounds.*

If present trends continue, the per capita consumption of such additives will be even greater. For example, in 1970, the FDA received some 476 new applications for food additives; it approved 62. The following year, the agency received 110 new applications and approved 51. Neither the FDA nor the USDA has demonstrated a willingness to apply the necessary curbs. On the contrary, these agencies have expressed the view that by discouraging new additives, progress may be stifled.

The food additive business is expected to boom throughout the 1970s. Early in the decade, sales of additives to food processors amounted to $500 million yearly. The projected figure for 1980 is $756 million.

Senator Gaylord Nelson noted that the American public is becoming "disenchanted and angry about the proliferation of chemicals in the food supply. . . . As scientists increasingly discover harmful effects of chemical additives that previously were considered safe, the public loses more and more confidence in the regulatory agencies that approve these substances for consumption."

Senator Nelson expressed the view that the crux of the situation is economic:

The profits of the food industry are being placed above the public health as regards the safety, nutrition, and necessity of food additives. Synthetic and convenience foods mean high profits and greater market control of the food industry. Additives mean that foods can be manufactured at low costs, shipped long distances, and remain on shelves longer. Many processed foods are not "real foods" at all, but a combination of chemicals. On an educational television program, it was demonstrated that a commercially marketed frozen lemon cream pie actually was composed of chemicals—no lemon, no cream, no flour. . . . Additives cut costs to the manufacturer, but not necessarily to the consumer.

The purpose of this book is twofold. As consumers, we need to know how tests on a food additive's safety are conducted and why present methods are inadequate. Equally important, we need to understand the past, present, and probable future policies and regulations of the FDA and USDA regarding food additives. After examining the facts, one is tempted to paraphrase William Henry Vanderbilt's infamous words; the official government policy of food additive safety is "Consumer be damned!"

2

The Consumer Is Misinformed

● . . . With inadequate scientific data, with fundamental scientific disagreement on technical issues and public disagreement on policy issues, with the necessity to act decisively and promptly, and with the assurance of widespread dispute about whatever action emerges, the agency [FDA] daily makes some of the most important public policy decisions that directly affect all of our lives. These obstacles have clearly taken their toll. Public and Congressional confidence in the ability of the Food and Drug Administration to carry out its statutory responsibilities has unquestionably been undermined. . . .

Peter Barton Hutt, Assistant General Counsel, FDA

● Some additives introduce a hazard without offering offsetting benefits. The use of nitrite in baby food is one example where slight effects on the color and taste are seen which are of no value to the baby. Nitrite is not used in baby food as a preservative nor added to increase the nutritional value or palatability. . . . Should a food additive be used in foods that does not benefit the consumer? . . . Additives that are risky and, as well, unnecessary should be avoided. BHA, BHT, and propyl gallate are all in this category. These are anti-rancidity additives used in many foods in which they are not needed, e.g., vegetable oils and shortenings. Animal tests show varying degrees of toxicity. BHA and BHT accumulate in body fat. Their safety is not yet established; safe alternatives are available.

Dr. J. David Baldock, Assistant Professor, Food and Science Technology,
Virginia Polytechnic Institute and State University

● We can live perfectly well without additives.

Jean Mayer, Ph.D.

● Since food dyes are nutritionally unessential constituents of foodstuffs, it seems reasonable to demand that any dye conveying even a minor degree of health, and especially, cancer hazard to the general consumer be eliminated from the list of permitted food additives.

Wilhelm C. Hueper, M.D., Chief, Environmental Cancer Section,
National Cancer Institute

• When one peruses the formidable list of substances embraced by [this] conference [Problems Arising from the Use of Chemicals in Food], one is struck by the fact that, however necessary these substances are today, not one of them is of the slightest value to the nutrition of the human organism. The corollary of this is: to what extent may these substances be harmful?

G. Roche Lynch, Toxicologist, Paddington, England

• *Senator Abraham S. Ribicoff:* Do you think that there would be resistance from industry toward an efficacy test on chemicals that go into the food products that we consume?

Samuel S. Epstein, M.D.: It depends on how you define efficacy. . . . If you import oranges from Florida, they are yellow. The consumer does not like having yellow oranges. He prefers having red oranges. Therefore dyes are put on the oranges to make them red. I would submit from the standpoint of efficacy, the dye does the job. It makes the yellow orange red. From the point of general social utility, this is ridiculous. This is [a] cosmetic food additive, and does not enter into my definition of efficacy. So the requirement has to be stated in terms of general special utility. . . . When you put cyclamates in soft drinks which you drink, it makes it sweeter without sugar. This is limited FTC [Federal Trade Commission] type of efficacy, which meets the narrow stated requirement of efficacy.

Senator Abraham S. Ribicoff: Are there other examples you would like to give us?

Samuel S. Epstein, M.D.: They are limitless. The whole question of food dyes—the whole field is replete with examples of cosmetic food additives, cosmetic agents added to foodstuffs which improve the appearance. For instance, the high levels of nitrites in meats are largely for cosmetic purposes, to make the meat look nice and red. . . .

• FDA is a very sensitive agency which has extremely important responsibilities for regulating products which affect the well-being and often the very lives of our people.

Congressman L. H. Fountain

When consumers concerned about food additives write to the FDA, they are sent a brochure, *Primer on Food Additives,* written by G. Edward Damon, a writer in FDA's Bureau of Foods. This brochure assures the consumer that any new substance undergoes strict testing before it can be added to food. The reader is told that industries must submit to the FDA any new additive's identity, its chemical composition, its intended use, information about how it is manufactured, the methods used to detect and measure its presence in food and the amounts expected to be used. The data submitted also must show that the proposed testing methods are sufficiently sensitive to determine compliance with FDA regulations.

According to the *Primer,* a new food additive cannot be used legally unless it affects the production, manufacture, or storage of the food in some way. In addition, the industry must supply data verifying that no more of the additive is used than necessary. The reader is informed further that scientific data must establish that the intended use of the additive is safe. Such evidence is generally obtained from feeding studies and other tests that use the proposed additive at various levels in the diet of two or more animal species.

The brochure poses the question: Can you really test for safety? It then replies that in a very real sense this cannot be done. One can test only for the presence of known hazards. If known hazards are not found, the additive is assumed to be safe. If someone discovers a new hazard, the testing must be repeated. The reader is assured that this is a typical pattern, repeated many times during the FDA's history, as scientific knowledge has increased.

The *Primer* was written to assure today's consumers, who "are very concerned about what's going into their food." It "recounts how the Congress and the Federal Government have responded to consumer demands for tight controls."

For veteran FDA-watchers, and especially for those who have closely observed the history of the FDA's food additive surveillance, the *Primer on Food Additives* appears to be a contrived public relations effort, characterized by misrepresentations and half truths.

The "strict testing" turns out to be a joke—at the public's expense. The FDA, by repeatedly pleading shortages of funds and personnel, has conducted far too few safety tests itself. Instead, it has relied heavily on summary assurances from food and chemical companies or from their contracted private laboratories. In this manner, the FDA has relinquished its mandated control of food additive safety testing to the very industries that it was supposed to regulate. The effects are significant insofar as such policies may affect the well-being and very lives of the entire population.

The FDA's abandonment of its responsibilities is reflected by the statement made by Winton B. Rankin, deputy commissioner of the FDA, in discussing which food additives may be included on the GRAS list:

The manufacturer is entitled to reach his own conclusions, based on his scientific evidence that a [substance] is, in fact, generally recognized as safe. And he is not required to come to us [FDA] then and get the material added to the [GRAS] list.

With such an official laissez-faire policy established, an industry spokesman announced:

It should be made clear that industry has the right to make its own decisions on the status of any substance whether or not the FDA has listed it and that it [i.e., industry] is under no obligation to request the FDA to express an opinion on unlisted materials.

Incidents frequently surface that give an inkling of the chaotic situation regarding the FDA's ignorance—or lack of control—of industry's use of additives:

—Swedish researchers found that DEP, a preservative used with certain beverages, posed health hazards. The facts came to the FDA's attention, but the agency admitted that it did not know to what extent the additive was being used in beverages. The best it could do at the moment was plan an industry survey.

—Canadian researchers reported certain toxic properties of BVO, compounds widely used as clouding agents in certain foods and beverages. The FDA admitted that it had no idea of how much BVO was being used in the food supply.

—Russian researchers reported adverse effects from amaranth, an extensively used food dye. The FDA ordered the food industry to provide lists of products in which the color was being used, as well as the levels of use, since the agency lacked the information.

—In recalling hair sprays containing the potentially hazardous vinyl chloride, the FDA admitted that it was "unaware" of any past or present use of this chemical compound in food aerosols.

The Primer assures the reader that proposed testing methods are sufficiently sensitive to determine compliance with regulations. This is not always the case. The FDA's approved test method for detecting diethylstilbestrol (DES) residues in edible meat tissue was shown to be impracticable for USDA regulatory purposes. Despite this shortcoming the FDA approved a new animal drug application for this synthetic hormone in 1970, doubling the permitted amount. It did not develop a practicable test method. This issue was only uncovered during a congressional investigation. The Committee on Government Operations commented:

Since the published test method was not practicable as a USDA enforcement method, FDA had the legal responsibility to require the submission of a practicable method of analysis before approving the application. But FDA ignored this requirement and approved the NADA [new animal drug application] and the food additive petition. . . . The repeated assurances by USDA and FDA officials that the new analytical method would soon be validated and published do not appear to have been justified. [As a result] FDA and USDA used a nonapproved test method for diethylstilbestrol regulatory purposes.

The *Primer*'s statement that industry must show that an additive has some physical or technical effect on the food and that the amount to be used is no higher than necessary to achieve this effect is also suspect. In fact, the 1972 congressional hearings on sodium nitrate and sodium nitrite (officially sanctioned preservatives) show that this statement is not necessarily true. The USDA's limitations on sodium nitrite's use was shown to be unrelated to the minimum quantity necessary to accomplish color fixation in processed meats. Although the USDA argued that the extra nitrites are essential to prevent botulism in processed meats, the congressional committee reported that it "did not uncover persuasive evidence that the nitrites are required for this purpose, except in special cases, such as canned ham."

The hearings also revealed a "careless and excessive use" of these compounds. Although the legal maximum limit for sodium nitrite with processed meat and fish is 200 parts per million (ppm), some smoked fish samples contained over 3,000 ppm. When questioned, Charles C. Edwards, then Commissioner of the FDA, admitted that such excessive nitrite levels could be fatal to children, could be detrimental to pregnant women and their fetuses, and could severely injure anemic persons. As a result, the FDA was charged with ignoring serious violations of its own regulations. The agency had failed to institute any actions against processors who used highly excessive levels of nitrite-treated products.

Congressional investigators also found that the FDA had established a *second* tolerance level above the regulation already set. In the case of smoked chubs, the FDA knowingly allowed 30 percent more sodium nitrite than the permissible allowance. In fact, smoked or cured fish were never seized unless the residues were above 260 ppm. For this offense, congressional investigators charged the FDA and USDA with failure to take action to reduce the use of nitrites, and with establishing maximum residue levels that are "not based on adequate scientific evidence, may be unnecessarily high, and . . . of questionable legality." Congressional investigators were shocked to learn that the FDA had no effective surveillance and enforcement program to assure industry compliance with the nitrite-tolerance limit.

The FDA does require safety data based on scientific evidence. If hazards are not found during testing, the additive is assumed to be safe. While the FDA has followed this policy, its assumptions may be risky. The public has often been exposed to "safe" food additives that later proved unsafe, and at times, even fatal. One flour bleach was used for 30 years before its harmfulness was uncovered; a harmful artificial flavoring was used for 70 years. The artificial sweeteners have had a particularly infamous history of wrongly assumed safety: dulcin was used for over 50 years; the cyclamates for over 20 years, and saccharin for nearly a century.

"If someone discovers a new hazard, the testing must be done again," says the *Primer*. But when new hazards of a specific food additive have been discovered, invariably they have not been found by the FDA but by scientists outside the agency—frequently ones from abroad. The FDA's reactions to these discoveries are predictable. If the findings come from outside the agency, the FDA tends to ignore or discredit them; if they come from within the agency, the FDA may bury them in the files.

In analyzing the FDA's handouts—such as the *Primer on Food Additives*—the informed individual develops a healthy skepticism. The baseless and untrue statements only further undermine public confidence in the agency's ability to carry out its responsibility of protecting the public from harmful substances.

3

The Very Small Tip of the Iceberg

• The question of the ultimate effect of food additives on man is still unanswered.
The Lancet

• Often, for what seem rather trivial benefits, risks of undetermined magnitude have been incurred by substantial fractions of the total population.
Philip H. Abelson, editor of *Science*

• Food additives . . . have increased 50 percent in the last decade. . . . What do we know about the long-term effects of these substances on the human organism? What do we know about their interactions?
John J. Hanlon, M.D., Deputy Administrator, Consumer Protection and Environmental Health Service, HEW

• Americans consume more chemicals in their food than any other nation. At the same time American forecasts are the gloomiest in the world about the continued rise of cancer, high blood pressure, heart disease, congenital abnormalities, etc.; in fact, all the degenerative diseases. The United States leads the civilized world in chemicalized food and in degenerative diseases.
Franklin Bicknell, M.D.

• [Chemical] pollutants may induce a wide range of adverse biological effects in man, which are generically and collectively termed toxicity. Acute or chronic toxicity *per se* may be expressed in fetal, neonatal, perinatal, childhood, or adult life, in effects ranging from impairment of health and fitness to mortality. More specific manifestations of chronic toxicity include carcinogenicity, teratogenicity, and mutagenicity [producing the states of cancer; monstrous fetuses or birth defects; and mutations]. The possibility that chronic toxicity is also manifest in immunological impairment or in psycho-behavioral disorders has yet to be explored.
Samuel S. Epstein, M.D.

• The 3,000 food additives with which mankind has had no biological experience prior to this century may prove innocuous, but prudence and a sense of self-preservation bid us to examine these potential threats to our own and subsequent generations, especially in view of the unexplained occurrence of cardiovascular, carcinogenic, and degenerative disease in younger and younger members of our society.

W. V. Applegate, M.D.

• There is no clear way for us to learn scientifically the extent to which all additives taken in during a lifetime cause damage—we don't know what to look for. . . . There is no way to ascertain what subtle changes combinations of additives might have in the body over a span of years.

Dr. Eleanor Williams, Clinical Dietetics Program, State University, Buffalo, New York

• With the frequent introduction of new foods and beverages into our diets . . . it is becoming more difficult to establish etiological factors responsible for hypersensitivity reactions. It has now been definitely established that hidden allergens in the form of flavorings, colorings, preservative agents, excipients, antioxidants, stabilizers, and emulsifiers cause a wide variety of hypersensitivity reactions.

Stephen D. Lockey, Sr., M.D.

• Food additives are being incriminated as a cause of an astoundingly large number of allergies. . . . A number of . . . allergists have documented the many mental symptoms and behavioral problems caused by food additives and food allergies. If mental illness caused by allergies were recognized more, and emotional factors not always sought to explain mental disturbances, a great deal of time and money could be saved and patients' mental conditions eliminated. There are millions of patients enduring needless suffering. One can only guess at the number of major and minor tragedies that are enacted daily because of misinterpreted symptoms. . . .

Howard G. Rapaport, M.D.

A pediatrician experienced a strange set of symptoms whenever he ate in Chinese restaurants. Fifteen to twenty minutes after eating the first dish, he would experience symptoms closely resembling a heart attack: general weakness, palpitations, and a numbness at the back of his neck which would gradually radiate to his arms and back. The physician described his symptoms in a letter to the editor of a medical journal and precipitated a flood of correspondence on monosodium glutamate (MSG), a flavor enhancer used extensively in Chinese restaurants, as well as in processed foods and in many homes. The physician was surprised to learn that many people suffered similar symptoms, and other symptoms: profuse cold sweating, a tightness on both sides of the head, and throbbing sensations in the head. The symptoms became known as the "Chinese Restaurant Syndrome."

In the 1970s, a six-month-old girl began to eat the regular family food. The child started to have seizures, resembling shuddering fits. The seizures grew in frequency, and by the time she reached one year of age, the child was experiencing more than a hundred seizures daily. She showed no signs of losing consciousness. Repeated electroencephalogram tests revealed no cortical disturbance.

The child, taken to a clinic for nervous and mental disorders, was found to be sensitive to MSG. Placed on a MSG-free diet, supported heavily with anticonvulsant medication, the child responded well. Gradually, the medication was withdrawn. Then, after the child was without symptoms for a year, she was fed one-half of a frankfurter. Within three hours, the child experienced a shuddering seizure. A week later, a bit of spaghetti sauce containing MSG induced a similar reaction.

A 58-year-old man noted that during the previous seven years he had developed severe headaches within a half hour after eating normal quantities of meat products such as frankfurters, bacon, salami, and ham—all of which are sodium nitrite-treated. These attacks, sometimes accompanied by facial flushing, lasted for several hours. No other foods or beverages produced headaches in the man, nor did he otherwise experience headaches. Nor had recurring headaches been noted in any other members of his family.

The man underwent a series of medical tests to determine whether the sodium nitrite was the cause of what he now termed his "hot-dog headaches." Headaches occurred 8 out of the 13 times the man ingested sodium nitrite. They never occurred after he ingested the sodium nitrite-free control solution.

By excluding nitrite-cured meats from his diet, the man was freed of headaches. When he inadvertently consumed a nitrite-cured product, the headache would return.

A 69-year-old physician had experienced moderate to severe arthritic pains sporadically for four years. He diagnosed his own ailment as a type of recurrent rheumatism brought on by an allergy. After carefully recording and analyzing the foods he had eaten prior to his attacks, he concluded that the additive sodium nitrate was causing his discomfort.

The physician enlisted the aid of a pharmacist to prepare identical unlabeled pills containing either sodium nitrate or control substances. He found that the control pills caused no discomfort, but the sodium nitrate produced moderately severe reactions for up to six days.

The physician remarked, "Though mine is only a single case, it is the first authenticated report in which hypersensitivity to sodium nitrate has been definitely established and also as the main cause of a case of palindromic [recurrent] rheumatism. It seems possible, however, that *a more intensive investigation may demonstrate that the sensitivity is not as uncommon as it seems to be.*" [emphasis added]

At breakfast one morning, a child ate a spoonful of cornflakes without any other food or beverage. Within minutes, the uvula (the pendant fleshy lobe in the middle of the posterior border of the soft palate) in the back of her throat swelled. She felt extreme fatigue and moved her limbs only with great effort. The child was tested for food allergies. Tests were negative. On another occasion, she ate some reconstituted mashed potatoes; the symptoms of swollen uvula, extreme fatigue, and weakness returned. Tests for potato allergy were negative. The antioxidants BHT and BHA, present in both the cornflakes and potatoes, were the common denominator. As long as the girl avoided foods containing these two additives, her attacks did not recur.

A woman suffered two violent episodes of hives and swellings in her lips and throat after eating cornflakes and instant mashed potatoes. Since she was having extensive dental work done at the time, her diet had been limited to these two items on each occasion. An allergist found that the only common denominator used in these foods was BHT. The woman was advised to eliminate foods containing BHT from her diet. She became an avid label reader. Her symptoms did not recur.

A seven-year-old boy stomped around, slammed doors, kicked walls, and charged oncoming cars with his bicycle. At school, he was disruptive, and his hyperactive behavior affected other children. His scholastic achievement was poor, and he was placed in a special learning class. Numerous pediatricians, neurologists, psychiatrists, and psychologists were consulted. In reviewing the child's diet, it was found that he was eating large quantities of convenience foods containing artificial colors and flavors. Many of these additives contain salicylates. The child was placed on a salicylate-free diet. Foods with naturally occurring salicylates, as well as those foods containing salicylates in artificial colors and flavors, were excluded. After a few weeks on this diet the boy displayed a dramatic personality change. He was well-adjusted both at home and at school. When he failed to follow the recommended diet, he immediately reverted to his former behavior pattern.

In 1960, some 100,000 people in Holland became ill quite suddenly, with fever and skin eruptions. Several hundred required hospitalization, and among them, there were a few fatalities. Investigation suggested that the epidemic was similar to one experienced two years earlier in Germany, also with some fatalities. The causative agent was thought to be a new type of emulsifier, added to margarine, as an anti-spatter agent.

The Rotterdam Public Health Authority broadcast a warning concerning the risks of eating the treated margarine, and directed margarine processors to withdraw their products. The processors complied and offered to compensate persons who suffered from the condition that became known as "The Dutch Margarine Sickness." The epidemic subsided after the emulsifier was withdrawn from use in margarine, although the Dutch Ministry of Health found no conclusive evidence, direct or indirect, that incriminated the emulsifier or the product.

Monochloroacetic acid was patented in France in 1933. Interest in this food and beverage preservative was soon carried to the United States. The preservative was studied by presumably competent investigators, including the dean of a leading American medical school, at the school's pharmacology laboratory. The preservative was tested and found to be safe. The dean was so convinced of the additive's harmlessness that he declared the preservative would be safe even if used daily by infants.

A great many foods—salad dressings and pickles, as well as wines and carbonated beverages—were preserved with monochloroacetic acid. Some 60 million bottles of an orange-type drink were distributed. Only after all of these products were marketed did it become apparent that the preservative was *not* innocuous. It irritated the cells of the gastrointestinal tract and caused extensive acute digestive upsets. Large numbers of persons became ill.

Repeated seizures, fines, and extended litigation followed, during which time the public continued to be exposed to foods and beverages containing monochloroacetic acid. Ultimately, in 1941, the FDA barred further use of this compound in foods and beverages. Even after notorious mass poisonings and the official curb, the dean, who had originally proclaimed the compound harmless, continued to contend that monochloroacetic acid should be used!

In 1950, a candy company made a quantity of Halloween pumpkin candy. In order to achieve the color of real pumpkins, the manufacturer used an extra heavy dose of a listed and certified food dye, FD&C Orange No. 1. A young boy became ill from eating the brightly colored candy. Later, a number of children who ate this candy suffered severe gastrointestinal upset. Pharmacological tests of the food dye showed that the color was not "harmless"; in sufficient concentration, it was quite capable of inflicting harm.

Four years later, some 200 children were made very ill from eating popcorn at a Christmas party. The popcorn was dyed with three "safe" dyes (FD&C Orange No. 1, FD&C Orange No. 2, and FD&C Red No. 32). A few months later, the FDA decertified the three dyes; but the agency allowed food and beverage manufacturers to continue using these dyes, with the cautionary explanation that foods containing excessive quantities could cause illness. Ultimately, all three dyes were banned.

Several decades ago, lithium chloride, contained in a "safe" salt substitute for low-sodium diets, was marketed after insufficient testing. Prolonged absorption of this substance can disturb the electrolyte balance, impair kidney function, and disturb the central nervous system. Action could be taken only after proof of harm was demonstrated. After the lithium chloride-containing salt caused several deaths, the additive finally was banned.

As recently as 1966, outbreaks of fatal heart disease among heavy beer drinkers in the United States, Canada, and Belgium, was attributed to cobaltous salts. Used in beer to stabilize the foam and to prevent gushing, these cobaltous salts had been judged safe. They had been used in European beers since 1956 and in the United States and Canada since 1963. After the deaths were traced to the cardiotoxic action of these compounds, breweries in the United States voluntarily stopped using the additive and one large brewery in Quebec City dumped more than $600,000 worth of beer. After a number of deaths finally were attributed to the cobaltous salts, the FDA banned these compounds from beer.

All of these incidents are linked together by a common bond: the adverse reactions resulting from exposure to a chemical additive intentionally introduced into food. In each case, the assumption was made that the additive was safe. Adverse effects were found only after public exposure. In some cases, highly sensitive individuals suffered temporary allergic discomfort or people suffered radical personality changes. In other cases, the effects were graver, resulting in toxicity or even in death. These incidents are well-documented. The adverse effects of these few specific food additives have been observed in human beings, and a cause-and-effect relationship has been established. But these form only the small tip of an iceberg that is still largely submerged. As it surfaces, we are gradually learning its enormous size.

While it is true that the early additives predated the 1958 mandatory pretesting requirements, even some of the more recent additives, which were pretested and judged "safe," have been banned later.

CHEMICAL ADDITIVES USED AND THEN BANNED FROM THE UNITED STATES FOOD SUPPLY

Agene (nitrogen trichloride) was used as a bleaching and maturing agent for flour for more than 30 years. Dogs fed bread made with the treated flour developed running fits. Agene was banned in 1949.

Cobaltous salts (acetate, chloride, and sulfate salts of cobalt), approved as "safe" stabilizers and antigushing agents in beer, were found to be a causal agent in fatal heart attacks. These cobaltous salts had been approved for use in beer in 1963 in the United States. They were banned for this use in 1966.

Coumarin, an artificial flavoring used in synthetic vanilla, chocolate, and other confections for nearly 75 years, was found to cause liver damage in rats and dogs. Its natural source, the tonka bean, was banned along with coumarin in 1954.

Cyclamates, artificial sweeteners approved for special dietary purposes in 1950, were on the GRAS list in 1958. Later found to induce bladder cancer in experimental animals, they were banned in 1970. Subsequent investigations have raised additional questions.

Diethylstilbestrol (DES), a synthetic hormone, was added to animal feed to promote growth. In addition, pellets of DES were implanted in poultry to caponize the birds. Even in 1954, when DES was first introduced, it was recognized as a powerful cancer inducer. But in 1959, under actual conditions of use, residues of DES were detected in the liver and skin fat of treated poultry. The

FDA responded by banning the use of DES in poultry. But DES was not withdrawn from liquid and dry premixes for animal feed until 1972. Existing stocks were to be phased out by 1973. Pellet implants in animals were also banned in 1973. But in 1974, DES manufacturers obtained a court order reversing the ban. The FDA announced that the court action would not be contested.

Diethyl pyrocarbonate (DEP) had been used as a preservative in many beverages since the early 1960s. Under certain conditions, DEP was found to combine with the natural constituents of beverages to form a carcinogenic compound. DEP was banned in 1972.

Dulcin (ethyoxyphenylurea), an artificial sweetener 250 times sweeter than sugar, was synthesized in 1883 and used for more than half a century in foods. When tested, dulcin was found to cause liver cancer in rats. Dulcin was banned in 1950.

Food dyes have an especially poor safety record. Although many have already been banned, the safety of those still in use is dubious. "U.S. Certified Color" merely means that a representative sample from each batch of a food dye is submitted to the FDA for chemical analysis to ensure that the batch is identical with the material used in animal feeding studies during the toxicologic testing program on which approval was based. *Certification is no assurance of safety.*

Even if an approved dye is found unsafe, its use is not always banned. In many instances, unsafe dyes are merely "delisted." Under certain conditions, they can still be used. To date, this is the shocking history of approved food dyes:

—Butter Yellow was approved for food use in 1918 and was delisted the same year. Later, when Butter Yellow was tested in Japan it was found to cause liver cancer in animals.

—FD&C Green No. 1 (Guinea Green B) was approved for food use in 1922. It was delisted in 1966 for "lack of economic importance." When tested, this dye was found to cause liver cancer in animals.

—FD&C Orange No. 1 (Orange 1) was on the original list of approved food dyes in 1907. Later, when Orange 1 was tested, it was found to cause organ damage in animals. It was removed from foods in 1956. However, it was permitted in externally applied drugs and cosmetics (as Ext. D&C Orange No. 3) until 1968.

—FD&C Orange No. 2 (Orange SS) was approved for food use in 1939. When tested later, it was found to cause organ damage in animals. Delisted for food use in 1955, its use in externally applied drugs and cosmetics (as Ext. D&C Orange No. 4) was permitted until 1963.

—FD&C Red No. 1 (Ponceau 3R) was among the food dyes on the originally approved 1907 list. At a later date, it was found to cause liver cancer in animals. Delisted for food use in 1961, its use in externally applied drugs and cosmetics (as Ext. D&C Red No. 15) was permitted until 1966.

—FD&C Red No. 4 (Ponceau SX) was approved for food use in 1929. When tested at high dosages, it caused damage to the adrenal cortex of dogs. Food and pharmaceutical interests exerted pressures against an outright ban of this dye. In 1965, the use of FD&C Red No. 4 was restricted to a specified level and could be used only with maraschino cherries and certain pharmaceutical pills.

—FD&C Red No. 32 (Oil Red XO) was approved for food use in 1939. When tested later, it was found to damage internal animal organs and was suspect as a weak carcinogen. Delisted for food use in 1956, its use in externally applied drugs and cosmetics (as Ext. D&C Red No. 14) was permitted until 1963.

—Sudan 1 was approved for food use in 1918 and was delisted the same year. When tested, Sudan 1 was found to be toxic; further testing showed it was also carcinogenic.

—FD&C Violet No. 1 (Benzyl Violet 4B) was approved for food use in 1950. During ongoing safety tests, its listing was made provisional. It was a suspected carcinogen. In 1971, this dye was officially cleared. In 1973, the clearance was reversed, and the dye was banned from food use.

—FD&C Yellow No. 1 (Naphthol Yellow S) was on the original approved food dye list. This dye was delisted for food use in 1959, but it is still used in externally applied drugs and cosmetics (as Ext. D&C Yellow No. 7). In later tests, high levels of this dye caused intestinal lesions in animals.

—FD&C Yellow No. 2 (Naphthol Yellow S, potassium salt) was approved for food use in 1939. It was delisted for food use in 1959, but it was still permitted in externally applied drugs and cosmetics (as Ext. D&C Yellow No. 8). In later tests, this dye caused bladder cancer in dogs; at higher levels, it caused heart damage. It was completely delisted in 1960.

—FD&C Yellow No. 4 (Yellow OB) was approved for food use in 1918. It was delisted for food use in 1959, but its use was still permitted in externally applied drugs and cosmetics (as Ext. D&C Yellow No. 10). Tests showed that the dye caused bladder cancer in dogs; at high levels, it caused heart damage. It was completely delisted in 1960.

Lithium chloride, a salt substitute, was banned after it caused several human fatalities.

Monochloroacetic acid, a preservative introduced in the late 1930s, was found to be highly toxic. It was banned in 1941.

Nordihydroguaiaretic acid (NDGA), an antioxidant, was on the GRAS list in 1963. At a later date, it was shown to cause kidney damage in test animals. The FDA removed NDGA from the GRAS list, and its use in foods was restricted. The USDA completely banned its use in foods in 1971.

Oil of calamus, a flavoring derived from the calamus plant root, was on the GRAS list. Later, it was shown to be carcinogenic. It induced malignant tumors in the duodenum, caused intestinal cancer, and damaged the liver and heart in rats. Oil of calamus was banned from food use in 1968.

Polyoxyethylene-8-stearate was an emulsifier widely used in baked goods. Animal tests showed that this emulsifier produced a high incidence of bladder stones and tumors, as well as gastrointestinal irritation, changes in intestinal flora, and disturbances in bile secretion. It was banned from food use in 1952.

Safrole, a flavoring substance extracted from sassafras bark, was used in the production of root beer and similar beverages. When tested, safrole was found to cause liver cancer in rats and in dogs. It was banned from food use in 1960.

Thiourea, an antibrowning agent, was used with frozen sliced peaches and apples. It was found to be highly toxic to rats, and to adversely affect thyroid function. It was banned from food use in the early 1950s.

Traditionally, spokesmen for both the food industry and the FDA have tended to view critics of food additives as crackpots, extremists, alarmists, lunatic fringers, or persons with an uninformed, irrational phobia against "chemicals." However, an increasing number of medical and biochemical authorities, cancerologists, oncologists [tumor specialists], geneticists, allergists, and other professionals are continuing to report various adverse findings from the use of food additives. Many of these experts have begun to perceive the impossibility of adequately testing, regulating, and monitoring the present number of food additives. These authorities are now taking a hard look, as congress has already done, at the current use of food additives which may be harmful to health, are highly suspect, and may be unnecessary.

4

The Mirage of Safety

• . . . the phase of mechanical performance of set exercises in animals has persisted to the present day—so much so that, even now, it is possible to complete the investigations necessary for clearance knowing virtually nothing, and understanding even less, about the intrinsic biological properties of a compound. Extrapolation of animal results to man has in many instances remained essentially guesswork. Thus, a mirage of safety evaluation has been created, in whose illusory green pastures browse the three sacred cows on which the faith is based: the "no-effect level," "safety factor," and "acceptable daily intake." They have been considered sacrosanct for so long that it comes as a shock to realize how truly weak is the rationale on which they are based.
L. Golberg, Institute of Experimental Pathology and Toxicology,
The Albany Medical College of Union University

• It was all very well to say "Drink me," but the wise little Alice was not going to do that in a hurry. "No, I'll look first," she said, "and see whether it's marked *poison* or not." . . . she had never forgotten that if you drink very much from a bottle marked "poison" it is almost certain to disagree with you, sooner or later.
Alice in Wonderland

• In spite of sophisticated analytical techniques, scientists are not sure that drug or additive reactions observed in laboratory animals will be experienced by people, nor whether all people will react in the same way to an agent. FDA safety decisions will probably become more, rather than less, complex as analytical techniques become more refined and pharmacologists discover more and more substances in tissues in ever smaller amounts.

Joan Arehart-Treichel

• . . . with synthetic substances that have never existed before . . . the tissues and cells of the body have no previous experience. The synthetic organic chemist today can prepare new substances much faster than they can possibly be tested.
P. R. Peacock, Director of Research, Glasgow Royal Cancer Hospital

• Even those animal tests that have become widely accepted by scientists frequently produce results that are variable and inconclusive. Every scientist knows that quite different results can be obtained from a standard test protocol using different animal species, different strains of the same species, different animal rations, different routes of administration, and a host of far more subtle variables. Different laboratories not infrequently obtain diverse results even trying to replicate identical testing procedures. The significance of much of the animal safety testing today is poorly understood, and the widely variable results obtained are subject to differing interpretations. Its usefulness in the design and execution of sound public policy under these circumstances is unfortunately limited.

Peter Barton Hutt, Assistant General Counsel, FDA

• Toxicology, as it is practiced in many centers, is still far from an exact science.

The Lancet

• The generally accepted criteria for evaluating the toxicity of food additives represents an unstable compromise between widely divergent scientific views and are subject to serious challenge.

Lewis Herber

Toxicology is the science of poisons and their effects on living organisms. It also deals with normally harmless substances that prove toxic under certain conditions. As a developing science, the main object of toxicology was to test the safety of drugs; but as food additives were developed, tests for their safety were included in the field of toxicology.

Although the toxicological principles involved in drug testing do apply to food additives, the use of toxicologic testing for food additives is unsatisfactory in several respects.

A segment of the population is expected to benefit from a controlled quantity of a drug administered over a relatively brief period of time. The risks of each specific drug are weighed against its benefits. However, the whole population may be exposed to relatively small, uncontrolled quantities of food additives over very long periods of time. Risks cannot be weighed against benefits: Those who take the risks are the consumers, and those who receive the benefits are, for the most part, the manufacturers of additives and food processors who use them.

Pharmacologists recognize that the rate of adverse drug reactions may increase enormously if several different drugs are administered to a patient at the same time. Since a large number of food additives may be ingested at any one meal, the potentials for adverse reactions are immeasurable. While the problems of drug interactions are considered, the problems of food additive interactions are uncontrolled.

Whereas human and clinical research are mandatory for drug safety testing, most food additive safety is based on animal testing. Human testing for food additives is uncommon.

Efficacy is a clear requirement for drugs but not for food additives. In a landmark decision, the United States Supreme Court ruled in 1973 that the FDA has the authority to remove ineffective drugs from the market and to impose stringent rules for assessing drug effectiveness. Many food processors speculate that such regulations could be extended to food components.

The enormous burden of testing food additives increased greatly with the proliferation and complex applications of these additives. Agencies, such as the FDA and the USDA, had to evolve or adapt experimental procedures for safety evaluation long before analytical chemistry, biochemistry, and other basic allied scientific disciplines had developed enough to give adequate answers to the problems. Dr. P. R. Peacock, Director of Research, Glasgow Royal Cancer Hospital, remarked, "The synthetic organic chemist today can prepare new substances much faster than they can possibly be tested."

Gradually, a set of standard routine investigations was recognized and approved for assessing the safety of food additives. In the light of present knowledge, the early tests were grossly inadequate. As newer concepts and testing procedures were developed, testing had to be expanded; yet, the tests always failed to keep up with developments. Unforeseen, and at times startling, information has been revealed. Cases such as cyclamates, saccharin, food dyes, and DEP reflect the limitations in present testing programs and the great gaps in our knowledge.

In addition to the several thousand intentional food additives, thousands of unintentional substances may contaminate food. Even less is known about these substances, either singly, or their possible interactions with each other, than about food additives.

Their sheer number obviously places an enormous burden on the body's ability to handle them.

Basic information about substances added to food is long overdue. Some, but by no means all, of the questions that must be answered satisfactorily about each intentional additive already in use, and each one proposed for use in the food supply, are:

—What are the chemical and physical properties of the additive? Does it have any impurities? If so, what are they? What are the chemical and physical properties of these impurities?

—Will the additive change chemically when it comes in contact with food? When the food is packaged? during transportation or storage? with changes in temperature or humidity? during cooking?

—What are the exact conditions under which the additive is to be used? What is its intended purpose(s)? Does the purpose serve a real consumer need, or does it only benefit the food processor?

In addition, many pharmacological questions must be asked:

—What are the pharmacological effects of the additive on test animals? What happens to the additive when it is ingested? Is it changed in the intestinal tract, or does it pass through the body unchanged? Does it produce diarrhea or constipation? Does it alter the bacterial flora in the intestinal tract, possibly rendering subsequent drugs partially or totally inactive? Does the additive influence the absorption of foods or food nutrients such as vitamins or minerals?

—Is the additive absorbed into the circulation? Is it changed by the kidneys? If it is excreted by the kidneys, does it produce injury while it is being excreted?

—Is the additive detoxified by the liver or other organs? If so, what are its effects on these organs?

—If the additive, in being detoxified, forms metabolites (breakdown products), what are they? How toxic are the metabolites as they are produced by actions within the body? What are their routes of excretion?

—Does the additive affect the blood-forming organs?

—Is the additive stored in the fatty tissues, the central nervous system, the brain, the spinal cord, the bones, the liver, the hair, the nails, or in other parts of the body? If so, where is it held and for how long?

—Are there any studies on humans who have ingested the chemical additive under the same conditions for which it will be used? If so, do the results demonstrate that humans handle the additive the same way as experimental animals?

There also are many difficult toxicological questions:

—What happens when humans ingest the food additive in small quantities, repeatedly, over their lifespan?

—How does a single additive interact with other additives? or with vitamins, minerals, trace elements or other substances?

—What are the effects of the additive on a fetus? on the pregnant or lactating woman? on the newly born? on the young child? on the malnourished? on the person under great stress? on the chronically ill? on the elderly? on the individual with severe allergies, respiratory ailments, diabetes, or other health problems?

Some questions are unanswerable:

—If a food additive is suspected of inducing cancer, how will we know that a malignancy was triggered by a substance ingested twenty years earlier?

—If a food additive is suspected of being toxic to an embryo, how can we prove that embryonic death or a birth defect was caused by transmission of the food additive from a pregnant woman to the fetus through the placenta?

—If a food additive is suspected of being capable of damaging chromosomes and harming the human genetic pool, how will our descendants ever suspect that their children have been denied a healthy body or mind because of a substance used several generations earlier?

—How can we know that subtle changes occurring in the human body—changes too subtle to detect or assess with current techniques—are being produced by a food additive?

Animal tests to establish the safety of food additives affect the lives of millions of humans. Yet many uncertainties remain. In formulating tests, researchers must make a number of decisions: the test's time span; animal species to be used; the strain, sex, age, and number of generations; how and when to perform routine tests; and suitable means of administering the additive. *Even one unwise choice made with any of these factors may invalidate test results.*

The time spans used for animal tests are divided to test for "acute," "subacute," and "chronic" toxicity. The acute and sub-acute time spans are used to reveal the effects of short-term exposure to substances. The techniques were devised for testing drugs and other substances. Such information is useful in dealing with problems such as accidental poisoning or short-term drug treatment. These tests are *unsatisfactory* for food additives, which are used over long periods of time. In the past, the acute toxicity test was frequently the *only* test performed on a food additive. But since an acute toxicity test gives only a crude idea of a substance's lethality, it should be used only as a quick screening device.

Animals are usually fed an additive orally either once or for a brief time period. The animals are usually divided into four groups. Three of the groups are given the additive at three different dose levels: high, intermediate, and low. The fourth group, the control, does not receive the additive. The tester hopes to find a level that *does* produce a toxic effect so that a "safe dose" can be established at a lower level, where these effects are *not* observed. With our present knowledge, this concept appears simplistic. We now recognize that many adverse effects may be inflicted which, at the moment are beneath the threshold of perception, and may not appear for 20, 30 or even 40 years, at which time the cause may be completely undeterminable. Hence, one of the basic principles of traditional toxicology, the myth of a "safe dose" level, needs to be discarded.

Another misconception, frequently expressed, is that "everything, even water, is toxic in some way if the amounts consumed are excessive enough. So the idea is to find a level that does not produce toxic effects and then to establish a lower 'safe dose' level where these effects disappear." This concept must be challenged, since *low doses of a chemical, such as food additives, can be even more harmful than large ones.* Dr. Jacqueline Verrett, research biochemist at the FDA, reported that "often the body just excretes large gulps of a substance whereas smaller amounts will be absorbed and metabolized." Verrett suggested that such absorption may occur in the case of the controversial food dye, FD&C Red No. 2.

To determine the degree of acute toxicity of the additive, animals are subjected to an "LD_{50}" test, a technique by which toxicologists attempt to find the lethal (L) dose (D) for 50 percent of the animals in the test group. Thus, when half of the animals die within a designated period of time after exposure to a certain dosage of the additive, the LD_{50} level is established. The lower the LD_{50}, the higher the toxicity of the substance. Generally, if the LD_{50} falls below the level of one milligram per kilogram of body weight of the test animal, the substance is considered to be "of extreme toxicity"; between 50 and 500 milligrams per kilogram, "of moderate toxicity"; and above that, "of low toxicity."

Again, such information is valuable for purposes of drug dosage, but its application to food additives is unsuitable. To obtain the LD_{50} for a food additive, the substance is tested *singly*. Results from such tests may grossly underestimate the true toxicity of a substance when it is combined with foods and other food additives. Hence, another basic principle of traditional toxicology, the LD_{50} level, does not apply to evaluations of a food additive.

Subacute toxicity tests yield somewhat more information. Animals are given the additive for a short time span, usually 90 days. During this time, blood samples are studied and enzyme activities are measured. Then, the animals are sacrificed, and about 30 different tissues from each animal are examined microscopically. If the additive has produced adverse effects, the harm is often observed in the liver, kidney or spleen. The limitations of subacute toxicity tests for additives (and pesticide residues) were discussed in a report by an advisory committee to the FDA. The report cautioned that such pathological (relating to the study of disease) and histopathological (relating to the study of tissue changes characteristic of disease) studies do not necessarily reveal the interference with normal functions of bodily systems. The committee warned that it is "illusory to place complete reliance on the thesis that a well-defined and well-conducted subacute toxicity study will detect changes in . . . biological systems."

In a chronic toxicity test, an additive is usually incorporated into the diet of the test animals for two years or for the animal's life span. At least two animal species, at least one of which is not a rodent, are used. After the first 6 and 12 months, some animals may be sacrificed and examined. If harmful effects have already begun to appear, the test may be terminated.

Chronic toxicity studies yield a variety of information. Growth rate, life span, appetite, behavior, and the condition of blood and urine can all be measured. These tests show whether the additive is excreted from the animal's body at a slower rate than it is ingested, and if so, how much must be accumulated in the body before a toxic reaction is observed. Upon autopsy, tissues are examined for possible changes in functioning and for pathological changes. Special attention is given to critical organs and systems and to the possibility of tumor formations.

Although it is true that chronic toxicity tests yield far more information than acute and subacute tests, the information is still limited. If an additive produces no observable effects from chronic toxicity studies, a "no-effect level" is established. The scientific validity of a no-effect level is shaky. Negative results do not prove that the additive under investigation is entirely harmless. Such studies only demonstrate the absence of any observed injury.

Compare the no-effect levels of some commonly used additives. Remember: *the lower the number, the higher the toxicity.* With compounds such as polyethylene glycol, the lower the molecular weight (mol. wt.), the higher the toxicity. Substances with low molecular weights are more apt to be absorbed within the body.

Additive	No-effect level at ppm	Purpose(s)
Ethoxyquin	120	Antioxidant
Octyl gallate	350	Antioxidant
Sodium bisulfite	500	Preservative, antioxidant
BHT	1,000	Antioxidant
FD&C Blue No. 2 [Indigotine]	1,000	Food dye
NDGA	2,500	Antioxidant
BHA	5,000	Antioxidant
FD&C Blue No. 1 [Brilliant Blue FCF]	5,000	Food dye
Sodium hexametaphosphate	5,000	Emulsifier, sequestrant, texturizer
FD&C Yellow No. 5 [Tartrazine]	10,000	Food dye
Propyl gallate	10,000	Antioxidant
Saccharin	10,000	Artificial sweetener
Sodium lauryl sulfate	10,000	Component of detergent for raw products followed by water rinse
Sodium nitrate	10,000	Color fixative with cured meat products
Tartaric acid	12,000	Emulsifier, sequestrant, acid
Polyethylene glycol (mol. wt. 400)	20,000	Defoamer in manufacture of sugar beets
(mol. wt. 1540)	40,000	Coatings' and bindings' component in tableted foods to increase resistance against oxidation and moisture
(mol. wt. 4000)	40,000	Component of defoamer in manufacture of yeast and sugar beets
Polyoxyethylenes:		
(20) sorbitan monolaurate	50,000	Flavor dispersant, defoamer
(20) sorbitan monopalmitate	50,000	Emulsifier, flavor dispersant, defoamer
(20) sorbitan monostearate	50,000	Emulsifier, flavor dispersant
(20) sorbitan tristearate	50,000	Emulsifier, flavor dispersant, defoamer
Sorbic acid	50,000	Fungistat
Glycerol	100,000	Humectant, solvent, thickener, plasticizer for edible coatings
Gum guaiac	250,000	Antioxidant

The establishment of a no-effect level for an additive does not assure its safety. In the past, no-effect levels *had* been determined for additives subsequently banned:

Additive	No-effect level at ppm	Purpose
FD&C Yellow AB	500	food dye
FD&C Yellow OB	500	food dye
FD&C Red No. 1 [Ponceau 3R]	5,000	food dye

While toxicologists frequently speak of "insignificant toxicological levels," numerous cases show that many substances with no *demonstrable* effect levels can exert profound biological effects:

—DES, the synthetic sex hormone used in animal feed, induced malignant tumors in treated mice at a level considerably below the official analytical sensitivity of two parts per billion (ppb).

—Prostaglandins, potent biological substances, cause smooth muscular contractions in animals with as little as one nanogram (one billionth of a gram) per milliliter. Researchers need detection methods sensitive in the picogram (trillionths of a gram) range to detect prostaglandins in tissue.

—Powerful carcinogens such as aflatoxin molds are present in certain foods at undetectable levels. A no-effect level of these aflatoxins is not reached in either the rat or trout even at 1 ppb.

—Dioxin, an impurity sometimes present in an herbicide, used with pregnant guinea pigs at levels far below those detected in their tissues, induced stillbirths or defective offspring.

To establish a safety level for food additives, toxicologists have adopted a time-honored—but arbitrary—arrangement known as "margin of safety." The "safe" level for humans is set no higher than 1/100th as much as the no-effect level for animals. The philosophy underlying this safety margin is that it allows for uncertainties in predicting human safety from animal tests. Also data indicate that the very young, the very old, or the sick of a species may occasionally be up to ten times as susceptible as normal mature individuals. The "margin of safety" formula was devised, then, by multiplying a tenfold allowance for species variability by a tenfold allowance for individual variability.

The safety margin may be inadequate for idiosyncratic dietary habits. From time to time, reports about such individuals with such diets appear in medical journals:

—A 25-year-old airline stewardess, admitted to St. George's Hospital in London, was suffering from photosensitive dermatitis (skin sensitivity to light) and severe renal (kidney) tubular acidosis, accompanied by an abnormally decreased level of phosphorus in the blood. Investigation revealed that the young woman had consumed habitually large quantities of cyclamate-containing soft drinks and had used 20 or more packets of calcium cyclamate daily.

—Allyl isothiocyanate, a toxic substance occurring naturally in mustard, is a legally permitted food additive in meat products, beverages, ice cream, candy, baked goods, pickles, and various other condiments. Mustard is used regularly, and in very substantial quantities, as an ingredient in food items such as mayonnaise and salad dressings.

As early as 1948, Jackson Blair, M.D., reported some 50 cases of high blood pressure in individuals who regularly ate large amounts of spices—including mustard, pepper, and ginger. Blair considered mustard as the worst offender. Blair warned that individuals who use mustard on cold meats, hamburgers, frankfurters, and sandwiches run unnecessary risks. He asserted that allyl isothiocyanate, a strong irritant, can inflict injury by ulcerating the arterial wall: "The oil of mustard has a strongly injurious effect upon the walls of the capillaries and consequently the mustard burn is very slow of healing." In more recent years, Blair has reported cases of coronary disease (coronary thrombosis as well as coronary attack with infection) associated with the ingestion of large amounts of mustard over a period of years.

—The active principle in licorice extract is an acid that is chemically and structurally similar to several adrenal gland hormones. Licorice extract is a food flavoring additive commonly used with beverages, ice cream, ices, candy, baked goods, gelatin desserts, chewing gums, and syrups. Thomas J. Chamberlain, M.D., reported the case of a 53-year-old man who had eaten 700 grams—about 1½ pounds—of licorice candy over a period of nine days. The man suffered from shortness of breath, swelling of his ankles and abdomen, weight gain, headache, and weakness. Although he previously had a record of excellent health, his respiratory distress required hospitalization for the developing heart condition. Chamberlain warned other physicians that overeating licorice-containing foods and beverages might result in congestive heart failure.

Three physicians from the University of Michigan reported that a 58-year-old man, who had eaten two to three bars of licorice daily for seven years, developed high blood pressure and paralysis of the extremities. The syndrome disappeared after the patient stopped eating licorice.

An elderly man suddenly developed heart palpitations after moderate exertion. After being hospitalized and examined, he was found to suffer from hypertension and malfunctioning of the intestine, heart, and kidney. In attempting to stop smoking cigarettes, he had substituted licorice. For a period of three months he had eaten approximately 124 grams of licorice daily. In all these cases, the safety margin was inadequate.

Even when the hundredfold safety margin is not abused by irregular diets, the margin may offer less safety than assumed. When saccharin was removed from the GRAS list, the FDA recommended that its use be limited to no more than a gram daily by the average adult. At the same time, the agency revealed that *some test animals developed bladder tumors at approximately 100 times the maximum permitted by the new regulation.*

On occasion, the FDA even has set safety margins far lower than a hundredfold. Although a hundredfold safety margin *had* been recommended for saccharin by the National Academy of Sciences (NAS), a mathematical error caused the FDA to establish only a *thirtyfold* safety margin. By a not-too-strange-coincidence, the thirtyfold margin met the needs of food and beverage processors, who were spared the burden of having to select and test new formulas for their products.

When the safety of a food dye, FD&C Red No. 2, appeared extremely doubtful, the FDA took the extraordinary action of revising the original no-effect level upward. The new safety factor was only *tenfold*, the smallest safety margin ever proposed in the FDA's history.

The concept of a hundredfold safety factor, frequently applied in cases of *reversible* toxicity, is totally inappropriate for covering *irreversible* damage inflicted by carcinogens, teratogens, or mutagens. An ongoing scientific controversy centers around the application of a no-effect level to additives that are known or suspected of causing irreversible damage.

Proponents of a no-effect level for these substances argue that all biological systems have a "threshold" below which these potent substances will not inflict harm. Opponents argue that, even if such thresholds exist—and it remains to be proven that they do—our present lack of information and relatively unsophisticated testing techniques make such determinations unscientific.

The controversy over the use of DES forms the basis for the repeated attacks against the Delaney Clause, which excludes carcinogenic substances in food. To solve this problem, scientists at the National Cancer Institute (NCI) have attempted to work out procedures to determine specific "safe" dose levels for carcinogens. One procedure, formulated by Dr. Marvin A. Schneiderman, is the "acceptable risk dose" (ARD). Schneiderman proposed that the safety factor for carcinogens be a millionfold. Schneiderman arrived at the millionfold safety factor by allowing a hundredfold safety factor for species differences. This was multiplied by another hundredfold safety factor to allow for interactions with other inducing factors. The resulting figure then was multiplied by another hundredfold safety factor as a hedge against the incorrect choice of "blow up" (weight or surface area) from animal to man.

Another procedure, the Mantel–Bryan Model, also was developed at the NCI. First reported in 1961, this procedure statistically assesses probable risks for carcinogens to arrive at a "virtually safe" dose level.

FDA scientists have been sharply divided on the acceptance or rejection of the threshold concept. In 1971, the agency established an advisory panel on carcinogenesis. Drawing largely on the Mantel–Bryan Model, the panel proposed the outlines of a testing program for carcinogens to the FDA.

At first, the FDA endorsed the report. However, Dr. M. Adrian Gross, Assistant Director for Scientific Coordination, Office of Pharmaceutical Research and Testing, FDA, used the Mantel–Bryan Model for analyzing an animal study of DES, and *the model established the carcinogenicity of this substance at extremely low concentrations*. When it became apparent that the Mantel–Bryan Model would *not* serve the purpose of establishing threshold levels for carcinogens, the FDA reversed its position, ignoring the recommendations of its own advisory panel.

The FDA then announced that it would follow guidelines established by the Food Protection Committee for estimating "toxicologically insignificant levels" of chemicals in foods. But the validity of these guidelines also became the subject of controversy. The report of the Surgeon General's Ad Hoc Committee on the Evaluation of Low Levels of Environmental Chemical Carcinogens repudiated the validity of these guidelines for evaluating carcinogenic additives. Scientists at NCI also strongly disagreed with the guidelines.

In a flurry of memoranda within the FDA, attempts were made to downgrade Gross' studies using the Mantel–Bryan Model and to reaffirm the concept of a threshold level. Gross answered the criticisms with a stinging memorandum, in which he charged that the safety factor for carcinogens, being considered by the FDA, would be to endorse "a policy which has been conclusively demonstrated time and again to be scientifically bankrupt." Gross charged that "no-effect levels," safety factors, and similar concepts were:

. . . eroded skeletons rattling in our closet. These are not just skeletons but actual monsters—by the very fact that one chooses to say nothing about the risks associated with estimates of unqualified "safe" levels, there is a considerable likelihood that such levels are markedly less "safe" than those which are estimated by some procedure that [a member of the FDA] has chosen to attack . . . they can be viewed therefore as actually "hazardous."

By July 1973, the FDA had developed a new approach. The agency proposed procedures under which the sensitivity of analytical methods for carcinogenic substances (in this case, animal drugs in foods) might be extrapolated from the results of toxicity studies. The agency proposed that industry test results be fed into a statistical system to extrapolate a "safe" residue level. And what statistical system did the FDA propose to use? The agency proposed the Mantel–Bryan Model, previously rejected, but with its own "slight" modification. Instead of demonstrating probable harm from low levels of carcinogens, the FDA's modification of the Mantel–Bryan Model distorted its findings so that it appeared to support the threshold concept. In fact, the modification distorted the original intention to such an extent that results would be interpreted *exactly the opposite.*

As coauthor of the original system, Dr. Nathan Mantel protested:

The modification [of the Mantel-Bryan Model] has the effect of vitiating the Delaney Clause, while our original procedure was intended to strengthen it. In fact, under the modification it may be true that the more carcinogenic an agent appears in laboratory testing, the higher will be its permitted residue level in edible animal products; further, the stronger the evidence for a carcinogenic effect in terms of the number of animals on which based, again the higher will be the permitted residue level.

Food additive proponents frequently attempt to apply a "benefit–risk" ratio to these substances. While this concept, long employed in evaluating new drugs, may be useful for the purpose of treating life-threatening health problems, it is totally inapplicable to food additives. No reference to any benefit–risk concept exists in the entire history of federal food additive laws. The FDA has never been authorized to balance the benefits of a food additive against the risks of its use to decide whether or not to approve an additive. In an FDA memorandum, Dr. Bert J. Voss, at the time Deputy Director of the Division of Pharmacology and Toxicology, stated: "There is no benefit versus risk consideration involved in food additives. They need only be safe and accomplish the intended purpose."

But since food additive proponents persist in making value judgments based on benefit–risk ratios, then the cold facts should be publicly available. Then, the informed public could be given the opportunity to decide whether the benefits really outweigh the risks.

Can the "benefit" of a food additive or other chemical, with a known or suspected quality of inducing cancer, birth defects, genetic mutations, or other forms of biologic harm offset the "risk"? Such problems are seldom raised by proponents of benefit–risk ratios.

In terms of genetic effects, it is completely impossible to even estimate the risks. No one can make a calculated guess as to how many future generations may be adversely affected by mutations. Nor can anyone know what mutations may inflict in terms of mental deficiency, increased cancer incidence, or a wide range of other possible effects. It is impossible to predict what types of mutations will occur, what form they will take, or how long they will remain in the human gene pool.

The concept of benefit–risk ratio was frequently applied to DES during congressional investigations of this additive, a potential carcinogen. Many cancerologists and physicians urged the elimination of DES from the food supply, irrespective of the economic costs involved. The likely economic costs, estimated in a report issued by USDA, suggested that retail beef prices might increase by as much as 3.5 cents per pound if DES were banned from use in commercial cattle feeding. Retail prices of other kinds of meat and eggs were also expected to rise as the public demand shifted away from the more expensive beef. Added costs for all meat and poultry products could be as much as $2.30 per person annually. *If consumers were given a choice of paying an additional $2.30 per person annually to keep a probable carcinogen out of the food supply, they might well consider it an outstanding bargain.* The average cost of treating a terminal cancer patient has been estimated to be more than $20,000. This financial burden in no way includes the suffering and anguish of the cancer victim or of his family and friends. These costs, intangible and unestimable, must nevertheless also be considered apart from the great financial burden.

Moreover, if a benefit–risk ratio ever is used to determine whether a food additive may be used, the people who take the "risks" must also be those who receive the "benefits." The consumer cannot be asked to take risks for the benefit of industry. "The problem is," noted Dr. Joshua Lederberg, "to ensure that the people who bear the risk and eventually pay the price, will also reap the benefits."

After a food additive has undergone a battery of tests, the results need to be evaluated. The public wrongly assumes that such assessments are based on objective scientific data.

The adverse effects of well-designed and well-executed tests even may be assessed differently by workers in the same laboratory, much less by different laboratories. For example, there may be an exceedingly fine demarcation between "statistically significant" or "statistically insignificant." Organ enlargement may be interpreted as a reaction to stress instead of a pathologically induced state. Tumor growths, behavioral changes, and even fatalities may be ascribed—rightly or wrongly—to factors other than the additive under scrutiny.

There have been numerous occasions that might be facetiously termed "Word Games Testers Play," except for the fact that policies based on such "games" are serious matters:

—Tests demonstrated that a group of emulsifiers produced bladder stones in test animals. Although bladder cancers resulted, both the testers and officials denied that the emulsifiers could be termed bladder carcinogens. The stones were not a "direct" cause.

—During the testing program to discover DES residues in meat samples, reports stated that the hormone was not found in "edible portions" of the meat. The edible portion concept was arbitrarily limited, in the minds of officials, to the carcass of the animal. It did not include any internal organs. Of course, the internal organs include the liver, which was found consistently to contain DES residues. Thus, with semantic assistance, livers were mysteriously dismissed, despite the fact that they are often eaten.

—Liver cancers, induced in test rats and mice by the administration of chlorinated hydrocarbon pesticides, were labeled with the neutral, noncommittal term "tumors."

—A published paper purportedly demonstrated that a specific pesticide does not produce birth defects in test animals. In fact, even low doses of the substance produce a very wide range of birth defects. The pesticide company had ingeniously *redefined* birth defects, limiting them to abnormalities inconsistent with survival or optimal function. By using this definition, cleft palates, heart lesions, and a very large number of other commonly acknowledged birth defects were automatically excluded.

Food safety tests are conducted mainly by food interests or by commercial laboratories they employ. The problems of evaluating such tests were discussed at the congressional hearings, "Chemicals and the Future of Man":

Samuel S. Epstein, M.D.: . . . the majority of the work done in this country is performed by special groups with client interests. Industry performs a lot of work in-house, or it is done for industry by commercial testing laboratories. These sources will tend to give industry the kind of answers that it thinks it needs. This often does a gross disservice to industry.
Senator Abraham Ribicoff: Under the present law, who does the safety evaluation of food additives?
Samuel S. Epstein: The FDA.
Senator Abraham Ribicoff: The FDA?

Samuel S. Epstein: For food additives, yes.

Senator Abraham Ribicoff: You have mentioned the conflict of interest, the safety evaluation of food chemicals. How big a problem is this?

Samuel S. Epstein: It is difficult to quantify this precisely. In my view, this is a major area of concern for several reasons. The example . . . with cyclamates suggests that you can get what you pay for. . . . Approximately half the research on cyclamates in this country, which was paid for by Abbott, showed that cyclamates are good for you. The other half, paid for by the sugar industry, showed that cyclamates are bad for you . . . Over and above this, within committees there are clearly conflicts of interest. Within expert committees of a wide range, committees on which I have sat with others, certain members of these committees speak in an advisory and consultant capacity, but it is often suspected that they are there as unofficial industrial spokesmen. They speak with an industrial viewpoint. I think it is absolutely essential that in any expert committee empowered to make decisions and recommendations with which the general public is concerned, there should be a clear statement of financial interest of individual members, and under certain conditions certain individuals in potential conflict should exclude themselves.

Commercial testing laboratories are neither licensed nor inspected. As a result, according to L. Golberg, Institute of Experimental Pathology and Toxicology, Albany Medical College, "Not infrequently the data produced speak for themselves, and shoddy work is readily apparent to the experienced eye." Regulatory agencies have accepted such results, on faith, without critical review. At times, the FDA even has recommended such laboratories to prospective clients.

"It is regrettable," says Epstein, "but it is a sad fact of life to say that one can buy the kind of information one wants." There is a common consensus in the food field that a laboratory which earns a reputation for finding hazards in substances ultimately finds itself without industrial clients. There are instances when scientists have been fired or have had their research terminated when their studies touched hazards associated with food additives or other products of commercial interest.

The able and conscientious tester in a commercial laboratory who finds and reports adverse effects may find that his recommendations are ignored. The tester, according to Golberg, is then "forced to follow the client's bidding, knowing that the resulting work will be inadequate, yet will possibly suffice to 'scrape by' the authorities."

Some additive testing is conducted at universities. Presumably, prestige is bestowed on tests performed at such institutions. However, as recently as 1963, no university in the United States even had a department of toxicology. Golberg has charged that some tests performed at universities may be shoddy due to "departmental chairmen who have built empires on the toil of underpaid and inexpert graduate students, producing data that were even less reliable than those [from commercial laboratories]."

An important factor contributing to the low standard of toxicological testing is that a very minute portion of the test results is ever published in open literature accessible to scientists. Industry regards any test results gathered from its experiments as trade secrets. The results, unlike those in other scientific fields, are *not* subject to peer review. Inadequate, erroneous, or distorted tests are not corrected as they would be if critically reviewed by independent scientists. The public has little assurance that test data submitted to the FDA or the USDA are reliable. FDA Associate Commissioner Kenneth W. Kirk admitted that the agency frequently did not bother to review industry research but depended largely on the summaries submitted.

In a memorandum to Dr. Herbert L. Ley, Jr., just prior to Ley's ouster as Commissioner of the FDA, Dr. Howard L. Richardson (who was facing transfer as chief pathologist in the FDA's Bureau of Science) charged that "on occasions too numerous to relate" the FDA had manipulated and censored laboratory data on food additives and pesticides to make them fit the agency's policies, rather than alter policies in view of the data. Richardson gave as examples old FDA slides and worksheets that revealed what Richardson termed a suspiciously high incidence of cancer in cyclamate-treated test animals. These findings were ignored by the

FDA and excluded from the agency's report. Richardson cited other cases in which lower-level bureaucrats within the FDA rewrote scientific reports and engaged in other activities that downgraded or concealed evidence that various food additives might be harmful.

Dr. Kent L. Davis, another FDA pathologist transferred at the same time as Richardson, had been concerned about food coloring safety. Dr. Davis had suggested that the eye damage that resulted when dogs ate FD&C Yellow No. 6 might warrant regulatory action. He also had recommended that FD&C Red No. 4 be reviewed for its possible carcinogenic qualities. Richardson commented, "all of these issues have gone unanswered and unresolved and remain potential health hazards."

Subsequent to these charges, a one-year study of the FDA by five professors from leading medical schools, issued in 1971, was harshly critical of the agency's performance in managing its scientific efforts and of the productivity of some of its scientists. The committee found that some of the agency's laboratories used advanced technology and gave every impression of being first rate. "On the other hand," the report continued, "one can also find laboratories so poorly managed that scientists seem to be unable to describe their work coherently or to produce interpretable data books containing their findings." The committee also noted an aura of secrecy around scientific work.

The secrecy of test data, locked in FDA and USDA files, has been criticized repeatedly. In 1962, a Citizens Advisory Committee on the FDA urged that scientific data be published. "It is doubtful," wrote the committee, "whether the degree of secrecy now maintained is compatible with the public interest." The agency ignored such criticisms and continued to treat data as "privileged," whether they were from the agency's own tests or had been submitted by food interests or commercial laboratories.

In 1969, the congress encountered the lack of access to FDA data. During drug hearings, Congressman Fountain requested from the FDA all recent files on its review of combination antibiotics.

There was considerable foot dragging before the congressmen were informed of an unwritten FDA policy that files would not be provided for congress in "potentially explosive situations."

In 1972, legal suit was brought by a university researcher and the Environmental Defense Fund, under the Freedom of Information Act, to force the FDA to open its safety data files on nitrite to the public. The lawsuit charged that the FDA, "has consistently and routinely countenanced violations of the law which have endangered the public health. . . . Both scientifically and legally, bureaucratic secrecy has made actions possible which could never stand the light of public review." The lawsuit succeeded in prying open the files on one food additive.

However, the secret-files policy was continued. The following month, a lawyer told a House of Representatives subcommittee on government operations that his request for information from the USDA under the Freedom of Information Act had been denied. He charged that the USDA had used tactics that he termed "fob-him-off-with-a-meaningless-summary-stratagem" or "delay-until-the-information-becomes-stale." The lawyer also alleged that the agency denied him information by using an "it's-exempt-because-it's-embarrassing" routine. (Under the Freedom of Information Act, certain categories of information disclosure are exempt.) In a third instance, a colleague of the lawyer was denied information by a "sue-us-again" tactic. The colleague contended that the right of access had been established by a court ruling, but the USDA insisted on having the issue decided in court again.

A month later, mounting pressures from these legal actions and the anticipation of new ones, as well as congressional criticisms, caused the FDA to announce a complete reversal of its policy. The agency proposed to make publicly available about 90 percent of its confidential data on the safety and efficacy of thousands of products, on adverse drug reactions, and on the results of factory and food plant inspections. Some 10 percent of the data, consisting of manufacturing methods, formulas, and commercial and financial information would remain unavailable to the public. Regarding food additives and food dyes, the policy called for public accessibility "unless extraordinary circumstances arc shown." The new policy proposed to make all completed reports of FDA testing and research available to anyone who knew what to request.

At the time of the proposal, spokesmen for the food and drug industries privately expressed alarm, but they withheld public statements. Shortly afterward, the Manufacturing Chemists Association (MCA) stated that the FDA's interpretation of a trade secret was too narrow and that industry should be allowed to justify information confidentiality when disclosure is requested. The MCA also stated that *research data on food and color additives should remain confidential.* To date, public disclosure of data on these substances has not become a reality.

Public access to data is, of course, an issue far larger than food additives. Epstein made an eloquent plea for public access to data on all substances relating to human safety and environmental quality:

Further legislation concerning public access to data is critically needed. All formal discussions between agencies, industry, and expert governmental and nongovernmental committees on all issues relating to human safety and environmental quality, and all data relevant to such discussions properly belong to the public domain and should be a matter of open record. Such records, including clear statements, by all concerned, of possible conflicts of interest, should be immediately available to the scientific community, scicntific and legal representatives of consumer, occupational, and environmental groups, and to other interested parties. Appropriate legal safeguards for the protection of patent rights should be developed.

In addition to open access of data on all issues of public health and welfare, and environmental safety, it is essential that the interests of consumer, occupational and environmental groups be adequately represented, legally and scientifically, at the earliest formal stages of such discussions. Decisions by agencies on technological innovations or on new synthetic chemicals after closed discussions on data which have been treated confidentially are unacceptable. Consumer, occupational, and environmental safety apart, such decisions are contrary to the long-term interests of industry, which should be protected from perforce belated objections.

Obviously, animal tests are inadequate for demonstrating food additive safety for humans. A logical question follows: Should testing be conducted with humans? While such studies might be useful, there are drawbacks.

Advocates for human testing say that if animal tests indicate additive safety, some of the evaluations of these tests should be carried further. Human subjects should be examined to see how the human body deals with small doses of the additive and what effects the additive has on the human enzyme systems. Toxicologists believe that if the results with human volunteers are similar to those obtained in one or more of the animal species tested, extrapolation of animal toxicity data to humans will be more meaningful. Proponents of human testing believe that the sensitive techniques now available make it possible to examine—with relative ease and little danger—human metabolism, storage, accumulation, excretion, and metabolic conversions of additives.

Humans are used commonly in skin testing of cosmetics and toiletries. In testing such consumer goods, any untoward side effects are apt to be brief, superficial, and reversible. The situation is different for food additives; testing by ingestion would be for longer periods, would have greater risks, and might create irreversible effects.

Humans are frequently used to evaluate new drugs, where trial is essential and where patients clearly need treatment. In such cases, the therapeutic effects as well as any unexpected side effects or other adverse reactions can be observed directly under carefully controlled conditions. In such situations, risks may be justified. But food additives are not generally life-saving substances, and such risks cannot be justified. Even food hazards such as trichinosis, salmonellosis, and botulism are better controlled by means of heat treatment than by the use of food additives.

Information about the harmful effects of food additives on humans can be gathered in three ways: by accident, from situations of occupational exposure where levels are far higher than those of the general population, and by using human volunteers. Each of these methods has limitations.

Accidental exposures to additives are infrequent, and they cannot supply the systematic and adequate information needed. However, some information has been gathered in a few rare incidents:

—The consumption of fish fillets, illegally treated with a dangerously high sodium nitrite level, resulted in severe illness in some individuals and the death of one boy.

—Children were poisoned after consuming processed meats (hot dogs and bologna) that contained sodium nitrite greatly in excess of the maximum permissible level.

—A man died after sprinkling his food in a restaurant with a substance labeled "meat tenderizer." The jar, mislabeled, actually had been filled with sodium nitrite.

More useful information can be gathered from cases of high occupational exposure levels. The drawbacks of this approach can be illustrated with food dyes. It would be nearly impossible to find a group of people who come in contact with a *single* food dye. The most meaningful information could be gathered from surveying populations which have had contact with a restricted dye group identical with, or similar to, some food dyes. Such groups might include food dye producers as well as those who used food and related dyes in foodstuff processing. People involved in the production or processing of certain other industrial substances and products (colored flares, smoke signals, fireworks, textiles, paper, plastics, rubber, linoleum, paints, shingles, chinaware, pharmaceuticals, cosmetics, sanitary goods, deodorants, insect repellents, gasoline, cleaning fluids, leather goods, colored prints) could also be used. Such studies could yield important data on potential cancer-inducing properties as well as on congenital malformations, allergies, and other adverse effects.

Most human test volunteers have been mature male prisoners. Some 70 percent of early drug trials are conducted with prison volunteers. On the basis of past testing experience, the use of prisoners has several drawbacks:

—As with other tests, any human test of relatively short duration fails to reveal potential long-term effects. Once the prisoner is released, there may be no medical follow-up.

—Mature male prisoners, with a carefully regulated daily regime and controlled diet, comprise a far more homogenous group than the normal population (composed of persons of all ages, both sexes, and with a wider range of physical conditions).

—Prison volunteers have been offered rewards ranging from candy, cigarettes, and cash, all the way to early parole and sentence reduction. Dr. Herbert L. Ley, Jr., while serving as commissioner of the FDA, remarked that such incentives to prison volunteers provided "a high stimulus not to report adverse side effects."

In addition, human experimentation raises serious ethical considerations. Individuals such as prisoners may not be afforded an opportunity for any truly "informed consent," and on occasions, they have been unknowingly subjected to unnecessary and extremely hazardous experiments. Well-documented instances of exploitation of human life make the use of humans for testing food additives neither reliable nor desirable.

5

The Toxicological Imponderables

• What originally started out as a suggestion, but was soon cultivated into a deep-rooted conviction, was the idea that by some mathematical magic formula, or factor, or other sleight of hand, animal data could be transmogrified into safe levels for human exposure. We recommend that this concept should now be formally, totally, and irrevocably abandoned.

L. Golberg, Institute of Experimental Pathology and Toxicology,
The Albany Medical College of Union University

• One really can't tell from animal testing how safe an additive will be in man. So the prudent thing to do, on the basis of the experimental data, is to lean over backward not to greatly increase risks.

Dr. Paul E. Johnson, Executive Secretary, Food Protection Committee,
National Academy of Sciences-National Research Council

• Since there is no certainty that a substance harmful to one species of animals will affect another, even when toxic effects are found for the test animals, it does not necessarily follow that human beings would be affected, although it is prudent to assume that they would be. On the other hand, one could argue that even when a test substance has no effect on animals it may still harm people.

Magnus Pyke

• No food additive should be used with blind reliance that man will not or cannot react in an unpredicted way.

H. C. Hodge, Department of Pharmacology, Rochester School of Medicine

• Our analytical investigators seem to have wandered away from the question they set out to solve; the more minutely they have subdivided this problem, the more difficult it is to rejoin its parts . . . the sum of the toxicologists' analytical data accruing from animal experiments is *far removed* from the situation confronting humans in their daily lives.

Theron G. Randolph, M.D.

The shortcomings of animal tests may be seen any time an animal species is chosen to demonstrate a food additive's safety. Substantial variations exist from species to species: Additives may be absorbed, distributed, stored, metabolized, and excreted in different ways. The site of these mechanisms may also vary. High doses of an additive given to animals during studies may impose metabolic stresses which are absent at lower doses. Or, the way in which an animal metabolizes a compound may differ at high and low dosages. Germ-free animals are difficult to obtain for laboratory testing. Such factors make it difficult to evaluate test results.

An animal species may not reflect human sensitivity to an additive. For example, different animal species convert quinic acid (from plant products) to hippuric acid (a detoxification product formed in the liver) in quite different ways. Similarly, different species metabolize propyl gallate (an additive used as an antioxidant and flavoring agent) in different ways. The results of tests on such additives may differ widely, depending on which animal species has been chosen.

Different animal species do not necessarily react in the same way to the test diet. For example, dietary sucrose (sugar) increases insulin concentration in human and pig blood, but it decreases insulin in rat blood. Obesity is best produced in the rat by fat-rich diets, but in humans it is produced by carbohydrate-rich diets. A specific food additive's action on intestinal flora also may differ from species to species.

Mice and rats are often used to test the safety of food additives. Practical considerations tend to favor their choice: they can be bought and maintained reasonably, they require little laboratory space, standardized lines are readily available from commercial breeders, they breed well in the laboratory, and they have a relatively short life span of 2 to 3 years. Comparatively, guinea pigs live from 6 to 8 years; rabbits live from 7 to 12 years; and dogs live from 9 to 15 years.

But even though these favorable factors have made mice and rats popular for laboratory work, their physiological responses may differ from humans. For instance, the antioxidant BHT was studied extensively in the rat, but it is metabolized and excreted differently by humans.

Dogs also are used for many chronic toxicity studies. Yet studies have shown that human metabolism of BHA may more closely resemble the rat's than the dog's.

The pig is closer to the human in its physiological responses than either rats or dogs, and it is considered to be a better research model. It is impractical to use an 800-pound creature in the laboratory, but miniature strains, weighing under 200 pounds, have recently been developed and are now used. However, even these pigs are too large and expensive for laboratory work. In the future, animal breeders hope to develop a breed of pigs weighing no more than an average dog.

Other species used in testing are the guinea pig and the rabbit. Although penicillin usually is not toxic to humans, it is fatal to guinea pigs. Ulcerative lesions, resembling human ulcerative colitis, can be induced in both guinea pigs and rabbits with carrageenan (a vegetable gum widely used as a food additive), but this additive apparently does not produce similar lesions in humans.

Primates are more closely related to humans—anatomically, biochemically and physiologically—than any other animal species. Their reproductive system as well as their hematopoietic system (the blood and the structures that function in its production) are similar. These qualities give primate test results advantages over those of other species. But primates are expensive and difficult to maintain. And wide variations among individual primates may cloud test results.

Although primates are more closely related to humans than other animal species, extrapolation of primate test results remains a problem. In a comparative study of the effects of ten pharmacologically active compounds, neither rhesus nor squirrel monkeys reacted the same as humans. In another case, the response of rhesus monkeys to large doses of BHT and BHA differed significantly from that of rats: these additives caused increased liver weights and interfered with enzyme systems. Different responses of the two species also were observed ultrastructurally (the invisible ultimate physiochemical organization of protoplasm).

Since there are substantial variations between species, comparative metabolic and excretion studies of two or more species give more reliable information. For example, rhesus monkeys were found to be more sensitive to two compounds (a rat poison and a chemotherapeutic agent) than humans. But both rhesus monkeys and humans were found to be able to tolerate more of the chemotherapeutic agent than dogs, which were unusually sensitive (even a small dose induced convulsions). On the other hand, the dog is one of the few species to react to the drug isoniazid in a way similar to humans; the rhesus monkey is unaffected by a proportionate amount sufficient to kill the dog. In the past, many people treated with isoniazid suffered from peripheral neuritis. Tests with dogs demonstrated that they are unable to acetylate the compound completely. It was learned that humans metabolize the drug in the same way as dogs.

In the early 1960s thalidomide brought into dramatic focus the difficulty of extrapolating data from animal tests to humans. In some instances, human beings may be far more sensitive than other species; in other cases, they may be less sensitive. Indeed, the comparative sensitivity for thalidomide showed a substantial species variation. Humans are far more sensitive to thalidomide than any other species tested. The human being was found to be 10 times more sensitive to thalidomide than the baboon; 20 times more than the monkey; 60 times more than the rabbit; over 100 times more than the rat; 200 times more than the armadillo and the dog; and 700 times more than the cat. Such species variations may exist for food additives as well.

It is because of the thorny problem of species variations that current tests with additives are conducted with at least two animal species, one of which is usually a nonrodent. Toxicologists believe that if humans are similar metabolically to one or more of the species studied, the animal toxicity data can be extrapolated more reliably to humans.

While the use of two or more species may yield more accurate information, additional obstacles beset testers of food additives. The tester must decide whether inbred or randomly bred strains of study animals will be used. The choice may be crucial in the results obtained.

Inbred strains of animals are produced by mating brothers and sisters for 20 to 40 generations. The most successful inbreeding was developed first with mice, and later with rats and guinea pigs. Theoretically, such strains have similar characteristics, and the individuals are as alike as identical twins. The advantage of using inbred strains is that the tester can work with similar individuals to duplicate and verify results.

Certain characteristics, such as proneness to a particular disease, can be bred into animals. Reliable statistical analysis can be gathered more readily with an inbred line of animals than with a randomly bred group. For example, the tester will know the incidence of spontaneous tumors to expect in a control inbred group of mice that is known to be tumor-susceptible. Any increase in the tumor production rate in the other test groups can then be attributed to the effect of the substance being tested.

There is no assurance that all strains within a species will react alike. Sometimes the results are surprising. For example, strains of white rats were *not* adversely affected by thiourea, while some strains of gray rats were killed by even moderate concentrations of the additive. In another case, some strains of rats were not affected by large amounts of sugar added to their diets, but one strain was carbohydrate-sensitive and became hyperglycemic. Other wide variations from strain to strain have been demonstrated with trypan blue in the rat, with cortisone in the mouse, and with vitamin A in the rat. After many tests conducted with rats and several strains of mice failed to show any mutagenic potential of a breakdown product of cyclamate (cyclohexylamine), one strain of mice (C57 B1/Fe) demonstrated a mutagenic property in this substance. Workers in experimental teratology (the study of birth defects) know that even within inbred strains, some animal litters are affected much more severely than others. Inbred strains of test animals may also vary widely in their individual susceptibility to cancer-producing agents or to infections such as tuberculosis.

Some testers criticize the use of inbred strains of animals. A group of genetically homogenous animals does *not* represent a typical heterogenous population of animals. It is even less representative of human beings who are *always* genetically heterogenous. These critics believe that randomly bred animals give more reliable results.

The choice of inbred versus randomly bred animals becomes particularly important in testing the cancer-inducing property in a food additive. The type of cancer which can be produced experimentally differs from species to species, and a carcinogenic property may be overlooked because the strain of animals selected happened to be cancer-resistant rather than cancer-prone.

An advisory committee to the FDA recommended that randomly bred animals be used in testing for the cancer-inducing properties of food additives and pesticides. Another group of cancer experts suggested a combined approach: the progeny of two different inbred lines of animals would be crossed and the offspring used for cancer tests.

The time of day in which tests are conducted may be a crucial factor. Responses from living organisms, including test animals, may vary considerably within the 24 hour day. Scientists, studying biological rhythms, have suggested that test results may be unreliable merely because data has been gathered at varying times within the 24 hour day, when the organism may be functioning with different degrees of efficiency. This fact suggests that testing should be conducted at some specified time in order to obtain valid results.

The age of the test animal may be an essential factor in obtaining valid results. At times, the newly born animal may be adversely affected by an additive, while a juvenile or an adult is not. In other instances, the reverse may occur.

Newly born animals, including humans, develop nonregenerating tissue cells—such as kidney, brain, and muscle cells—very rapidly during the early days of their lives. If these cells are damaged by some chemical food additive at this crucial stage, they cannot be repaired later.

The importance of using newly born animals to test substances was demonstrated by tests on the flavor enhancer monosodium glutamate (see page 101).

The effects of other additives also depend on the age of the test animal. The additive thiourea is now banned. It was not acutely toxic to young rats, but it was highly toxic to old rats.

In a test series using infant and juvenile monkeys, the livers of infant monkeys were far less responsive to doses of the antioxidants BHT and BHA than the livers of juvenile monkeys. It is thought that the infant monkeys responded less because of the low activity of drug-metabolizing enzymes at that age. The enzymes are far more active in the juvenile.

Young rats and chicks were adversely affected by heat-labile substances (substances which have undergone changes due to heat) in soybean products, but mature dogs apparently remained unaffected.

Tests suggested that newly weaned mice were more susceptible to cancer-inducing qualities of specific chemicals than mice only a few weeks older. Test mice less than one day old were extremely sensitive to the cancer-inducing qualities of certain viruses that failed to induce cancer in older mice. Younger animals also have been shown to be more susceptible than adults to induced tumors. In the past, animal tests had been conducted with newly weaned animals. But in testing monosodium glutamate newly born animals were used. The cellular damage inflicted on the newly born animals was not observed on mature animals. The damage would have been overlooked in earlier testing procedures using only mature animals.

The detoxification mechanisms, efficient in the mature individual, may not be developed yet in the infant. This is illustrated by nitrate. Although some nitrate is naturally present in certain foods, it is also a serious contaminant of foods and water, as well as an intentional food additive.

While certain levels of nitrates may present no particular health problem to adults, bacteria within the body may convert these nitrates to nitrites. The nitrites react with the hemoglobin in red blood cells so that the cells lose their ability to carry oxygen, and the body is threatened with asphyxiation. This condition is called *methemoglobinemia.*

A number of circumstances make infants particularly susceptible to methemoglobinemia. Infant gastric juices have a low pH (high acidity); such a highly acidic environment is especially suitable for the conversion of nitrates to nitrites. And the infant's intestinal flora is far more apt to include nitrate-converting bacteria than an adult's. An infant's hemoglobin is also more reactive with nitrites. At the same time, infants are deficient in those enzymes which reduce methemoglobin to hemoglobin. As a result, foods and water with high nitrate content is a real hazard to infants. In the past, numerous infant deaths from water with high nitrate levels were recorded.

Infants and juveniles must not be regarded merely as miniature adults. Infant and juvenile anatomy, physiology, and body responses differ from those of adults. Some of the infant's organs are not completely developed yet and may be affected adversely by certain food additives. Since the infant is growing, he needs more energy than the mature adult. Hence, interfering with an infant's energy requirements is more dangerous than interfering with an adult's. Any toxicologic or other noxious insult results in an energy deficit. If the noxious agent continues to act, the energy deficit cannot be overcome. Growth retardation and developmental defects (both obvious and not so obvious) may result.

Furthermore, introducing a substance such as a food additive to an infant raises the possibility that the substance may be ingested throughout a long life span. This situation raises safety issues quite apart from short-term adult use.

Testing should include both sexes, since male and female animals may react differently. The female kidney cells of rhesus monkeys, in contact with the antioxidant BHT for 24 hours at very low concentration, were twice as sensitive as male kidney cells. It is thought that the effect varied according to sex because of the more rapid metabolism of BHT in male cells.

Marked discrepancies have been observed in the relative incidence rates of many cancers in male and female animals. Results suggest that the differences are attributable, at least in part, to the sex-conditioned differences in metabolism. Certain activity in the liver (hydroxylation) in untreated rats is greater in males than in females. The length of sleeping time produced by the sedative (hexobarbital), given to female rats, depended on the female's estrus cycle.

Where obvious differences, such as size and weight, between male and female animals are known to exist, due allowances must be made in evaluating experimental test results. It is possible, however, that unknown sex differences could invalidate test results.

The relative liver and kidney weights differ significantly between male and female animals. In testing, when the organ weights of treated males and females were compared separately with those of control animals of the same sex, differences caused by exposure to the test substance were often apparent. The combined male and female organ weights failed to reveal any differences. Quite often, the organ weights of only one sex were different from its controls, while no such difference was detectable in the other sex. The results of this test demonstrate that the data obtained in organ-to-body-weight studies must be considered separately for each sex.

Since tests use a limited number of animals, low incidences of adverse effects may go undetected. In practice, each dose level of a specific additive may be tested with but few compared to the millions of people who may consume the additive. Under these circumstances, the possibility is exceedingly poor that adverse effects with a low incidence, including weak carcinogens (see page 153) and weak teratogens (see page 171), will be revealed.

To illustrate, let us assume that the human is as sensitive to a particular carcinogen or teratogen as the rat or mouse. Assume further that this particular agent will produce cancer or teratogenic effects in only 1 out of 10,000 humans exposed. The chance of detecting these effects in a group of only 50 rats or mice is only 1 out of 200. Indeed, samples of 10,000 rats or mice would be required to reveal only one incident of cancer or teratogenic effects (over and above any spontaneous occurrences). For a significant test, some 30,000 rodents would be needed.

Because adverse effects may easily escape detection by conventional biological tests, it is important that food additives be administered to test animals at maximum dose levels. This should offset the gross insensitivity of testing small numbers of animals. Although this feature is widely recognized and accepted by toxicologists, unfortunately it is poorly understood by the public. Frequently, the high dosage in testing has been ridiculed by the uninformed:

—"The rats received cyclamate in doses . . . equal to what an adult would have gotten before the cyclamate ban from drinking 200 to 400 bottles of diet cola a day."

—"A woman would have to eat about 3,600 lipsticks per month to obtain an equivalent amount [of the dye administered to test animals]."

—"If DES were present in the liver at 2 ppb, you would have to eat 500 pounds of that liver to get an amount of estrogen equivalent to the daily estrogen production of a premenopausal woman."

Such statements reflect a lack of understanding that high doses are necessary because of the small number of animals tested.

To overcome the difficulty of detecting low incidences of adverse effects, "mega-mouse" tests have been suggested. Such studies would make use of as many as 100,000 mice per experiment to detect low incidences of biological damage (such as a substance's tumor-inciting properties). Proponents of mega-mouse tests hope that such studies will reveal threshold doses for carcinogens, thereby making it possible to establish "safe" doses. Opponents charge that mega-mouse experiments—estimated to cost about $15 million per study—would be prohibitively expensive. Furthermore, most of the problems in evaluating carcinogenic hazards would remain unsolved.

A standard "reproduction test" studies fertility and pregnancy in a single generation of parents–offspring. Such studies are useful. They show the effects of a substance upon the maternal uterine environment, lactation, post-weaning growth, and the offspring's development. Animals which are exposed to the additive continuously from conception should show any changes occurring during embryo growth, infancy, puberty, and reproductive maturity. The accumulation of a potentially toxic additive can be observed in the maternal reproductive performance, as well as in the offspring's growth and development.

But standard reproduction tests also should include a study of the progeny of parents which themselves have been exposed to the test substance from conception to reproductive maturity. Occasionally, effects are only observed in later generations that did not appear in earlier ones. Such effects may *not* be noted if the test is limited to a single generation of parents–offspring.

"Multigeneration tests," using three or four generations of animals, may demonstrate certain types of pathological or histopathological effects not demonstrated in other types of testing. At times, multigeneration tests have been more sensitive in demonstrating the hazardous nature of a substance than any other type of tests.

Multigeneration tests can answer many questions about the specific effects of an additive during different stages of the reproduction cycle. In recent years, there has been increased awareness of the importance of such effects:

—Is the LD_{50} toxicity of the additive the same for the mother and the fetus?

—Does the additive affect the immature animal differently than it affects the mature animal?

—Does the additive concentrate in the reproductive system, the placenta, the gonads, or elsewhere?

—Are there specific histopathologic or gross effects in organs such as the pituitary, male or female gonads, or secondary sex organs?

—Does the additive affect the libido of the animals?

—Does the additive affect the formation and maturation of the gonads, gametes (mature germ cells, as sperms or eggs), combination of gametes (fertilization), implantation (attachment of embryo to maternal uterine wall), or the continued function of corpus luteum (an endocrine body present during pregnancy) and the placenta?

—Is the onset and completion of parturition normal?

—Is lactation normal and is the milk quality satisfactory?

—Are there any congenital malformations or abnormalities in the offspring?

Multigeneration tests can provide an overall view of reproduction function which is not achieved by single specific tests. In some animal reproduction studies with a number of different chemical compounds, effects were shown to include stunted growth, as well as depressed fertility, viability, and lactation. These effects had *not* been demonstrated in chronic toxicity studies.

In another set of multigeneration studies (with pesticides and certain combinations of pesticides), the viability of mice was not reduced until the second or third generation. In one group of mice, no reduced viability was observed in the first three generations; but in the fourth generation, viability of the first and second litters was reduced.

In evaluating the no-effect level of chemical compounds, multigeneration studies were crucial. Although one of the substances (administered at relatively high doses for a year) failed to produce an effect in rhesus monkeys, the same compound administered at a very low dosage (0.025 percent of the diet) caused dramatic interference with parturition in subsequent generations of rats.

Unfortunately, multigeneration studies require more time and money than standard reproduction studies. But multigeneration tests are important. Any interference with the reproductive process is undesirable, and no segment of the human population should be exposed to food additives capable of producing such effects.

The route by which a substance is administered to animals is another important factor in testing. The substance may be administered by injection (subcutaneous, intramuscular, or intraperitoneal), skin painting, gavage (a tube to the stomach), ingestion, or inhalation. Only certain methods may be appropriate for the substance being tested. Obviously, since food additives are eaten with food, the ingestion route is commonly used. However, other routes also may yield valuable information. In each case, the tester must choose what he considers an appropriate method. Test results may depend upon the choice. For example, one study found both quantitative and qualitative differences in brain lesions induced by monosodium glutamate administered by two different routes (oral and subcutaneous) in each of two different species (mice and monkeys).

The appropriateness of certain routes of administering substances and the validity of test results from various routes have created a scientific furor in recent times. The resolution of this furor affects the health and welfare of 200 million Americans.

The Delaney Clause provides that "no additive shall be deemed safe if it is found to induce cancer when ingested by man or animal, or if it is found, after tests which are appropriate for the evaluation of the safety of food additives, to induce cancer in man or animal." The phrase "tests which are appropriate" became crucial. A year after the Delaney Clause became effective, the Food Protection Committee of the Food and Nutrition Board issued a report, "Problems in the Evaluation of Carcinogenic Hazards from Use of Food Additives," in which the various methods of administering carcinogenic tests were discussed. The report was critical of subcutaneous injection, charging that the technique "does not withstand a critical appraisal," and several characteristics "throw doubt on its usefulness." The report stated that subcutaneous tests, used repeatedly with large doses of substances, were "of limited value and of dubious interpretation."

The downgrading of subcutaneous injection was done by a "scientific" panel that included industry-associated individuals. The report permitted industry to repudiate subcutaneous tests for determining the cancer-inciting properties of many consumer goods, including food additives.

Traditionally, cancer specialists had considered a substance carcinogenic if it produced cancer in any species of test animals, regardless of the route used. As a rule, subcutaneous injection had been found to be the *most sensitive* method: it was the method which had been used to find the majority of carcinogens.

Dr. Wilhelm C. Hueper, then chief of the Environmental Cancer Section of the National Cancer Institute, disputed the arguments set forth in the Food and Nutrition Board's report. He charged that the widely accepted subcutaneous tests were downgraded only after environmental chemical carcinogens had become a serious, practical, and economically important issue. Up to that time, objections had not been raised against the scientific and practical validity of this procedure. Its appropriateness was challenged only when subcutaneous testing became unsuitable for industries' needs. Hueper stated:

[The policy] has opened, intentionally or unintentionally . . . the door to a legalized inclusion of carcinogenic chemicals in consumer goods, especially foodstuffs, and thereby has become the pernicious instrument in perpetuating the avoidable and needless exposure of the general public to certain environmental chemical cancer hazards.

Hueper's prediction proved correct. The downgrading of subcutaneous tests has resulted in the FDA justifying the use of actual or potential cancer-inciting substances in foods and other consumer goods. The Delaney Clause does not justify a distinction between oral and subcutaneous carcinogenicity. This interpretation, made by the FDA, has been branded as "arbitrary and unscientifically unsound."

By rejecting subcutaneous test results, the FDA has sanctioned the continued use of food dyes which are known to be cancer-inciters. Repeated subcutaneous injections of triphenylmethane dyes (FD&C Blue No. 1, also known as Brilliant Blue FCF; FD&C Green No. 3, also known as Fast Green FCF), investigated both here and abroad, have induced malignant tumors in rats. This evidence has been sufficient to prohibit their use in foodstuffs in several European countries, but the FDA considers the evidence "inadequate."

Another scientific furor about the appropriateness of administration methods has developed more recently. In this case, the appropriateness of pellet implants was questioned.

Dr. George T. Bryan and coworkers at the Division of Clinical Oncology at the medical school of the University of Wisconsin had devised carcinogenicity tests with sodium cyclamate. Pellets composed either of pure cholesterol or sodium cyclamate and cholesterol were surgically implanted in the bladders of mice. The bladders' exposure to sodium cyclamate was very brief, since half of the compound disappeared from the pellets in about one hour. The animals in each group were allowed to survive for 13 months; but the bladder of any animal surviving for more than 175 days was examined microscopically for the presence of cancer. The sodium cyclamate-treated mice had a high incidence of urinary bladder cancer. Bryan pointed out that *it was only after this demonstration of the carcinogenic activity of sodium cyclamate for mouse bladder that any attention was drawn to the urinary bladder as an organ susceptible to the carcinogenicity of this compound.* Bryan reported that the pellet implant technique was highly sensitive and was a useful predictive tool with bladder carcinogenicity of orally administered cyclamate. Pellet implant studies were then extended to saccharin.

Subsequent to the publication of Bryan's studies with cyclamates and saccharin the Food Protection Committee downgraded the pellet implant technique for carcinogenicity tests:

Tests for carcinogenic effects by applying saccharin to the skin, by subcutaneous injection, or by implanting pellets into the bladder have no known relevance to the safety of saccharin consumed orally. In light of present knowledge, positive results by any one or a combination of these tests, as they have been conducted thus far, cannot be accepted as evidence of a positive effect through dietary intake. Nor, conversely, can negative results of such tests be accepted as reliable evidence of the noncarcinogenicity of a substance when consumed in the diet. In the case of saccharin, we feel that negative results in well designed and properly executed long-term feeding tests in two species of animals would indicate the absence of any carcinogenic hazard and would override the finding that bladder cancer is produced by pellet implantation.

On the basis of this report, the FDA announced that methods which did not involve oral administration were considered inappropriate indices to the cancer-inducing properties of saccharin. Despite the official downgrading, Bryan is supported by other authorities who assert that the pellet implant technique *is* a valid method of assessing the carcinogenic potential of a food additive.

Administration methods deemed inappropriate by some may still yield useful information. This point was made by Samuel S. Epstein, M.D., a cancer researcher, who added that extrapolation from such data to human experience should be done cautiously. However, to demonstrate weak carcinogens (see page 153) in the environment, Epstein said that using *the most sensitive* available test system is essential and that the comparability administration methods should be subordinated to the sensitivity requirement. After an effect has been clearly established, *then* the quantitative relevance of the experimental data to the human situation should be considered before limits can be reasonably proposed:

Only at this stage does it become appropriate to weigh factors such as route of administration. To use such factors in a limiting sense, and to insist on precise comparability between test systems and human exposure before the problem of hazard is established, may effectively limit the possibility of detecting weak environmental carcinogens.

Epstein's emphasis on using the most sensitive available test system should be applied to teratogens, too. In recent years, the chick embryo test (a quick screening preliminary method to detect potential teratogens) was developed by researchers in the Division of Toxicology and Evaluation of the FDA. The test substance is injected into chick eggs. At the end of the incubation period the chicks can be examined for possible birth defects. Since there is no placental barrier to cross, this technique assures that the embryo comes into direct contact with the test substance.

The chick embryo test was instrumental in exposing thalidomide as a teratogen. The test demonstrated the teratogenic effects of some agricultural chemicals (captan; folpet; and the contaminant, dioxin, in 2,4,5-T) and food additives (FD&C Red No. 2; monosodium glutamate; cyclamates; and cyclohexylamine, a breakdown product of calcium cyclamate).

The chick embryo technique is relatively inexpensive. It can give a large sampling, since thousands of eggs can be used to test a single chemical. It is also remarkably rapid. For example, it is estimated that chick embryo studies could have warned scientists about thalidomide's dangers in *three weeks;* epidemiologists needed *three years* to make the discovery.

The chick embryo technique has been downgraded by its detractors, including a cyclamate manufacturer, and the Food Protection Committee. In reviewing nonnutritive sweeteners, the committee reported: "Chick egg injection teratogenic experiments cannot be extrapolated to man in the face of other mammalian feeding experiments in which no evidence of fetal malformation was found." However, such claims have never been made by proponents of the chick embryo test. Researchers using chick embryo tests are aware of their limitations. The absence of a placenta makes it difficult to extrapolate results when any morphologic changes are noted in the chick embryo. However, the chick embryo is *extremely sensitive* to noxious substances and has revealed toxic effects not demonstrated by other tests. Thalidomide's malforming effects had been demonstrated with the chick embryo technique, whereas these effects had not been revealed in rat experiments. Consequently, the sensitivity of this test should be regarded as an asset. If a substance demonstrates an effect by means of this technique, the relevance of the data to humans can then be studied.

Toxicological hazards increase as the number of compounds introduced into the environment increases. The need for improved, sophisticated testing techniques and tools for analyzing substances such as food additives has become urgent. That present testing methods are inadequate for the task is illustrated by the testing programs used to monitor additives used in the production of food animals.

FDA regulations required a two-part test for detecting DES residues in edible tissue. The first part was a biologic test, a bioassay. This procedure determined the relative strength of a substance by comparing its effects on test animals with those of a standard preparation. The sensitivity of the bioassay test, at a level of only 2 ppb for DES, was not sufficiently low, nor could it identify the specific estrogen present.

The second part was a chemical test, which served to determine whether the estrogen present was DES. But this method was impractical for regulatory purposes because it took three to four weeks to complete. Also, for residue monitoring purposes, such tests required large numbers of animals. This method of detecting DES residues had been approved prior to the enactment of the food additives amendment. Dr. Van Houweling, director of the Bureau of Veterinary Medicine of the FDA, acknowledged that if such a test method were submitted today, it would not be approved by the FDA.

Despite this shortcoming, the FDA approved a new animal drug application for DES in 1970. Since present test methods were impractical for the USDA to enforce, the FDA had the legal responsibility to require submission of a practical method of analysis before approving the application. But the FDA ignored the requirement and consented to use a nonapproved test method for DES regulatory purposes. Both the FDA and the USDA failed to follow federal regulations requiring approved and published methods of analysis for detecting carcinogenic substances in the edible tissues of animals.

The USDA chemist responsible for methods development characterized chemical analysis for DES and other hormone residues as "a vagrant concept of a few regulatory chemists." He termed the difficulty of regulating these residues as "a regulatory control chemist's 'nightmare.'"

After evaluating the testing methods, Dr. M. Adrian Gross, assistant director for Scientific Coordination, Office of Pharmaceutical Research and Testing of the FDA, warned the agency about their inadequacies. In an internal FDA memorandum, Gross wrote:

The chemical [test] used by USDA is one which, to our knowledge, has never been evaluated as to sensitivity by a collaborative study and Dr. [Daniel] Banes [Director, Office of Pharmaceutical Research and Testing, Bureau of Drugs, FDA] informs us that it is his impression that the chemical method may in fact have a sensitivity . . . comparatively poorer than the biologic method, and we have [demonstrated] that the latter is not nearly good enough.

Gross then described work in progress to increase the sensitivity of the biologic method, and then added:

It is extremely unlikely, if not well-nigh impossible, that under the best of circumstances and with the best of fortunes, the sensitivity of the analytic procedure would approach anything of what is needed. . . .

A number of growth-promoting hormones other than DES used in the production of food animals also are suspected carcinogens. And their testing programs also are inadequate. Both dienestrol and estradiol are officially sanctioned for use in the production of food animals. In September 1969, the USDA and the FDA jointly discussed the possibility of including these two hormone drugs in the USDA's planned 1970 monitoring program. The agencies decided against their inclusion since "no analytical methods that are acceptable are available."

Melengestrol acetate (MGA), another sex hormone used extensively for the same purpose, is another suspected carcinogen that cannot be monitored adequately at present. The current testing method is incapable of detecting MGA in tissue any lower than 25 ppb. USDA researchers believe that the method of detecting hormones such as MGA should be accurate to 2 to 4 ppb.

In 1970, the USDA initiated a monitoring program for MGA residues in meat. The program was quickly dropped when it became apparent that the FDA-approved testing method resulted in erroneous findings. Both agencies agreed that the official testing method should not be used for enforcement purposes.

The congressional committee investigating DES and other drugs used in food-producing animals harshly criticized both the FDA and USDA for using public funds to improve inadequate testing methods for drugs such as MGA and DES. The congressmen charged that *if a practical testing method had been required of the manufacturer when these drugs were approved, as the law demands, there would be no need now to expend public funds to develop a satisfactory regulatory method.*

In addition to growth-promoting hormones, antimicrobial drugs (such as furaltadone, furazolidone, or nihydrazone) are used in the production of meat animals. Although residues of these drugs or their breakdown products have been found to accumulate in the edible tissues of treated animals, the FDA and the USDA do not have practical methods of detecting them.

A wide range of antibiotics is used in animal feed, but present analytical methods lack the specificity to identify individual antibiotics or their breakdown products as residues. Residues of these substances found in edible animal tissue are regarded as potential human health hazards. Clayton Yeutter, assistant secretary of the USDA, reported:

One of the problems showing up in the objective samples [of meat animals] is the frequency of antibiotic residues in veal calves. Somewhere between five and ten percent of all veal calves have such residues in their tissues. Most of the materials are residual traces of treatments given during the short life of these animals and can be readily identified. Others cannot be identified with present test methods, and we don't know what they are. Under these circumstances, it is very difficult for our people to discuss the problem with other federal and state agencies and to try tracing the residues back to their origin in order to stop whatever practice may be causing them.

Nitrosamines and their derivatives (see pages 88–91) are another example of substances for which present testing methods are inadequate. These potentially hazardous compounds may be in a wide variety of foods. Yet the analytical methods used to detect them lack both sensitivity and specificity.

Toxicologists recognize that different analytical methods are not equally valuable. Also, the use of a single analytical procedure is rarely, if ever, adequate to establish a substance's chemical identity. Therefore, more than one method should be used to examine a test substance.

Newer equipment and techniques developed for other fields could be applied to food additive testing. The mass spectrometer, used with the gas-liquid chromatograph, is a powerful analytical tool. A procedure termed mass fragmentography could be used to solve many toxicological problems, such as the detection of nitrosamines, or the detection of chemical additives migrating from food packaging materials into foods. Such equipment and techniques are not generally used in toxicology (except for pesticide measurement). Yet, they could help scientists cope with the needs for greater sensitivity and specificity in food additive testing.

6

The Intricate Interrelationships

- We know so little about many [food additives], and what we do know tends to raise one's doubts rather than allay them.

G. Roche Lynch

- Are the results of . . . chronic toxicity studies to *one specific chemical*, made in animals and under ideal laboratory conditions, applicable to *humans* who are daily subjected—often during their lifetime—to *this* chemical and to many related chemical exposures? Is not modern man's increasing chemical environment impinging on his health and general welfare? [emphasis supplied]

Theron G. Randolph, M.D.

- Even when . . . chemical substances have passed through a battery of tests from the point of view of toxicology, unexpected harmful results have often ultimately been demonstrated. Medical science often cannot give adequate answers to questions of toxicological action, not only as regards new compositions but even in the case of substances long in use. Indeed, to the medical man unpleasant surprises are constantly being revealed, in the case of both drugs and of chemicals used in food preparations.

Sir Edward Mellanby, M.D.

- As Dr. [René] Dubos has pointed out, the traditional laboratory approach which is designed to minimize the influence of extraneous factors is "extremely effective for the discovery of agents of disease and for the study of some of their properties." But it may even delay "recognition of the many other factors that play a part in the causation of disease."

William D. Ruckelshaus, Administrator of the Environmental Protection Agency

- Some of the most troublesome chemical exposures have not been adequately described and there is no general knowledge of their potential *hazards*. The chief reason for this is that these materials have become integral parts of our current existence. Not being readily avoided accidentally, they are not usually suspected. Not being suspected, they are not usually avoided deliberately. [emphasis supplied]

Theron G. Randolph, M.D.

Test animals are raised in a controlled environment. To obtain valid data, they must be well fed and have clean air, pure water, adequate room, and a minimum of stress. If any of these factors are altered, they are done so by design. Humans live in an uncontrolled environment. They may be poorly fed, or they may be exposed to polluted air and water or other noxious substances such as tobacco, alcohol, and drugs. They may live in crowded conditions or be exposed to many other daily stresses. With such divergent living conditions, how meaningful is it to extrapolate animal test results for humans?

The importance of laboratory animal diets was discussed recently at a conference concerned with carcinogenic testing procedures. Discussion centered around the diets of rodents used in carcinogenicity tests and how such diets can influence test results. A comparison was made of the test results from different laboratories, and emphasis was given to the need for study and standardization of test diets, so that experiments are repeatable. The conference participants recommended the use of semisynthetic diets, free of known enzyme inducers and antioxidants, and diets with standardized levels of protein, fat, carbohydrates, vitamins, and minerals.

The dietary choices made in animal experiments, whether testing for cancer-inducing properties or other forms of biological harm, are important. Even minor alterations in diet can change test results.

Evidence demonstrates that well-nourished animals can withstand the assault of chemicals better than malnourished ones:

—Sulfites, a group of commonly used preservatives, are recognized as destroyers of thiamine (vitamin B_1). Animals on nutritionally adequate diets withstood the destruction of thiamine, even when fed high levels of sulfites.

—The growth of cancer was tenfold greater in animals lacking riboflavin (vitamin B_2) in their diet than with control animals fed adequate amounts of this vitamin.

—Diabetic hamsters were more sensitive to the adverse effects of calcium cyclamate than healthy ones.

—The magnitude of peak concentrations of saccharin in blood and tissue levels depended on whether the animals had been fed or starved prior to the administration of the additive.

—Dietary malnutrition or some metabolic disturbance of the body can alter the type of metabolite formed. For example, dietary conditions altered the metabolism of a recognized cancer-inciter (o-aminoazotoluene) in rats. Rats fed a low-protein diet had a decreased ability to destroy this harmful dye, and the level of the dye, which became bound to the protein in the animal's liver, was increased. However, when the rat received a diet containing high levels of protein and riboflavin, the animal became increasingly resistant to the liver cancer-inducing property of the dye.

—In the case of another dye (paradimethylaminoazobenzene), formerly used in foods and drugs, quantities failing to induce cancer in well-fed test animals induced cancer in animals on less adequate diets.

—Laboratory animals deficient in vitamin A were more susceptible to liver cancer from aflatoxin molds than animals on nutritionally balanced diets. Both laboratory animals and birds suffered from the toxic effects of aflatoxins when their diet was low in protein.

—An emulsifier (polyoxyethylene-(40)-stearate) caused an abnormal increase in the number of stomach cells (often indicative of cancer) when rats were fed a diet deficient in vitamin A, but not when they were fed a normal diet.

Dietary manipulation by testers may alter an experiment so that it becomes difficult to evaluate the results. For example, adverse effects from the antioxidant BHT were found in rats when lard comprised 20 percent of their diet. Since the lard constituted an abnormally high and stressful level in the diet, were the results valid?

An increase of fat in the diet is known to influence the toxicity of substances such as DDT and derris (an insecticide of plant origin). A high proportion of fat in the diet of experimental animals increased the incidence of neoplasms (a new growth of tissue, serving no physiologic function, and potentially malignant) induced in the skin and mammary glands.

Protein deficiency may also increase a substance's toxicity. Some "relatively safe" pesticides were shown to be extremely toxic on single or multiple administration to protein-deficient animals.

Dietary manipulation also has been shown to affect results with human volunteers. The antioxidant BHA was more rapidly absorbed when it was administered to humans with a milk–olive oil suspension. When the BHA breakdown product was administered, also in the milk–olive oil suspension, most of it was excreted from the body in half the time it took without the suspension. The remaining portion was also excreted more rapidly with the suspension.

Obviously, an individual's reaction to a specific additive depends in part on his nutritional state. Testing food additives in well-nourished laboratory animals cannot give accurate information concerning possible adverse effects on the general human population since many individuals live on diets with marginal or submarginal levels of essential nutrients. The implications that can be drawn from pesticide tests are especially important to those living in countries where the general diet is low in protein or to people who, for a variety of reasons, may have low protein diets.

Even the diets of well-fed people may not be comparable to those eaten by test animals. Foods for the animals may not be prepared under conditions identical to those used in preparation of meals for human beings. Foods for humans, for example, are heated or cooked in fats. Such treatments may destroy nutrients, form toxic substances, or modify the foods in other ways.

Animal studies have shown the beneficial effects of dietary fiber in counteracting the toxic effects of some food additives, other chemicals, and drugs. When high levels of food additives such as emulsifiers (polyoxyethylene compounds), sodium cyclamate, and FD&C Red No. 2 were fed to animals on purified, low-fiber diets, the additives were toxic. However, animals fed diets containing adequate amounts of dietary fiber were protected. Since current dietary fiber intake of Americans is estimated to be only 20 percent that of the mid-19th century, the researchers suggested that:

Serious questions arise as to whether the ingestion of drugs, chemicals and food additives that may be without deleterious effects when ingested by persons on high-fiber diets may not constitute a hazard to health for a substantial portion of the population. . . .

The general human population contains a certain percentage of anatomically, functionally, metabolically, or nutritionally abnormal or defective persons. Hueper suggested that animals with artificially altered function of metabolically important organs (the liver, kidney, gastrointestinal tract, thyroid, adrenal, and pancreas) should be included in tests. Hueper said that such experiments are needed because abnormal humans may react differently to carcinogens than normal ones. They may produce metabolites that differ in their biologic properties from those normally generated. For example, impaired function of certain organs may cause some people to retain dyes over longer periods of time than normal persons; these people may even excrete the dyes through channels which are not ordinarily used. Such individuals may respond to the carcinogenic quality of a food dye or other substance differently than the majority of the population.

Others have pointed out additional shortcomings of animal test diets. For example, obesity (prevalent in humans but not usually present in laboratory animals) can affect the metabolism and storage of toxic compounds. A toxic substance is of special concern whenever it is stored in fatty tissues. In a lactating woman, the substance may be transferred to the infant during breastfeeding. In an individual who undergoes a period of severe, moderate, or even mild starvation, the substance may be released and induce acute intoxication long after ingestion or exposure to the substance has ceased.

If an individual's diet contains only a bare minimum of an essential nutrient, an additive may create a dietary deficiency where none had previously existed. For example, when food treated with an additive is cooked, the additive may adversely affect a vitamin or other essential nutrient either by destroying a portion of it or by combining with it to form a nonabsorbable compound or one with a different metabolic function. The substance also could compete with the vitamin in certain of the body's metabolic reactions.

An additive may affect changes in the body's absorption and utilization of nutrients. Sorbitol, a rare sugar sweetener, can affect the absorption of vitamin B_6. Sodium lauryl sulfate, a surfactant, can affect the absorption of food constituents such as glucose or methionine. Toxicologists admit that this is a neglected area of research.

The fatalities of heavy beer drinkers (see page 19) resulting from cobaltous salts dramatized the need to recognize special risk groups of individuals. The cobaltous salts were used in both bottled and draft beer. But the bottled beer was treated with sulfur dioxide, which destroyed the thiamine. In experiments with rats, thiamine-deficiency has been found to be more important than protein-deficiency in increasing cobaltous-induced heart lesions. Even if the cobaltous salts were primarily responsible for the fatalities suffered by heavy beer drinkers, a predisposing factor was the high alcoholic intake accompanied by a poor nutritional status with a low level of thiamine. This combination made heavy beer drinkers especially vulnerable to the cardiotoxic action of the cobaltous salts.

Examination of infants ingesting high nitrate levels from community water supplies showed that their health had a significant effect on the methemoglobin levels. Infants with respiratory illness or diarrhea had the highest levels. No acutely ill infants were examined, but it is possible that they would have suffered far more from methemoglobinemia.

Although maltol and ethyl maltol occur naturally in some foods, they have also been synthesized. They are used to enhance the flavor and aroma of fruit-, vanilla-, and chocolate-flavored foods and beverages. Individuals with thalassemia (an inherited anemia) may be adversely affected by foods treated with maltol and ethyl maltol since these additives lower the hemoglobin levels in blood and deposit additional hemosiderin (a breakdown product from the red blood cells). Thalassemic children and adolescents, who commonly consume large amounts of chocolate desserts and fruit-based drinks, are exposed to even graver risks from eating foods and beverages containing maltol and ethyl maltol.

Even well-nourished animals may be affected by additives that interact with constituents in their food:

—Ethylene oxide, a fumigant, destroys almost completely many fractions of vitamin B (thiamine, niacin, riboflavin, pyridoxine, and folic acid). It may also destroy two amino acids (histadine and methionine). Rats failed to grow on specially purified gas-treated diets.

—Methyl bromide is a widely used fumigant for stored grain, dried milk, meat, and dried fruit. Although it is toxic, when fresh air is permitted to enter the fumigated area, methyl bromide evaporates quickly and leaves but little residue. Hence, it was considered fairly innocuous.

However, Japanese physicians reported that more than 10,000 Japanese now suffer from subacute myeloptic neuropathy, a condition which produces many symptoms (lowered resistance to infection and stress, gastrointestinal disturbances, impaired vision, and spinal cord degeneration). The physicians believe that the condition is caused, not by any methyl bromide residue on the foods, but rather by pantothenic acid-deficiency induced by methyl bromide fumigation. Using infrared spectrophotometry, investigators analyzed food before and after fumigation. They discovered that fumigation changed pantothenic acid into another, as yet unidentified, compound.

The nutritive destruction in methyl bromide-treated foods was confirmed by another study. Farmers filed legal suits against many seedsmen in the United States and claimed serious losses when fumigated seeds failed to germinate. Pantothenic acid occurs naturally in nearly all growing things and is regarded as a natural growth stimulant. Investigation showed that seed fumigation interfered with germination of every type of seed tested. Even seeds which were still viable after methyl bromide treatment showed signs of abnormality.

—Although chlorine dioxide, a commonly used flour bleach, does not form toxic substances, it does injure the flour. Both chemical and biological tests have demonstrated that flour treated with chlorine dioxide at about the ordinary commercial level causes almost complete destruction of the vitamin E in the flour. (Up to 90 percent of the vitamin E in grain is also destroyed by flaking, shredding, puffing, and other cereal-producing processes.)

—Solvents, used in some types of food processing, may react with certain protein components and either destroy nutrients (essential amino acids) or produce toxic compounds which remain in the food. At various times, and in different countries, trichloroethylene was used to extract oil-bearing seeds, especially from dry soybeans. Almost invariably, cattle fed the extracted beans developed aplastic anemia. The toxic factor was *not* due to the solvent residue in the oil meal or to any product formed by the solvent. Rather, the toxic factor was a reaction product formed from the protein in the soybean and liberated in the solvent's presence. After this formation became recognized, the commercial production of trichloroethylene-extracted soybean meal was abandoned.

—Sulfites (sulfur dioxide, sodium bisulfite, sodium metabisulfite, etc.) are widely used as preservatives in foods and beverages. These compounds destroy dietary nutrients, such as thiamine, and interact with another vitamin, folic acid. Recently, test-tube experiments demonstrated that sulfites were capable of modifying the ribonucleic acid (RNA) system to such an extent that it no longer functioned as a messenger for protein synthesis.

—EDTA (ethylenediamine tetraacetic acid) is an additive used to trap metal impurities. It is listed on the labels of many salad dressings, margarines, sandwich spreads, and canned shellfish; but it also is used in many other items where it is not declared on the label: processed fruits and vegetables, beer and soft drinks. Individuals who consume many processed foods have a high intake of EDTA. EDTA combines with calcium, iron, and other essential nutrients and prevents them from being utilized. It may interact with essential as well as nonessential metals in the body at different sites and under different conditions.

—Polyoxyethelene derivatives, used as emulsifiers and defoaming agents, may alter absorption from the intestine. In animals, these compounds caused abnormally large amounts of iron to be absorbed from ordinary foods and deposited in the cecum, spleen, and liver. Excessive iron storage in these organs can lead to cirrhosis and other diseases.

—Various studies with cattle, sheep, pigs, chickens, and rats showed that nitrates and nitrites inhibited intestinal absorption, causing decreased liver storage of vitamin A. High levels of these compounds in animal forages led to vitamin A deficiencies even when the livestock was fed adequate amounts of carotene (a vitamin A precursor).

—Mineral oil is another food additive that interferes with the absorption of essential nutrients from the digestive tract and may lead to nutritional deficiencies. At one time, mineral oil was used as an ingredient in salad dressings for individuals who wished to restrict their fat intake. Between 1941 and 1945, clinical research showed that mineral oil, ingested before mealtime, interfered with the absorption of various fat-soluble vitamins (especially A and D) from the digestive tract, consequently interfering with the utilization of minerals (especially calcium and phosphorus). Researchers recognized that the use of mineral-oil salad dressings could lead to deficiency diseases. The hazard was of special concern to pregnant women, since the use of mineral oil predisposed the newborn infant to hemorrhage disease. The substance could no longer be viewed merely as a substitute for a valuable food ingredient, but rather as a potentially harmful one. It became clear that mineral oil should never be used with food. After a series of protracted, strongly contested legal actions, the FDA finally prohibited the use of mineral oil as a food ingredient. Ironically, the agency still permits the use of mineral oil as a food additive: it is used as a release agent, binder, coating agent for fruits and vegetables, and a component in defoamers.

An additive safety test must investigate all of the additive's salts because different salts may produce different biological effects. Unless all of the salts are examined, test results may be misleading. For example, the teratogenic quality of the dye carmine was found to vary, depending on the salt being tested. The sodium salt of carmine, injected subcutaneously into pregnant mice, produced only a slight teratogenic effect; the lithium salt of carmine produced a pronounced one. In another case, the sodium salt of saccharin demonstrated a possible mutagenic effect. However, saccharin acid and its ammonium and calcium salts failed to show this effect.

Impurities in a food additive may result in erroneous or contradictory test results. For example, orthotoluene sulfonamide, a common contaminant of saccharin, is closely related to a known cancer-inciting substance. Karaya and tragacanth, two vegetable gums widely used as food additives, have induced a variety of allergic reactions in individuals. When tested with skin patches, these additives have produced positive reactions. However, allergists suspect that the reactions are due to gum contaminants, rather than from the gums themselves.

Accurate testing of artificial food flavorings and food dyes has often been hampered by the presence of impurities. The potential teratogenic hazards of FD&C Red No. 2 remain uncertain, in part, because of the impurities of this dye during testing. Two food dyes, Yellow AB and Yellow OB were banned because some of a highly potent human carcinogenic substance (beta-naphthylamine), used in producing these dyes, remained unreacted and appeared in the finished dyes as an impurity.

Safety tests on a food additive should include a study of the breakdown products formed during processing or storage of a treated food. Unless all of these compounds are examined, test results are incomplete.

Breakdown products sometimes produce surprises. Although the original "parent" compound may be relatively innocuous, the newly formed one may be toxic:

—Agene (nitrogen trichloride), a flour bleach used for over 25 years, was assumed to be innocuous. However, tests discovered that it combined with methionine, an essential amino acid present in flour, to form toxic methionine sulfoximine.

—Trichloroethylene is a solvent used in food processing. It can combine with cysteine, a common constituent in protein, to form toxic S-dichlorovinyl-L-cysteine.

—Ethylene and propylene oxides are used as gas fumigants when steam sterilization is impractical (see page 78). Ethylene oxide (used with spices, cocoa, flour, starch, dried egg powder, desiccated coconut, dried fruits, and dehydrated vegetables) reacts chemically with foods containing components of inorganic chlorides. The reaction product ethylene chlorohydrin is toxic and remains in the food. Propylene oxide is less reactive than ethylene oxide, but it also forms a toxic reaction product, propylene chlorohydrin. Being nonvolatile and chemically nonreactive, chlorohydrins form long-lasting residues.

A food additive may break down to unknown or unidentified new compounds. In 1973, officials of the Animal and Plant Health Protection Service (APHIS) of the USDA reported an unidentified antimicrobial compound as residue in veal calves. Officials suspected that the unidentified substance might be a breakdown product of a group of antibiotics, tetracyclines, used in the calves' feed. The hazards of such compounds must also be evaluated.

Food contaminants sometimes form breakdown products that add to already existing problems:

—Ethylene bisdithiocarbamates are fungicides (substances used to destroy fungus) used on many food crops since 1934. One of their breakdown products is ethylene thiourea (ETU). Although this substance was recognized as a potential health hazard as early as 1948, it was not until 1969 that researchers demonstrated that ETU fed to test animals in large doses over long periods caused thyroid cancer. As late as April 1972, William D. Ruckelshaus (then Administrator of the Environmental Protection Agency) announced that the fungicide manufacturers had agreed to reduce levels of the parent compound in their products and assured the public that there was no evidence that ETU residues occurred in commercially marketed crops. By September 1972, however, Canadian officials reported finding ETU residues at measurable levels in apples and spinach shipped from the United States. ETU was found to have formed while the crops were being stored. Researchers admitted the difficulty of setting any new tolerance level for ETU, since the level of the breakdown product fluctuated.

—Certain pesticides have been found to convert to more toxic forms after their application. Aldrin, recovered in the soil, was found to convert to the more toxic dieldrin. Another pesticide, heptachlor, after being in the soil or in plant and animal tissues, was found to convert to a far more toxic form, heptachlor epoxide, after a brief time.

—Certain pesticides change into more toxic substances in the presence of sunlight. Heptachlor, exposed to sunlight, forms a compound 20 times as toxic. Parathion, a nonpersistent but highly toxic pesticide, changes in sunlight to a substance which may increase the toxic effects of the remaining parathion.

Another unanticipated effect of breakdown products was discovered in testing DDT. In the presence of sunlight, DDT converts to polychlorinated biphenyl. The polychlorinated biphenyls (PCBs) are industrial chemicals suspected of widespread environmental contamination. PCBs have been found in fish, eggs, poultry, vegetable oils, milk, meat, cereal, baby food, animal feed, food packaging, and drinking water. In turn, some of the compounds formed when PCBs themselves break down are more toxic than the original PCBs. Such data emphasize the need to study breakdown products of food additives and other substances before they are introduced into the environment.

There is at least one case of a food dye degrading to another. Canned white cherries are sometimes colored with the food dye erythrosine (FD&C Red No. 3) by adding the dye to the covering syrup. Erythrosine is the only food dye permitted for this purpose. Samples of such artificially dyed cherries, processed in unlacquered cans, were found to appear greenish-yellow after being stored for two weeks at room temperature. After nine months of storage, the product contained considerable amounts of this new dye, fluorescein. Upon investigation, it was discovered that fluorescein was formed in the presence of metallic iron and/or tin and an organic acid. By a strange coincidence, all three substances were present in the cherries packaged in unlacquered cans. An electrochemical reduction had taken place, and erythrosine had degraded to fluorescein. Fluorescein is not certified for food use. Since it is a photo-sensitizer, continued ingestion of fluorescein may produce a sensitivity and a consequent allergic reaction to sunlight.

Food packaging materials are approved for safety and monitored by the FDA because chemicals in food packaging may react with food. Newer safety tests make use of tritium or carbon-14 as tracers to study the migration of plastic additives from packaging materials or of waxes from the linings of glass containers. The interaction between chemicals used in packaging food constituents is a potential problem. Some convenience foods are packaged in plastic bags which also serve as cooking containers. This practice may not be as safe as is commonly assumed. Cooking heat is usually high enough to decompose the plastic material and release certain toxic substances from the plastic into the food. Such toxins include highly poisonous hexamethyleneamine, slightly toxic hexylamine, and methylamine (of unknown toxicity).

In 1970, professionals at Johns Hopkins reported that two phthalate plasticizers (often used in polyvinyl chloride plastic bags used to store human blood and in the tubing through which blood is passed into heart, lung, and kidney machines) may be leached out of the plastic and into the blood. These plasticized polyvinyl chloride packaging materials are also used in food wrap film and closures, as plasticizing components of pesticides, and in consumer goods such as cosmetics.

Do these phthalic acid esters present a human health hazard? The plasticizers have been found localized in the mitochondria of heart muscle cells of cows, dogs, rabbits, and rats. It is unclear whether the phthalate esters occur naturally or are picked up as an environmental pollutant. Other studies have found further effects of phthalic acid. It can be synthesized in the rat's liver, and some bacteria can make diesters of phthalic acid. Chick heart cells in a culture medium stopped beating when exposed to microscopic quantities of the plasticizer, and almost all of the cells died within

24 hours. Phthalate esters have also been shown to be teratogenic in chickens and in rats.

Recently, tragic human evidence revealed that industrial workers exposed to polyvinyl chloride for from 10 to 30 years have developed fatal angiosarcoma, a rare liver cancer. In view of these findings, the "prior sanction status" granted polyvinyl chloride plastic by the FDA for food-contact applications was revoked until its safety or toxicity can be established. The problem is not with the plastic polymer itself, but with residues of a vinyl chloride monomer (a simple, unpolymerized form of a chemical compound having relatively low molecular weight) that may remain in the plastic after manufacture. The FDA established a 10 ppm tolerance for the monomer in polyvinyl chloride resin used in food contacts and required proof that the monomer will not be transferred to food. These new regulations apply to food packaging, as well as to equipment and piping that comes in contact with food. These steps were taken after reports of two European tests in which rats developed cancer after exposure, respectively, to 30 ppm of vinyl chloride monomer by inhalation and 250 ppm by ingestion. Companies are now conducting safety tests on vinyl chloride.

The liver angiosarcomas of industrial workers presumably resulted from inhalation exposures. This indicates that the chemical was transmitted from the lungs throughout the body. If tests confirm this fact, polyvinyl chloride will be banned from food-contact applications under the Delaney Clause. The FDA has allowed a two-year period to conduct standard animal-feeding studies with a single species, a strain of rats known to be sensitive to vinyl chloride monomer. The problem is to devise a method of incorporating vinyl chloride (a gas at normal temperatures and pressures) into animal foods. The packaging industry has expressed doubts that tests can be completed within two years and already has suggested that final results may require several additional years. Meanwhile, public exposure continues.

In 1973, polyvinyl chloride plastic bottles were found to react with the alcohol in alcoholic beverages to form a product suspected of being toxic. Some 30 American distilling companies had been using plastic containers for their products experimentally for as long as four years, and the industry was on the verge of rapid expansion of plastic container use. The exact nature of the reaction was unclear. Sources in the distilling industry said that the alcohol had been reacting with the plastic to form, as one source reported, "something nasty." Tests showed that up to 20 ppm of vinyl chloride was leached from the plastic bottles by distilled spirits stored in such containers. The FDA reported that it had no indication that this level of the newly formed compound would harm humans. Nevertheless, the FDA as well as the Treasury Department suspended use of the plastic as an alcoholic beverage container until further study.

The PCBs (see page 83) were recognized as contaminants of food packaging as well as of food and feed. The FDA found high levels of these chemicals in cardboard food packaging. Some of the contamination was traced back to the use of recycled cardboard from different types of waste paper, including carbonless copying paper made with PCB. However, some was also traced to virgin wood pulp. In the production of pulp, PCBs can be picked up from contaminated process water from affected lakes and streams. The FDA proposed residue tolerance levels and announced that present PCB residue levels were unavoidable and would remain in food packaging, food, and feed until the proposed restrictions ultimately would reduce the contamination levels.

Safety testing may miss the potential hazards of an additive because of unanticipated interactions that take place at the testing time. Two recent discoveries illustrate how additives may be capable of forming surprising new combinations after being introduced into the food supply.

Diethyl pyrocarbonate (DEP) was first observed in Germany. Isolated and identified in 1938, it was hailed as "an ideal food preservative." DEP could kill microbes, yeasts, molds, and bacteria. It could be used for "cold sterilization" or "cold pasteurization" of some foods and beverages, such as still (nonbubbling) wines, unpasteurized malt liquors (draft beer), noncarbonated soft drinks, and fruit-based beverages.

DEP is colorless and has a fruity or esterlike odor. In the quantities used, it does not impart any taste or color to a beverage. Although it is poisonous, DEP breaks down into relatively non-toxic substances when added to aqueous solutions.

The "safety" of DEP was acknowledged by many official and prestigious groups. It was used with FDA approval in certain beverages between 1963 and 1968. In evaluating DEP, the Expert Committee on Food Additives of the World Health Organization had suggested that the use of DEP should be limited to beverages with a pH below 4.5 and with a low content of proteins and amino acids. This cautionary recommendation should have sounded an alarm to federal and state food and beverage control agencies.

DEP is known to react with ammonia in aqueous solutions in the pH range of 4 to 9 to form urethan (also called urethane, or ethyl carbamate). The carcinogenic property of urethan has been well-established. Ammonia is commonly found in plant and animal tissues. Citrus juices, wine, and beer all contain ammonia. *Thus, it is very likely that beverages treated with DEP contain the carcinogen, urethan. Once urethan is formed in the beverage or food it remains.* Even the recommendation of the Expert Committee on Food Additives for a minimal pH value of 4.5 was an inadequate safeguard.

Knowing that DEP may combine with ammonia to form urethan, two Swedish scientists tested the effects of adding DEP to orange juice, white wine, and beer. The orange juice had been imported in closed bottles from the United States. The wine was from Turkey. The beer was a DEP-free Swedish product, since it is illegal to treat beer with DEP in Sweden.

The experimental addition of DEP yielded urethan in all three beverages. The amounts varied with the pH, the concentration of ammonia, and the amount of DEP added. The urethan yields in the white wine and beer were up to ten times higher than in the orange juice.

In February 1972, the FDA initiated the first step to ban the use of DEP. The agency took no further action for 60 days, during which time interested parties might file comments before the proposed revocation would become effective. The FDA's failure to act promptly and decisively appears to be in clear violation of the Delaney Clause, which forbids the use of any amount of any substance that induces cancer when ingested by either animals or humans. Ultimately, the ban became effective.

Nitrates are natural constituents of plants. They are present in large quantities in vegetables such as spinach, beets, radishes, eggplants, celery, lettuce, collards, and turnip greens. Large accumulations of nitrates from heavy applications of nitrogen fertilizers also concentrate in the soil and plants. Some water supplies have high nitrate levels from agricultural fertilizers, from nitrogen fixation by microorganisms and plants, and especially from the decomposition of plant and sewage wastes followed by the leaching of nitrates from the groundwater. In addition to consuming nitrate from these sources, individuals may consume as much, or more, from cured meats and fish treated with sodium or potassium nitrate.

A high intake of nitrates constitutes a hazard when the nitrates are converted to nitrites. In cattle, this conversion may occur from the microbial environment in the rumen or from eating damp forage material, high in nitrate, which may convert to nitrite. In the human infant under about four months, nitrite conversion may occur due to the infant's low stomach acidity (see page 77). For the consuming public, the threat of nitrite toxicity may occur from the total sum of water and foods high in nitrate.

Originally, meat and fish products were cured in potassium nitrate-curing brine. In 1925, the actual curing agent was found to be the nitrite produced by bacterial reduction of the nitrate salt. Nitrite, substituted for nitrate in the curing solution, was quicker, and produced a more uniform product. Nitrite has been used as a curing agent for several decades, even though its toxicity at high levels is recognized.

But in recent times, a new, unanticipated hazard has been

discovered. Nitrites may interact with secondary and tertiary amines and amides to produce nitrosamines. Amines and amides are common in food, as well as in man-made consumer goods (fishmeal, cereals, tea, tobacco and tobacco smoke, wine, improperly brewed beer, meat- and bread-flavoring agents, some commercially canned foods cooked with steam, therapeutic drugs, and even toothpaste). Nitrosamines, a class of compounds termed "the most potent cancer-causing agent known to science," are present in many food materials and have been shown to act throughout the body.

The interaction of nitrites with amines or amides is called *nitrosation.* Such interaction is generally promoted by mildly acidic conditions. *Is it possible that humans synthesize nitrosamines within the body?* Constituents normally present in the body, including thiocyanate in saliva and acidic gastric juices in the digestive tract, may be favorable for nitrosation.

As yet, there is no direct evidence that nitrosation in the *human* body causes cancer. However, there is indirect evidence, based on animal tests. Cancer has been produced in animals simultaneously fed nitrites and certain secondary amines. Nitrosation occurred in the stomach of the cat and the rabbit when these animals were fed a secondary amine (diethylamine) and sodium nitrite. These two substances combined to form a powerful carcinogenic nitrosamine (diethylnitrosamine). This nitrosamine produced liver cirrhosis in several species (rabbit, dog, and pig). A 2 ppm dose of this nitrosamine administered to rats induced malignant tumors. A no-effect level for this compound has *not* been established; no dose, however low, has been found to be innocuous.

A striking characteristic of some nitrosamine carcinogens is that these compounds are capable of inducing cancer in animals after they are *treated with a single dose.* Some of these compounds, such as dimethylnitrosamines, cause severe liver injury. In 1961 and 1962 in Norway, the fatal liver poisoning in sheep was traced to the formation of dimethylnitrosamines in the fishmeal animal feed, which had been treated with nitrites.

Nitrosation probably occurs in the human body when nitrates or nitrites are consumed simultaneously with secondary or tertiary amines or amides. A German study with human volunteers fed nitrate and a secondary amine (diphenylamine) demonstrated that nitrosation *did* occur, and that nitrate *is* reduced to nitrite in the human body. But the extent of nitrosation remains unknown.

To compound the hazard, nitrosation also occurs in nitrited foods outside the body. This problem was raised by Dr. William Lijinsky and Dr. Samuel S. Epstein, two cancer researchers who pioneered in attempting to make federal agencies responsive to the hazards of nitrosation. The FDA and the USDA considered the problem of nitrosation as hypothetical. However, once a testing program was finally initiated, the presence of nitrosamines in nitrite-treated foods selected randomly from supermarket shelves was a reality. The USDA and the FDA found low levels of carcinogenic nitrosamines in samples of cooked sausage, dried beef products, cured pork, ham, bacon cooked in the conventional manner, dried blood used in making blood sausage, and in nitrite-treated smoked salmon. The USDA also reported that nitrosamines formed during the cooking of sausage containing 2,000 ppm or more of nitrite (a level far higher than legally tolerated).

The present official nitrite tolerance in the United States is much too high. Far lower limits are enforced on European sausage makers and meat provisioners. *Our present nitrite tolerance has no scientific basis. The level was established in the 1920s on the basis of the amount of nitrite residues found in the meat—not on toxicological studies.* Since nitrite-cured meat contained lower nitrite residues than nitrate-cured meat, at that time the investigators had no objection, from a health standpoint, to the substitution of nitrite for nitrate. Not only is the nitrite tolerance level excessively high, but the FDA has ignored repeatedly serious violations of these official levels. Even when products have exceeded levels, the FDA has failed to seize the products or institute any regulatory action.

An additional source of nitrosation was discovered recently in premixed ingredients used to make luncheon meats, wieners, and other processed meat and poultry products. These premixed ingredients include spices, such as pepper and paprika, and nitrate/nitrite curing agents. Some manufacturers used a chemical "buffer" to prevent the ingredients from interacting before the premix was added to the processed products. Nitrosamines were found to form when the nitrate/nitrite in the curing mix combined with the amines naturally present in the seasoning. Levels of nitrosamines ranging from 24 to 231 ppb were found. After this discovery, the FDA ordered manufacturers of unbuffered premixes to package the nitrate/nitrite and the seasonings separately or with a chemical buffer to prevent nitrosation.

Many agricultural compounds have the potential to form nitrosamines. Many derivatives of urea and carbamic acid are used in agriculture and horticulture as pesticides and herbicides. When these compounds (with seemingly innocuous structures) become incidental food additives as residues on plants, they react readily with nitrite at moderately acid pH to form nitrosamines.

Drugs are another source of nitrosation. Many drugs contain secondary and tertiary amines as well as amides and hydrazines. In some instances, test animals fed combinations of nitrites and these drugs developed tumors. One of the drugs tested in combination was frequently recommended to be taken by patients at breakfast. But if taken in combination with foods frequently consumed at breakfast (nitrite-containing bacon, ham, or sausage), nitrosation is a potential hazard.

The revelations concerning both DEP and nitrites demonstrate that food additives may act in completely unanticipated ways. In the case of nitrosation, especially, the hazards created are too complex to be monitored adequately.

In testing a food additive, the summation effect cannot be ignored. Test animals may be exposed to only a *single* source of the additive, while the human body may be burdened by a great number of sources.

Numerous sulfur compounds (sulfur dioxide, sodium and potassium sulfite, bisulfite, and metabisulfite) may be included in the daily diet. Sulfur compounds are used as bacteriostatic agents, bleaching and antibrowning agents, preservatives, and antioxidants. In the presence of water and food or beverage constituents, sulfur compounds are capable of a variety of chemical reactions. They may create many new compounds in greater concentration than normally would be found in foods. (The actual amounts of ingested unbound sulfite are unknown. In view of recent findings that free sulfites are capable of producing genetic mutagens, studies regarding the fate of any free sulfites in the body are needed.) In addition to ingesting sulfur compounds, many individuals are exposed to sulfurous fumes as air pollutants. The summation effect for humans is so high that the actual daily intake of sulfur dioxide per person is believed to be very close to the upper "acceptable daily intake" limit.

Similarly, the summation effect of nitrite is high because nitrite compounds are found in air, water, soil, plants, and nitrite-treated foods. An adult who consumes three to four ounces of processed meat containing 200 ppm of sodium nitrite ingests enough nitrate to convert from 1.4 to 5.7 percent of his hemoglobin to methemoglobin. Under ordinary circumstances, this percentage may be insignificant. But if the individual eats spinach, beets, or salad greens at the same meal, the amount of nitrite may become significant. These vegetables contain naturally high levels of nitrates, which may be converted to nitrites. The nitrite level may be raised further as a result of treating the crops with nitrogen fertilizers. Sodium nitrite is highly toxic in relatively small amounts. An adult lethal dose is about four grams. Only a small safety margin exists between the nitrite amount that is considered safe or hazardous. The safety margin for children is even lower because they have lesser quantities of blood and hemoglobin. Currently, some infants' diets *exceed* the recommended nitrite limits.

Infants and small children from low economic groups are at especially high risk to the summation effect of lead poisoning. These children may be fed inexpensive canned milk. Such milk has traditionally been processed with an outmoded technique that may contaminate the milk with lead. The problem was recognized only recently and is under current investigation. In addition, these children are apt to live in delapidated houses where they may eat lead-contaminated paint peelings. And they are likely to play in congested urban areas, where car exhausts spew high levels of lead into the air.

Allergies are also increased by summation effects. An individual who is sensitive to a specific additive may have only a mild reaction to a single exposure. But the same individual may suffer a severe reaction if he eats several different foods containing the same additive, or even different ones that induce the same effects, at one meal. For example, some people are sensitive to the food dye tartrazine (FD&C Yellow No. 5). If a tartrazine-sensitive person eats imitation strawberry jelly, the individual may be unaware that yellow-colored tartrazine is one of the dyes present. If a grape-, lime-, or lemon-flavored carbonated soft drink is consumed at the same time, the individual might ingest additional tartrazine. And, if, at the same meal, the person swallowed a yellow-coated vitamin pill, it would add to the total amount of tartrazine ingested. The summation effect could then cause a more severe reaction.

Both intentional additives and unintentional contaminants can result in summation effects. Individually, the levels of antibiotic residues in meat, arsenic in chicken liver, polychlorinated biphenyls in fowl, mercury in fish, pesticide residue on produce, lead in canned milk and fruit juices, and strontium$_{90}$ in milk may be low. But the sum total—the body's burden—may be significant. Indeed, scientists concerned with the problem of summation effect believe that low-level exposures, each in itself perhaps not very important, may be shortening the human life span. Eventually, the sum of these low-level exposures may produce disease states that, at present, we do not recognize.

Synergism is a mechanism whereby the total effect is greater than the sum of two or more independent effects. This mechanism, sometimes called *potentiation*, is well-recognized with drugs. Synergism also may apply to food additives, but its effects are less recognized than with drugs.

Food labels on vegetable oils or packaged dry cereals show that several antioxidants frequently are used together. These additives show significantly greater activity when combined than when used singly. For food processors, handlers, and distributors, such combinations extend the shelf life for foods that normally turn rancid quickly. Synergism of the antioxidants permits the use of lower concentrations of the individual antioxidants, giving higher activity at lower cost. Whether they benefit consumers is another question. But such combinations may create potentially hazardous, unrecognized cases of synergism.

Food dyes in a colloidal state generally do not pass through the intestinal mucosa. When ingested simultaneously with food additives known as surfactants, synergistic action probably occurs. In tests, surfactants caused the dyes to be absorbed and produce widespread staining of tissues.

Silicon is an additive used to prevent foaming in the production of evaporated milk, concentrated fruit juice, caramel color or other manufacturing processes. In itself, silicon is physiologically inert and is not absorbed from the intestine. However, in animal tests, when silicon was fed simultaneously with a harmless emulsifier, the silicon severely damaged the liver, kidney, and middle ear of the animals. (The amount of silicon given was only 25 times as much as that which may be added to foods, thus shattering the myth of a hundredfold safety margin.)

Ascorbic acid, used as a food additive, potentiates the effect of many substances, including food additives such as sodium nitrite and drugs such as antibiotics and insulin. Sodium cyclamate interacts with citric acid or caffeine.

Unexpected synergism of two food additives was recently noted in the case of Aspartame, a new low-calorie synthetic sweetener. The manufacturer had conducted extensive testing, FDA reviewed the data, and in July 1974, FDA approved Aspartame. The agency had not called public hearings prior to its approval.

The safety of Aspartame was promptly challenged by a neurophysiologist, Dr. John W. Olney, and others, who suggested that the sweetener had several potential dangers, especially to children, which could result from the synergistic action of Aspartame and another food additive. In studies, Olney had found that Aspartame produced the same kind of brain damage as glutamate, with approximately equal potency. Olney, who had previously reported that subcutaneous doses of monosodium glutamate (MSG) induced brain lesions in newborn and infant animals in several species, now reported that Aspartame and glutamate are both acidic amino acids, and chemically resemble each other. If the two are ingested simultaneously, a synergistic effect can be produced. Olney charged that FDA was either unaware of the toxic synergism of glutamate and Aspartame, or failed to comprehend the implications of toxic synergism. He added:

If it is seriously questioned whether children will be exposed significantly to a high combined glutamate/Aspartame intake, consider the following projected scene in a typical American home after Aspartame goes on the market: A young child awakens in the A.M. and has Aspartame-sweetened cereal and dry base imitation juice, then chews 3 wads of Aspartame-sweetened gum and drinks several glasses of Aspartame-sweetened Kool Aid before lunch, consumes a bowl of MSG-seasoned soup, 100–200 g of MSG-seasoned processed meat and vegetable mixture or MSG-seasoned potato chips and MSG-seasoned wieners, etc. for lunch topped off with Aspartame-sweetened pudding. He returns to his Aspartame-sweetened gum and beverages all afternoon. When father comes home at 5 P.M. to find junior chewing on Aspartame paper packets and scolds him for eating sweets before dinner, mother says it won't hurt him because FDA has approved it as a very safe low-calorie sugar substitute. Then to the table for the MSG-seasoned fish sticks, meat balls, canned or frozen vegetables, Colonel Sanders' chicken (loaded with MSG) etc. etc. before the Aspartame-sweetened Jello or cake and Aspartame-topping for dessert. Obviously it is untenable to assume that human children will not be ingesting substantial quantities of both glutamate and Aspartame. It is also untenable to assume that the two compounds will not act synergistically in the hypothalamus to destroy neurons since the neurotoxic ingredients of Aspartame (aspartic acid) when taken with glutamate has been shown to augment its neurotoxicity.

Olney and others have urged FDA to conduct public hearings for further deliberations on the toxicity of Aspartame. They insist that such hearings should be conducted before this new synthetic sweetener becomes widely marketed and consumed.

Like the summation effect, synergism of food additives must be viewed as part of a larger problem of multiple chemical exposures in a wide range of consumer products and environmental contaminants. Frequently, synergistic effects occur when food additives combine with other substances. Pronounced mutational synergistic effects with caffeine (sometimes used as a food additive) and ultraviolet have been demonstrated with bacteria. In other tests, particles similar to asbestos fibers penetrated the cells of the gastrointestinal tract of animals much more rapidly if consumed with caffeine or nicotine.

The principle of synergism is employed in formulating pesticides. The potency of pyrethrins (insecticides of botanical origin and of low toxicity) is enhanced by other chemicals. When packaged as aerosols, the addition of pressurized fluorocarbon propellants causes pyrethrins to form highly hazardous combinations.

At times, the synergistic effect results in unexpected chance combinations. The herbicide 2-4D was formed by various waste materials discharged simultaneously into the water. In another instance, the insecticides endrin and methyl parathion were applied simultaneously and produced a highly toxic mixture. There is a whole range of unstudied reactions which can take place between chlorine and other water contaminants. Of special concern is the possible chance formation of chlorinated hydrocarbons.

Synergistic effects have been noted with a variety of alcoholic substances. Alcohol enhances the ability of aspirin to penetrate the stomach mucosa. Alcohol may potentiate the effect of tranquilizers and pain-killing drugs. Well-documented cases demonstrate that a combination of alcohol and barbiturates or of alcohol and pesticides may be deadly.

Consumer goods demonstrate synergistic effects. Optical brighteners (also known as fluorescent whiteners), found in detergents, paper products, and fabrics, enhance human susceptibility to skin cancer caused by sunlight.

Occupational hazards may potentiate the hazards of certain consumer goods. Radiation exposure combined with cigarette smoking increases health risks tenfold. Asbestos workers who smoke have an increased risk of lung cancer death about 90 times greater than nonsmoking asbestos workers.

In 1967, a task force recommended that the FDA "must be able to evaluate the synergistic effect of food additives so that the consumer is protected from the threats that cannot be detected by separate analysis of individual food additives." Although synergism is an acknowledged problem, a testing program for all possible synergistic combinations of additives, as well as of additives with other substances, is a sheer impossibility. The task force recommendation was highly unrealistic. Such a testing program would be infinitely time consuming, prohibitively expensive, and require more toxicologists than are available. And ultimately, we still would be left with many toxicological imponderables.

Food additives may interact with other substances, interfering with their activity. Such interactions may be overlooked or unknown in additive safety tests.

The risk of drug interaction is well-recognized. A computerized study of prescription history of nearly 42,000 California patients suggested that drug interactions could have occurred in 1 out of every 13 prescriptions.

The possible interactions of food additives and drugs is a largely unexplored area. For many years, it was believed that the only physiologic effect of cyclamates was that ingesting large amounts produced stool softening and diarrhea in humans. It was only after extensive testing that cyclamates were found to interfere with the therapeutic effectiveness of certain commonly used drugs:

—Pretreatment of rats with cyclamates reduced the hypoglycemic effect of an oral antidiabetic agent (tolbutamide), but similar pretreatment increased the hypoglycemic effect of another oral hypoglycemic agent (chlorpropamide).

—Cyclamates potentiated the effects of diuretic drugs (thiazide), possibly resulting in excessive loss of potassium.

—Cyclamates potentiated the effects of anticoagulant drugs (coumarin) in some animal species, suggesting that exaggerated responses to anticoagulants might occur.

—Cyclamates bound to plasma protein; thus, they might displace other drugs similarly bound, rendering the drugs ineffective.

—Cyclamates reduced the absorption of an antibiotic (linomycin).

When the various ways cyclamates interfered with drugs became known, a medical advisory group to the FDA cautioned the agency that special care must be taken when cyclamates were used by patients being treated with other drugs.

A lesser-known case of a food additive decreasing drug activity was observed in an English hospital. Several patients on anticoagulant drugs continued to show abnormal coagulation. Test results seemed to indicate drug underdosage to a considerable degree.

Before attempting to increase the dosage, the physicians questioned the patients about their diet. All of them had been eating French fried potatoes. Upon investigation, the physicians discovered that the cooking oil used to fry the potatoes contained methyl polysiloxane. This substance, which is added to some cooking oils to give potato chips a crisp, dry, and attractive appearance, was suspected of having interfered with drug absorption. About a week after the patients stopped ingesting the oil, a repeat blood test showed a return to normal therapeutic values of the anticoagulant drug. The dose did not have to be altered.

The potential hazards of ingesting nitrite-treated foods along with drugs that combine with nitrites to form nitrosamines has already been discussed (see page 91). A congressional committee held hearings on sodium nitrite and criticized the FDA's failure to consider the drug-interference potential of this food additive.

The paucity of information on food additive interference with drugs does not necessarily mean that such interactions do not occur frequently. It may mean that such interactions have not been looked for or detected in the testing program.

The interaction of food additives and drugs also needs to be viewed within a larger framework. Some food constituents also combine with certain drugs in the gastrointestinal tract. These combinations may be harmful—or even fatal—to the patient. Food–drug combinations which are already recognized are cheese, wine, beer or liver with a group of tranquilizers (monoamine oxidase inhibitors); dairy products with an antibiotic (tetracycline); fats with certain antibiotics (griseofulvin and neomycin); leafy green vegetables with anticoagulants; and vitamin C with a sedative and antinausea agent (pentobarbital) or an anesthetic (procaine). Such findings further demonstrate the limitations of any safety testing program that examines a single substance without considering the total environment.

7

The Interference with Vital Processes

• There is a hierarchy of complexity that runs from atoms through molecules, cells, tissues, organs, individuals, specific populations, communities, and comprehensive ecological systems to the whole realm of the organic and its environments in space and time. . . . Each level of the hierarchy includes that below.

George Gaylord Simpson

• A change at one point, in one molecule even, may reverberate throughout the entire system to initiate changes in seemingly unrelated organs and tissues.

Medical Research: Unresolved Clinical Problems in Biological Perspective

• It is becoming increasingly clear that untoward effects in people, stemming from food additives, are exceedingly difficult to recognize or even establish with any degree of certainty once suspicion has been aroused. It has been amply demonstrated in the experimental laboratory and in a few cases of human disease that subtle and long-range chronic effects are real events which can be related to specific external causes. However, we must still learn how reliably to associate effects, namely, disease seen in the human population, with causes that have acted early in life and are now gone, or which have been acting subtly by slow accumulation of a deleterious factor or effect.

Leo Friedman, Ph.D.

• Men are naturally most impressed by diseases which have obvious manifestations, yet some of their worst enemies creep on them unobtrusively.

Dr. René Dubos

• It is known that while certain chemicals may be taken in substantial quantities for a month or a year without producing demonstrably injurious effects, nevertheless the continued use of the same substance, even in smaller quantities, will eventually undermine the health. . . . Man is a comparatively large animal. In addition, he is provided with an efficient mechanism for eliminating from his system poisonous or useless products which are taken in from without. . . . It is therefore not particularly remarkable or significant that chemicals sufficient to kill millions or billions of bacteria can be poured daily through this relatively large animal for weeks and months without producing a demonstrable effect. That this same big animal may be more or less damaged without the effect being known, demonstrably, or detectably, is also a fact. . . .

Otto Folin, Ph.D.

● Long-delayed effects are frequently difficult to relate to their specific causes. Thus, it is conceivable that injuries due to unrecognized causes have been produced by common materials that have long been considered safe as foods or for use in foods. In this regard we are concerned with cancer, genetic damage and birth defects, premature old age, cardiovascular, endocrine and mental disorders, and other human ills of unexplained etiology.

Julius M. Coon, M.D.

● The subject of food additives and their safety has generated much interest and concern recently. Part of this concern is due to the lack of basic knowledge about how these various chemicals behave in the body and the fear that we may be doing irreparable damage to ourselves without realizing it.

W. B. Gibson and F. M. Strong

"Living cells, although remarkably efficient in dealing with many toxic substances, are nevertheless often vulnerable to new molecules which may differ only slightly in chemical structure from biologically harmless substances," noted R. M. W. Cunningham. Toxic substances, interacting with constituents in the cell, may alter the cell and result in biochemical derangement. These alterations, subtle and difficult to observe, may precede gross pathological changes.

All too often in the past, cellular damage went unrecognized. More recently, researchers have begun to investigate the possibility of cellular damage inflicted by toxic substances. For example, by means of microscopic examination, Dr. John Olney discovered cellular brain damage in newborn animals fed monosodium glutamate. This cellular damage had not been found in earlier studies because it had not been looked for. It is axiomatic that what has not been investigated is not apt to be found.

Presently, scientists at the Massachusetts Institute of Technology are studying the subtle cellular effects of nonnutritive food additives consumed by humans over extended periods. The group has noted that surprisingly few data exist about the interactions of these additives with living cells. Even fewer data exist about long-term consequences.

Elsewhere, a series of studies was done on antimicrobial food preservatives. Although it had been assumed that these substances are not toxic to humans, the studies demonstrated that antimicrobials may reduce the amount of nutrients that enter human intestinal cells.

Antimicrobial compounds are used widely to kill bacteria that cause food spoilage. Commonly used antimicrobials include sodium nitrite (for frankfurters, luncheon meats, ham, bacon and other cured meats, and smoked fish), sodium propionate (for breads), sorbate (for cheeses), propyl paraben (for ice creams and foods in paste form), methyl paraben (for beverages and jams), acetate (for pickled food), benzoate (for beverages), octanoate (for cheese wrappers) and sulfites (for wines). All of these antimicrobial compounds are fatty acids. They have been found to prevent the growth of human cells by inhibiting the transport of molecules into the cells.

The effects of antimicrobials were studied with cells from human livers and intestines, as well as from chicken embryo cells grown in laboratory tissue cultures. At certain concentrations, the additives were found not to act selectively against the bacteria; they inhibited mammalian cell growth just as effectively. In fact, a substance, such as an antimicrobial, that is toxic to one form of life (bacteria) is very apt to be toxic to other forms of life (including humans).

At higher concentrations, the antimicrobial compounds altered the shapes of both human and animal cells and destroyed them. The effective concentration of these compounds in tissue surrounding the gut may be reduced by several mechanisms. Since the pH in the stomach is low (acidic in character), weak acids can be absorbed rapidly by ion trapping and distributed throughout the body by blood circulation, thus decreasing their local concentration. Some of the absorbed compounds can be metabolized. In addition, the mucous membrane may protect the underlying cells against the direct effect of insoluble free acids.

The researchers concluded that since these antimicrobial compounds inhibited all human cells tested in the study, at least as effectively as they inhibited bacteria, "present evidence would urge caution in eating large quantities of food containing such additives. There may be a mechanism whereby stomach tissue in a whole organism is able to detoxify the compounds in humans, but even in that case, ingesting too much might overload the mechanism and still pose a danger."

An additive may interfere with cellular metabolism, and inhibit the number of cells formed in an organ. The inhibition of cell formation may result either from cell death or from a sublethal depression of cellular metabolism. This may adversely affect the rate of DNA, RNA, and protein synthesis.

The antioxidant BHT is a highly lipid-soluble (fat-soluble) compound. It can combine with lipids of the plasma and intracellular membrane systems to disturb lipid metabolism. Normal metabolic systems are situated in part, or wholly, in these membranes. If this lipid combination alters the membrane water structure, either by changing the biochemical configuration or structural components, it might interfere with the normal metabolic systems.

The kidney cells of test monkeys were used to demonstrate this effect of BHT. A dose level of BHT was found which stopped all increase of cell numbers. After the doses of BHT were discontinued, the synthesis rate of RNA returned to normal.

Other tests showed that relatively large doses of BHT ingested by rats interfered with the normal cellular metabolism of fatty acids involved in the transport of both total serum cholesterol and phospholipid levels. This resulted in increased levels of both these fatty acids in the animals.

Cellular death may not be a passive phenomenon or end result of a general decline of vital processes from endogenous sources (sources within the body). Rather, it may be an active process in which the loss of cellular vitality is induced from assault by an exogenous source (source from outside the body). Two notable exogenous sources are toxic chemicals and irradiation.

Slight, unnoticed modification of cell structures may culminate in cancer. Dr. Otto Warburg has stated that the prime cause of all human diseases, including cancer, is impaired cellular respiration. According to Warburg, all growing body cells need to be saturated with oxygen. Whenever the active groups of respiratory enzymes are removed from food, cellular respiration is impaired. When the active groups are returned to the food, cellular respiration is repaired. Warburg claimed that cancer was preventable if cellular respiration could be kept intact.

Some additives interfere with cellular respiration by decreasing the oxygen-transferring enzymes. For example, methemoglobinemia results when nitrite impairs the oxygen transport in the blood. The presence of methemoglobin in the blood alters the affinity of oxygen for hemoglobin in nearly the same way that carbon monoxide makes more difficult the oxygen release from the blood to the tissues.

Since 1953, DNA and RNA have been recognized as the keys to all life. DNA, a gigantic molecule by chemical standards, carries the genetic code which specifies what a living creature will be. Every cell in the human body contains DNA molecules, which are "blueprints" for the entire body, down to the smallest detail.

Although much is known about DNA, including its chemical composition, its blueprint still remains an enigma. What is known is that an enzyme called *DNA polymerase* reads the correct section of the blueprint whenever a cell needs to build protein. Moving along the DNA molecule, somewhat like a phonograph needle on a record, the enzyme constructs a "carbon copy" of the needed information. The copy is an RNA molecule. Eventually, the RNA manufactures protein.

The cellular process is incredibly complex. Decades of research still may be required to clarify the way in which a human cell functions. Meanwhile, evidence is accumulating that some food additives are capable of interfering with DNA and RNA. For example, test-tube experiments demonstrated that sulfites interacted with nucleic acids (similar to the strands of DNA, and found in the chromosomes). This raised the possibility that sulfites may interfere with the double-helix formation (the double-coiled structure) of DNA and inactivate RNA. Ethylene oxide, a fumigant used with certain foods, reacts with DNA of living cells. Ethylene oxide is an acknowledged mutagen, and a possible carcinogen.

An astonishing number and variety of biological and chemical reactions are controlled by intricate enzyme systems. Any interference with their proper function may disturb profoundly a number of vital body processes. Toxic substances can interfere with enzyme systems.

An enzyme molecule consists of a pure protein part (an apoenzyme) and a nonprotein part (a coenzyme). Often the coenzyme is a vitamin or closely related molecule.

The total number of different enzymes functioning in the human body is believed to be sizable. Every bodily function requires enzyme action. Each enzyme has a highly specific role in promoting either a specific reaction or a closely related group of actions. For example, the enzyme protease will digest only certain proteins. Protease will never digest carbohydrates (which are digested by amylase) or fats (which are digested by lipase). Specific enzymes control the chemical reactions by which food is digested, absorbed, and metabolized. Enzyme systems also control the synthesis of structural materials used to repair old tissue, as well as the energy release needed for vital bodily functions and for all forms of physical and mental activity.

The living cell is composed of well-regulated arrangements of particles, crystals, membranes, and fluids. Within this structure, enzymes, coenzymes, mineral salts, fuel storage substances, and many other elements are interrelated in orderly fashion. They are regulated by hormonal substances and nerve signals. The transformation of nutrients, which proceeds continuously in every body cell, is subject to many local checks and balances. All of these regulating influences result in a dynamically balanced state. This mechanism makes possible the remarkable constancy of the adult organism's size and composition, despite the ceaseless turnover of a variety of substances. If uncontrolled, these substances would lead to the disintegration of the organism.

A series of enzymes—together with their coenzymes, activators, and other components—may be structurally united in the form of microscopically visible particles called *mitochondria*. The mitochondria include all the enzymes necessary for oxidation to occur. They are the powerhouses in which most energy-producing reactions of the body take place. Any disruption of the mitochondria interferes with the orderly succession of the vital enzymatic functioning—and mitochondria can be disrupted by toxic substances.

Over and above the cellular structures and metabolic processes is a network of regulating mechanisms that control the timing of reactions in the body. This system keeps the body functioning efficiently. It prevents reactions from ending before their function is actually finished, and it regulates energy production for the body's needs at any one moment. Enzymes are involved in all of these regulating mechanisms. This system permits the organism to adapt so that it can function at extremes of temperature, during times of starvation or overfeeding, when overworked, or when beset by illness or injury. By means of these regulating mechanisms, life processes continue to function, despite serious assaults or handicaps.

One function of enzymes is to serve as catalysts. Enzymes initiate and speed up reactions, but they are not used up during the reactions and remain essentially unchanged when the reaction is completed. Thus, enzymes are able to repeat the same reactions endlessly. However, interference with this function may result from the introduction of certain substances into the body. Such substances are called *enzyme inhibitors.*

Some naturally occurring enzyme inhibitors are present in foods of plant and animal origin, notably in raw legumes and raw egg white. The antienzyme factor in these foods is deactivated largely when foods are cooked before they are ingested.

Of far greater concern are the enzyme-inhibiting qualities of many chemicals added to foods. Some food additives interfere with enzyme systems by depressing them:

—Saccharin was shown to inhibit the action of an enzyme that helps to regulate blood glucose levels. Under acidic conditions, both saccharin and cyclamate compete with a normally reacting substance for access to the enzyme, and thus retard the reaction.

—Sorbic acid, another food additive, was shown to interfere with the functioning of numerous enzyme systems and to inhibit the activity of a large number of bacteria, algae, and fungi.

—Methionine sulfoximine, the compound formed in flour processed with agene, was shown to inhibit an enzyme in the brain.

—Sulfur dioxide, sodium nitrate, sodium nitrite, food dyes, certain hormones used to stimulate plant and animal growth, antibiotics used in food production, fluorides used in water for processing foods, and pesticides are all acknowledged enzyme inhibitors.

Some substances interfere with enzyme systems by stimulating rather than depressing them. When the body takes in poisons, it is called upon to produce more enzymes to aid in the detoxification process. Every cell can be induced to manufacture more than a normal supply of enzymes. The antioxidant BHT was found to be a powerful stimulant of enzyme activity in the liver of the rat. DDT and most persistent pesticides also were found to induce the body to produce more detoxifying enzymes.

Although toxicologists believe that such increased enzyme activity represents a response to stress rather than a pathological change, this interpretation may be faulty. At what point does stress end and a pathological change commence? Ultimately, through prolonged and repeated demands, such stress upon the enzyme system may lead to cellular exhaustion. Excessive enzyme production may cause premature cellular aging.

A human's response to a specific food additive may be determined, in part, by the efficiency of the individual's enzyme systems. As the organism ages, the body's enzyme systems tend to become weaker. In some studies, the elderly had only $\frac{1}{30}$ of the enzymes in their saliva that young people had. In other studies only half the number of enzymes present in the urine of people in the prime of life were present in the urine of the aged.

Certain genetic diseases are known to result from an inadequate supply of enzymes or from the presence of abnormal enzymes. In some cases, the enzymes may have diminished activity. An abnormally structured apoenzyme cannot combine readily with its coenzyme. Enzyme inhibitors may further impair the efficiency of enzyme systems which—due to health problems, age, genetic defects, or other factors—already may function poorly.

Enzyme inhibitors increase the body's needs for nutrients. For example, B vitamins are part of the enzyme systems. A large number of coenzymes are either identical with or are derivatives of certain B vitamins. All vitamins must be supplied continuously in the diet because the body cannot manufacture them from simpler substances. Unless they are available, several enzyme systems fail to function. When this happens, many important chemical reactions in the body are retarded or fail completely.

Enzyme inhibitors may break down the body's natural immunity mechanism. Microsomal enzyme systems, for example, are responsible for metabolizing and detoxifying a wide range of foreign substances in the body, including toxic chemicals. They are the first line of defense for the body. Microsomal enzyme systems are present in the small intestine, the skin, the placenta and other organs. However, they have been studied mostly in the liver because this organ is large and easily accessible. With the exception of the polycyclic hydrocarbon enzymes, relatively few of these enzyme systems have been studied in tissues other than the liver.

The stimulation or inhibition of microsomal enzyme systems caused by food additives can alter metabolism. This action may affect various normal body constituents such as steroid hormones, thyroxin, and bilirubin (present in bile, blood, and urine). Food additives that alter microsomal enzyme systems also may interfere with the safety and efficacy of certain drugs. Among the food additives capable of such interference are polycyclic hydrocarbons (a group which includes many synthetic flavors, food dyes, and substances used for the smoking of food), food preservatives, safrole (a flavoring agent now banned), and beta-ionone (a synthetic flavoring). In addition, many substances used in food production have the capacity to alter microsomal enzyme systems. Such substances include insecticides (both halogenated hydrocarbons and organic phosphates) and herbicides (from urea).

Metabolic interactions can occur among food additives, drugs, insecticides, and a variety of other environmental chemicals. A common denominator governing these effects is the versatile nature of the liver microsomal enzymes. These enzymes metabolize chemicals with diverse structures and biological activities. They can be stimulated or inhibited by two or more chemicals given simultaneously. Discovered in the late 1950s, the study of liver microsomal enzymes laid the groundwork for research on metabolic interactions. A considerable amount of information has been obtained on the metabolic interactions of environmental chemicals and drugs. More needs to be known about food additives, especially for basic studies of tissue enzymes.

Enzyme inhibitors may destroy the enzyme systems which protect the body from harm. Enzyme inhibitors increase demands upon the body's prime detoxification mechanism, the liver. This organ also performs an incredible number of other vital functions: It provides bile for fat digestion, keeps the blood sugar level normal by storing sugar as glycogen and releasing it as glucose, builds body proteins, maintains a proper level of serum cholesterol, inactivates excessive sex hormones, and stores vitamins. Because the liver functions in so many ways, even the slightest damage inflicted on the liver must be viewed with concern.

Many of the poisonous breakdown products of metabolism are detoxified quickly and efficiently by the liver. Additional toxic substances, such as food additives introduced into the body add to the liver's burden of detoxification. A continuous need to detoxify an overburdening number of substances may impair the normally functioning healthy liver.

A damaged liver weakens the body's defense against poisons and hampers a whole range of other liver functions. Although the consequences of such a breakdown may be far reaching and varied, they may not be apparent immediately. By the time they are noted, it may be difficult to relate cause and effect.

Enzyme inhibitors interfere with enzymes responsible for keeping the body's oxidative processes functioning properly. The body receives its energy from these oxidative processes. Each step is directed and expedited by a specific enzyme. When even a single enzyme is weakened or destroyed, the oxidation cycle ceases within the cell. If enzyme destruction occurs at any point in the cycle, oxidative processes stop and the function of various organs is impaired. Such blockage may initiate the slow and irreversible changes that ultimately lead to cell malignancy.

Catalase is an enzyme found in almost all living cells of bacteria, plants, animals, and humans. This particular enzyme plays many vital roles. It is intimately related to cell respiration. It buffers the cell from toxic substances, infection, virus, radiation, and cancer. The normal cell maintains a specific balance of catalase and hydrogen peroxide. Catalase controls the amount of hydrogen peroxide present in the cell and converts it into oxygen and water. However, many substances, including some chemical food additives, destroy catalase. When this occurs, the level of peroxide rises. In turn, the electron-transport system of the cell slows down or ceases altogether. Cellular abnormalities may then develop, and the cell becomes predisposed to tumor formation and cancer.

R. A. Holman, M.D., who has been particularly concerned with catalase–peroxide balance, stated:

It is obvious . . . that if this fundamental biological mechanism is interfered with for a long time by physical and chemical agents present in our environment, whether in food, drink, drugs, or in the air we breathe, then we shall see in races so exposed a progressive increase in the incidence of cancer. By contrast, in those primitive communities where such agents are not used or encouraged, the incidence will remain at a very low level. In my opinion, most of the chemicals added to food and drink for preservation or coloring could and should be abolished.

In the healthy body, impulses pass from nerve to nerve with the assistance of acetylcholine, a substance that performs its necessary function and then disappears. This transmitting chemical needs to be destroyed as soon as a nerve impulse has passed. If not, it continues to transmit impulses with increased intensification. If acetylcholine remains unchecked, the body's movements become uncoordinated and are accompanied by tremors, muscular spasms, and convulsions. Ultimately, death from acetylcholinosis ensues.

Normally, acetylcholine is controlled by the enzyme cholinesterase, which prevents acetylcholine from building up to dangerous levels. Consequently, any substance that inhibits cholinesterase from functioning properly, interferes with the destruction of acetylcholine. Certain pesticides are known cholinesterase inhibitors, and some food additives may also be cholinesterase inhibitors.

Recent tests demonstrated that monosodium glutamate inhibited cholinesterase. Fourteen human volunteers were given one large oral dose of monosodium glutamate (150 mg/kg). Thirteen suffered from neck numbness, headache, thoracic and abdominal discomfort, and nausea. These symptoms, frequently suffered by individuals who are sensitive to monosodium glutamate, are also induced by decreased cholinesterase activity accompanied by increased acetylcholine. Blood samples were taken an hour after the volunteers had ingested the monosodium glutamate. *Cholinesterase activity was decreased some 30 percent.*

These test results prompted an individual to write a letter to the editor of a medical journal, suggesting that a hazard might result from the ingestion of monosodium glutamate and exposure to any organic phosphate pesticide. The writer raised the possibility that unsuspected combinations of these two types of chemicals might explain the adverse effects suffered by individuals who are sensitive to monosodium glutamate.

An additive cannot be regarded as safe merely because it does not react chemically with food nutrients. Such so-called "inert" additives *may accumulate in the body tissue until they become toxic.* The reason that such tissue accumulation is not discovered as soon as it should be, according to Dr. Hans L. Falk of the National Institutes of Health, is "due to the short time the experiments have been run to test the toxicity of many such chemicals."

Studies showed that a dose of saccharin takes 72 hours to clear from all tissues in treated male rats. When "safe" daily doses of saccharin were given to the animals at several low doses, significant concentrations of saccharin occurred in certain tissues of the kidney and bladder. These concentrations were mostly, but not completely, cleared by the following day. What effects, if any, such daily peaks would have on the kidney and bladder over an extended period is presently unknown. Data indicate that prolonged use of normal doses causes saccharin to accumulate in the human bladder. When withdrawn from the diet, saccharin clears rapidly. The National Institute of Environmental Health Sciences has recommended that regular saccharin users occasionally discontinue saccharin use for several days to allow for tissue clearance.

The above-mentioned saccharin studies were unable to determine whether or not saccharin is metabolized. The studies failed to show the presence of any saccharin metabolite. The researchers suggested that the multiple low doses, used daily for a prolonged period, "could have masked the presence of trace metabolites."

In animal tests, saccharin was found to be rapidly absorbed from the gastrointestinal tract, distributed throughout the body, and excreted mainly in the urine. The concentration levels in blood and tissues peaked within 15 minutes after the saccharin was administered and then decreased. The magnitude of peak concentrations depended upon whether, prior to being given saccharin, the animals had been fed or starved.

An additive may be stored in the body's adipose (fat) tissues for many years. The lifetime exposure can be estimated by postmortem analysis of adipose tissue. At times, this has been done with humans.

The antioxidant BHT has been found to accumulate in human adipose tissue. Many tests on this additive have been conducted with rats, but human metabolism differs from that of the rat. BHT has *a higher degree of concentration* in the fatty tissues of humans than of rats.

Human tissue analyses for BHT adipose accumulation have been revealing. Extensive use of foods and food packagings with BHT has been permitted officially in the United States. In Great Britain, its use has been severely restricted. The policy differences of the two countries were reflected with data released in 1969. The accumulation of BHT in the adipose tissue of the average American was more than six times greater than that of the average Britisher. The American carried some 3.19 ppm BHT in adipose tissue, contrasted to 0.49 ppm for the Britisher.

The significance of adipose accumulation of an additive is uncertain. BHT is not the only foreign substance being stored in adipose tissue. DDT, PCBs, and other substances are also known to accumulate in the body's fat depots. In addition, other unrecognized substances may be stored. What is the sum total? What are the interactions, if any? It is known that any sudden reduction of body fat—resulting from dieting, fasting or illness—can release these accumulations from the body's depots *in toxic quantities.*

A food additive may interfere with endocrine functions. The breakdown product of the food dye erythrosine (FD&C Red No. 3) was found to release iodine, which concentrated in the human thyroid gland. Erythrosine is used widely in candy, confections, beverages, dessert powders, cereals, maraschino cherries, pet food, bakery goods, ice creams, sherbets, dairy products, sausages, snack foods, meat inks, pharmaceuticals, cosmetics, and miscellaneous consumer goods.

An additive may affect the level of blood cholesterol. This was demonstrated with surfactants, food additives that make oil and water more mixable. Surfactants are commonly used in foods such as commercial mayonnaise, ice cream, chocolate and baked goods. Surfactants, added to the diet of rabbits, monkeys and dogs, at levels ordinarily used in American foods, made the animals' blood cholesterol levels rise.

An additive may interfere with the body's muscular system. In tests, the antioxidant BHA inhibited contraction of the smooth intestinal muscles in the ileum of guinea pigs. The interference mechanism was complex and probably involved very strong or irreversible binding of BHA to the smooth contraction muscle. The inhibition was detectable even at relatively low concentrations of BHA. The effect was not entirely reversible even after the additive was withdrawn. The highest BHA concentration used in the tests only approached the level presently permitted in food under FDA regulations. Other phenolic antioxidants also have been shown to inhibit smooth muscles from functioning.

Neuromuscular disturbances also have been reported in tests on another group of food additives: sodium nitrate and sodium nitrite. Creatinine, a naturally occurring compound in the body, is part of a regulatory mechanism that controls the relaxation of muscle fiber. This control permits cells to recover from extended activity and metabolic depletions by reducing the transmission of messages between nerves and muscle fibers. In the stomach, the food additives sodium nitrate and sodium nitrite were found to react with creatinine to form a new compound, creatinine-5-oxime. When injected into rats, this newly formed compound caused neuromuscular disorders. The rats suffered from loss of alertness, muscular weakness, pelvic droop, twitches, tremors, and convulsions. When injected into mice, the compound caused similar neuromuscular disorders. Increased dosages caused tonic spasms and convulsions which could result in death.

Although some food additives may undergo changes with food constituents or other substances (see pages 77-91), others may undergo metabolic changes during absorption within the body. Such modification, termed *detoxification*, is a misnomer. The metabolites that form may be just as toxic as the original additive, or they may be even more toxic.

At times, intermediary metabolites formed during metabolism are later converted into further forms. Such intermediary metabolites are not necessarily innocuous. For example, intermediary metabolites of azo food dyes, xylidines, were shown to damage the liver of rats and dogs.

It is important to know the formation, site, and biological significance of *all* metabolites. Food additives have different metabolic patterns in different species. Therefore, it is important to know the metabolic pattern in several different species, strains, ages, and sexes of test animals and to know which of the various patterns applies to humans. Different biological effects may be demonstrated if a metabolite is toxic for one species, strain, age group, or sex, but not for others.

The problems of analyzing metabolites of a food additive and examining their effects on humans was illustrated with cyclamates. If cyclamates are excreted from the human body unchanged, they create no problem. But if they are converted to the compound cyclohexylamine or other metabolites, they are hazardous to humans. Cyclohexylamine is highly toxic. It is known to induce tumors in rats and is a suspected carcinogen for other species. Another form of cyclohexylamine is dicyclohexylamine. This metabolite is *even more toxic* than the original breakdown product.

Three adult men, previously on a cyclamate-free diet, were each given three grams of cyclamates daily. Initially, none of them converted cyclamates to cyclohexylamine. After about seven days, however, one of the three began to convert up to 17 percent of the cyclamate. After withdrawing from cyclamates for seven days, he lost his ability to convert to cyclohexylamine. This finding suggested that human gut bacteria can *learn* to metabolize cyclamates. However, even after a steady cyclamate diet for a month, the two other subjects failed to metabolize even one percent of the cyclamate dose. Therefore, the metabolism of cyclamates by human gut bacteria is not a universal problem.

Cyclamate metabolism was studied in rats, guinea pigs, and rabbits. After a steady diet of cyclamates for three months, all of the rats excreted cyclohexylamine in the urine. On the other hand, the guinea pigs had little ability to convert cyclamates to cyclohexylamine. One of six rabbits studied became a cyclamate converter and excreted about seven percent of the cyclamate in the form of cyclohexylamine.

Metabolic pathways also may vary from species to species. While a substance such as benzidine, used in dye manufacture, primarily induces bladder cancer in humans and dogs, it may produce leukemia as well as cancer of the liver, eustachian tubes, and intestine in rats. Food dyes have been known to choose different metabolic pathways, have affinity for different organs and tissues, and choose different excretory routes.

At times, human metabolic pathways may differ from individual to individual. For this reason, a cancer-inciting agent that damages the liver of one individual may damage quite a different site in another individual.

Metabolites of an additive are likely to be formed by gut bacteria in the gastrointestinal tract. Although the mammalian gut is sterile at birth, it becomes colonized by a multiplicity of bacteria types within the first week of life. The intestinal microflora are important to the person's nutrition and to his response to foreign compounds ingested. The metabolic activity in the gastrointestinal tract is potentially as high as that of the liver.

The intestinal microflora have a unique capacity to adapt, since the composition and range of acidity level can be altered by exposure to a foreign compound which stimulates or inhibits the multiplication of specific types of bacteria. The microflora are capable of metabolizing many food additives (as well as drugs). In doing so, they modify the toxicological or pharmacological effects of these substances.

Major differences exist between the microflora of different mammalian species. The rat, mouse, monkey, and hamster harbor far more microflora than either the human or the rabbit. The microflora of the rabbit's intestinal tract are comparable to those of the human gut, but there are major qualitative differences. Although for much of the time, the human upper intestinal tract harbors very few bacteria, it cannot be assumed that no bacterial metabolism occurs in this area. Whenever food is eaten, the bacterial numbers in the stomach and upper ileum increase.

Consequently, food additives and other foreign compounds ingested with food are exposed to a fairly large population of microorganisms.

Eating habits affect bacterial populations. Most types of animals eat more or less continuously. This is believed to play a role in maintaining large bacterial populations throughout the gut. In contrast, humans—who eat sporadically—have almost sterile conditions in the upper alimentary tract.

Hueper cautioned especially about human use of any chemical suspected of even a remote relationship with cancer of the human digestive tract. Cancers most frequently attack the "narrows" through which our food passes—a clear suggestion that prolonged contact between food chemicals and the intestinal lining could be a primary cancer mechanism. Although this is only a theoretical consideration, it is supported by the known fact that body tissues "remember" even brief encounters with "starters" and accumulate the ill effects over long time periods before a malignant growth actually appears. Hueper suggested that there is a crowding of substances at sites of the alimentary tract (the narrows, sphincters, and curvatures) where the food, chyme, or fecal matter moves slowly and/or remains stationary for prolonged periods (in the pyloric region of the stomach and in the rectum).

Chemicals with low molecular weights are likely to cause bodily reactions because they are broken down and absorbed quickly, while those with high molecular weights are apt to be excreted unabsorbed. Many food additives—including synthetic flavors and food dyes, antioxidants such as BHA and BHT, rare sugars such as sorbitol and xylitol, thickeners, leaveners, and sweeteners—have low molecular weights. The differences in the absorption or excretion of a food additive by different species may be determined by the substance's molecular weight.

In an article concerning food additives, *The Lancet* suggested that whenever food additives are considered for use, those *most poorly absorbed* by the intestine are possibly the preferable ones.

An ingenious process is being studied by a private corporation to make low molecular weight food additives nonabsorbable through the intestine. By binding certain food additives to molecules called *polymers*, the size of the molecules would be increased. Ongoing experiments are being conducted with food dyes, antioxidants, and sweeteners. The corporation's studies demonstrated that absorption into the cell does not have to take place with one group of additives (hormones) to produce a reaction. The active part of the hormone molecule merely needs to be locked onto a particular receptor site on the cell's surface; this sets off a chemical chain reaction that relays the hormonal message to the cell's interior.

Although metabolism may take place within the gut, the liver and kidneys are the main organs for metabolic absorption. They are also the most likely target organs for any toxic effects.

Many of the food additives that have been banned showed liver or kidney damage in animals. Among those that showed liver damage were many food dyes, the flavorings coumarin and safrole, the artificial sweeteners dulcin and cyclamates, and the preservative thiourea. Among those that showed kidney damage were ethylene glycol, a solvent and humectant, as well as the antioxidant NDGA.

Liver changes have been noted in cyclamate-treated animals of several species, including the guinea pig, mouse, and monkey. Liver damage was inflicted in guinea pigs with 2.0 percent cyclamate in the diet. At a lower dose of 0.5 percent, histological changes (changes in structure of the organism's tissues seen microscopically) were associated with changes in the blood levels of enzymes. This caused the NAS–NRC report on cyclamates to state that "serious considerations [should be] given toward potential liver damage and eventual liver disease in man, especially under conditions of continuous ingestion."

Among currently used food additives, the antioxidant BHT has displayed a wide variety of effects on the liver of different species of test animals. The long-term consequences to humans ingesting compounds such as BHT, capable of producing varied physiological effects, presently are unknown. For example, BHT-treated animals develop enlarged livers, accompanied by increased amounts of smooth endoplasmic reticulum (membranes); increased activity in liver cell division; and increased activity of at least seven liver enzymes and decreased activity of three other liver enzymes. In addition to these effects on the liver, BHT has been shown to increase the rate of urinary excretion of ascorbic acid and to elevate serum cholesterol.

Other effects may result if food additives are capable of forming chemical combinations, bindings, or complexes with components of the liver. For example, a food dye may have an affinity for protein elements in the liver—such as albumins and globulins—to form dye–protein complexes.

Prostaglandins are local hormonelike regulators in many tissues in the human body. They have been intensively studied only as recently as the late 1960s, and they have been shown to be incredibly potent compounds with a variety of biological functions. Among other tasks, prostaglandins shunt the capillary flow from poorly or nonaerated alveoli (air cells of the lungs or glands in which the secretory cells are gathered about a central space) to distended and well-aerated alveoli. Food additives, such as the dye tartrazine, can inhibit directly the synthesis and functioning of the prostaglandins.

Food additives also can affect prostaglandins indirectly. The body normally converts essential fatty acids into biologically active prostaglandins. The individual with a reasonably varied diet is apt to possess adequate amounts of essential fatty acids for this function. But the individual who chooses to eat a large number of highly processed foods containing additives is likely to be deficient in essential fatty acids, reducing prostaglandin production.

The gallbladder may be affected adversely by food additives present in the diet of people in Western industrialized countries. The number of cholecystectomies (operations to remove the gallbladder) in 1961 and 1971 was studied in three similar towns in Canada, France, and England. The incidence of gallbladder disease was six times higher in North America than in Western Europe. The operation was nine times graver for patients below age 35. The number of cholecystectomies had doubled in all three countries over ten years. In France, the majority of gallbladder patients were in late middle age, while in Canada the disease was most prevalent among lean and fit individuals between 20 and 29 years. No consistent relationship could be found between obesity, high carbohydrate diets, or even diets high in fat and protein. However, a common link was suggested by the investigators:

Prepared or processed food seems to be consumed more in North America, to a lesser extent in England, and hardly at all in rural France. *The Lancet* in 1969 commented that the average English person consumes 3 lb (1350 g) of chemical substances that are not the normal constituents of food. Are there chemical substances in food and beverages which, especially if consumed in excess, in some way alter the enterohepatic [intestinal and liver] circulation or directly affect the microsomes [minute protoplasmic granules] of the hepatocyte [liver cells]? Many food additives are powerful liver-enzyme inducers.

A food additive may affect adversely the central nervous system, inducing neurological and mental disturbances. To date, few toxicological tests have studied the possible psycho-behavioral effects inflicted by food additives. Environmental pollutants— including mercury, lead, sulfur dioxide, and certain pesticides— have been related to central nervous system disorders and mental diseases. Data suggest that certain food additives may inflict similar damage.

One of the earliest incidents of central nervous system disturbances caused by a food additive was observed in the mid-1940s. Strange animal behavior aroused interest in the southern United States, where dogs developed epilepticlike running fits. The animals lost interest in their surroundings, ran or walked more slowly, had dry mouths, sought shade, were frightened easily, and appeared unfriendly. In time, they frothed at the mouth, collapsed, and had ataxia and epileptiform fits. This canine hysteria grew in intensity and spread to other areas.

A miller, who requested anonymity, suggested to a British physician, Sir Edward Mellanby, that agene (nitrogen trichloride) might be responsible for this canine hysteria. Mellanby discovered that he could produce hysterical outbreaks in dogs at will by exposing them to flour containing agene. Mellanby wrote, "The abnormal behavior of the animals affected by the agenized flour suggests that the central nervous system is primarily affected by some toxic agent, but other organs may also be involved." Mellanby's published report was followed by a film in which he showed the animals' symptoms after they ate agenized bread.

When agene's toxicity was suspected, long overdue experiments confirmed its harmfulness (see page 81). In 1927, the British Ministry of Health recommended that agene be banned for use with flour. But official restraints were not actually instituted, and millers continued to use the bleach. Dr. J. J. Coglan, a British physician, presented clinical evidence of the damaging nature of agene to the British Ministry of Food, but no official action was taken. Decades passed, and agene was still in use in Great Britain and in the United States. Mellanby's findings in the 1940s prodded the FDA to conduct tests. The agency's tests confirmed Mellanby's data. In 1949, the FDA banned agene as a flour bleach. The following year, the British Ministry of Health agreed to discontinue the use of agene at an unspecified date and to replace it with another bleach. Ultimately, this was accomplished.

After agene had been banned in both countries, the reason for its harmfulness was revealed. Nitrogen trichloride combines with methionine, a naturally occurring amino acid present in flour, to form methionine sulfoximine. Tests with several animal species demonstrated that this compound interferes with brain enzymes, and in turn, adversely affects the central nervous system. Methionine sulfoximine inhibits brain protein metabolism by inhibiting methionine from being incorporated into brain protein.

In rat studies, methionine sulfoximine displayed some promise as an anti-tumor agent. For this reason, the compound was given to seven human patients with inoperable cancer. Methionine sulfoximine failed to arrest the tumors; but it caused psychosis, marked by "frank hallucinations, disorientation, and marked agitation which continued for from one to three days after administration of

the compound was stopped." In humans, heavy doses of methionine sulfoximine caused changes in electroencephalogram recordings.

More recently, there have been a few studies on the possible
effects of food additives on the brain and behavior. In 1972,
researchers fed diets containing large quantities of BHA or BHT to
pregnant mice. BHA or BHT was added to the diet at the level of
0.5 percent of the food's total weight. This is only five to ten times
as much as may be present in processed foods eaten by humans,
and it is only 25 times the maximum concentration that the FDA
permits in foods for humans.

The chemical analysis of the brains of the newly born offspring
of the mice treated with BHA or BHT showed that the amounts of
two important brain chemicals were well below normal. Little more
than 50 percent of the normal level of cholinesterase and about 60
percent of serotonin was present. These drastically reduced levels
produced pathological brain changes and altered behavior in mice.

When the mice were approximately 30 days old, they were
studied for motor activity, isolation-induced aggression, learning
ability, and social behavior. The offspring of the treated mice
differed significantly from the controls. There was a marked
decrease in their exploratory reflex. There was weight reduction.
The offspring of BHT-treated mice slept less and fought more than
the control mice. They groomed themselves less and did not sleep,
compared to the controls, which groomed and slept normally.

These results, according to the researchers:

. . . indicate that these antioxidants can no longer be viewed as innocuous
substances. Our results indicate that there does not appear to be too great
a difference between BHA and BHT. The safe use of these additives must
be reevaluated. . . . This work demonstrates the possibility of an
environmental threat from food processing practices.

Elsewhere, a researcher demonstrated that the preservative
sodium nitrite produced seemingly permanent epilepticlike changes
in the brain activity of treated rats. When sodium nitrite was fed

regularly to the animals, the electrical recordings of their brains indicated "outbursts" that resembled epileptic seizures. When the dosage was increased, these outbursts persisted even after the chemical feeding was discontinued. The researcher considered the results "disquieting," especially since the same tests also showed that sodium nitrite passed through the placenta of pregnant rats. At the higher levels, sodium nitrite causes a high mortality rate among offspring and a depressed growth rate among surviving offspring. (For a fuller discussion of placental transfer, see pages 167–69.) Although the researcher reported his findings to the FDA in 1971, the agency has not reduced the permissible level of this additive, much less banned its use in food.

Ben F. Feingold, M.D., has reported the possibility that the synthetic flavorings and food dyes used in many processed foods and beverages may be an unsuspected cause of behavioral problems, such as learning disabilities and hyperkinesis, in children. Feingold, an allergist and pediatrician, believes that the effects of these substances are *not truly allergic, but rather pharmacologic* (druglike reactions).

Feingold became suspicious of synthetic flavorings and dyes after having treated a psychotic woman for allergies. When he found that she was salicylate-sensitive, he eliminated her intake of aspirin and other salicylate-containing compounds, including synthetic flavorings and food dyes. The woman's allergies *and* psychosis cleared up. When Feingold tried the salicylate-free diet with other patients, he found that both hives and asthma sufferers gained relief.

Feingold then tested the salicylate-free diet on children with allergies and/or behavioral problems. He had found that some 1,610 components in synthetic food flavorings and some 34 components in food dyes induced similar symptoms. Aspirin, indomethacin (a drug), and tartrazine (FD&C Yellow No. 5) inhibit the synthesis of prostaglandins. In turn, the formation of kinins (hormonelike substances that trigger powerful physiological effects at high dilutions and, at times, with great rapidity) is also inhibited. Interference with this normal sequence may account for the similar adverse reactions to chemical compounds that bear no structural relationship to each other.

Hyperactivity, or *hyperkinesis,* interferes with a child's attention span, leading to learning difficulties and disruptive behavior. The disorder, which occurs almost exclusively in boys, is often treated with amphetamines and other drug stimulants (which have a reversed, calming effect on hyperactive children).

Feingold traced a parallel between sharp increases in hyperactivity and other learning difficulties and the rise in the sales of synthetically flavored and dyed foods and beverages in the past decade. Although there are only 11 basic synthetic colors, there are some 2,500 to 3,000 flavoring agents. Together, these two groups of additives constitute about 80 percent of all food additives. They have proliferated especially in convenience foods and soft drink powders.

Feingold cited a California study that showed the incidence of hyperkinesis in certain school populations increased in the last ten years from an average of 2 percent up to 20 to 25 percent, and in some cases, up to 40 percent.

To date, Feingold has treated successfully a number of hyperkinetic children, and his results have been duplicated and confirmed independently by other physicians. Feingold reported that even a slight violation of the diet can cause symptoms of hyperkinesis to emerge within a few hours and to persist for 24 to 48 hours.

Feingold speculated that chemical additives ingested by a pregnant woman might lead to hyperkinesis in her offspring, since additives can cross the placental barrier to the fetus (see pages 285–86). Feingold suggested that increased consumption of food additives by a pregnant woman could be an important factor in adversely affecting the fetus so that later, during childhood, a hyperkinetic behavioral pattern is likely to develop.

Both mental and physical illnesses caused by chemical additives were reported by Lawrence D. Dickey, M.D., in 1969. Ready prepared ice tea, which often contains several chemical additives, induced an epileptic seizure in one of Dickey's patients. In another patient, the tea induced tunnel vision (narrowing of the visual field).

There is growing awareness of the assault from an ever-expanding number of chemicals on the body and their potential harmfulness. "In the past 40 years, the environment in which we live has been altered to an extraordinary extent," wrote Dr. E. Cuyler Hammond and Dr. Irving J. Selikoff jointly in a background paper for the American Cancer Society's annual seminar for science writers in 1974. Among the environmental changes, the two doctors singled out food additives for special comment: "Our food has chemicals, designed to improve its taste, freshness, appearance—but which are strange to our intestines, livers, kidneys, blood."

8

Individual Susceptibility

• Protection of the most susceptible individual in the population is the basis for design of a program of disease control.

Jesse L. Steinfeld, Surgeon General of the United States

• When a husband and wife disagree on the temperature of the soup or on the amount of bed coverings, or if their sleep patterns do not jibe, this is evidence of inborn differences in physiology. . . . Organ weights may differ by as much as twofold, the free amino acids in the brain may vary fivefold, and certain hormone levels may vary as much as seven-, sixteen-, or even thirty-two-fold.

Professor Roger J. Williams, Clayton Foundation Biochemical Institute

• Have animals in the course of . . . long-term toxicity studies been tested with the excitant under investigation during a phase of adaptation in which reactions on the basis of *individual susceptibility* are accentuated? Or has the occurrence of aberrant responses indicative of individual susceptibility been averaged out . . . ? The medical problem involved [with] individual susceptibility is *not* concerned with the *middle* of the distribution curve, but with the *far end* . . . *!* Acute and chronic toxicity studies of new chemicals in animals . . . should be regarded as a *prelude to observations in man*—especially in susceptibility-prone individuals. Where are these reports? The few that exist tend to involve intermittent exposures and to appear some time *after* the production and distribution of a new chemical has become a "profitable venture." [emphasis supplied]

Theron G. Randolph, M.D.

• The reports on clinical patterns representing adverse reactions to food chemicals are extremely limited and do not reflect the incidence of this problem that would be anticipated in view of the very wide distribution of these chemicals in our food supply. An important factor contributing to the paucity of clinical reports is the lack of recognition that food additives are a relatively common cause of adverse clinical patterns.

Ben F. Feingold, M.D., Chief Emeritus, Department of Allergy, Kaiser-Permanente Medical Center, San Francisco

● Many of the things that pollute foods are also found in drugs. There is, however, a physician's reference book that lists exactly what goes into each drug. There is nothing comparable for foods. It is hard to estimate how many people who already have allergies are suffering from food additives. I think the less chemicals you put in a person's environment the better off he is, whether he eats them or breathes them or soaks them in. The more different chemicals you put in his environment, the more apt he is to be sensitive to more chemicals.

William C. Grater, M.D., Assistant Clinical Professor of Medicine, Medical School, Southwestern University

● The attention to date on the problem of additives has been focused primarily upon the carcinogenic potentials, hematopoietic effects, intestinal flora changes, and other physiological alterations. Except in a few cases, search of the literature has revealed no interest in the potential allergenic effect of excipient vehicles and additives.

Eugene Cowen, M.D., Assistant Clinical Professor of Medicine, Medical Center, University of Colorado

● The practical applicability of . . . knowledge concerning food additives and contaminants should alert all physicians to maintain a critical and sober attitude to the potential hazard of these agents. An increasing number of patients have been observed in clinical practice with diffuse hair fall, chronic urticaria [red patched skin], toxic epidermal necrolysis, pemphigus [spotted skin], and other such illness in which ingested drugs or predisposing factors can be excluded in the etiologic investigation. It is common practice to consign these diseases to causes unknown or to classify them as idiosyncratic.

Thomas H. Steinberg, M.D., Department of Dermatology, University of California Medical Center, and Stanley M. Bierman, M.D.

● A number of . . . allergists have documented the many mental symptoms and behavioral problems caused by food additives and food allergies. If mental illness caused by allergies were recognized more, and emotional factors not always sought to explain mental disturbances, a great deal of time and money could be saved, and patients' mental conditions eliminated. There are millions of patients enduring needless suffering. One can only guess at the number of major and minor tragedies that are enacted daily because of misinterpreted symptoms and inappropriate therapies.

Howard G. Rapaport, M.D., former President of the American College of Allergists and Associate Clinical Professor of Pediatrics for Allergies, College of Medicine, Albert Einstein University

In the susceptible individual, food additives may cause allergic reactions that can go unnoticed for years. Such individual susceptibilities to specific additives possibly represents a far larger segment of the public than is generally acknowledged. In the United States, some 100 million persons—half of the entire population—are believed to suffer from allergies ranging from serious to mild. One out of every five to ten people has a major allergy of disabling proportions and consequences. Although the remaining allergies may be less debilitating, nevertheless they may impair bodily functions. Allergens do not always affect a limited area of the body. Frequently, a mixture of patterns occurs, with practically every major body system being adversely affected. If an individual is susceptible to two or more allergens—as most allergic sufferers are—one allergen can add to another and reinforce its effects.

Food additives form part of a very large, ever-growing list of allergens. The FDA does not require any allergenicity tests for food additives, and besides, present testing methods have *rarely* demonstrated individual susceptibility to the allergenic qualities of a food additive. The frequency of clinical intolerance by the susceptible individual is often low. Consequently, the acute and chronic toxicity animal studies are usually inadequate to detect such hypersensitivity. The allergenic quality of an additive may be demonstrated only after the chemical has been released and is in widespread use.

The problem is further complicated by the lack of any adequate objective laboratory procedure for detecting individual human susceptibility. Experiments to develop such testing techniques are being attempted in at least one hospital. Common allergy tests (skin tests) do *not* measure intolerance to food additives.

One set of animal tests *did* demonstrate an allergic reaction to an additive. Using sulfa drugs to produce allergies in 42 rabbits, researchers were able to induce degenerative arterial changes in 31 animals within eight months. The changes closely resembled arteriosclerosis in man. The findings suggested serious disease conditions, such as arteriosclerosis, might be promoted by allergenic substances, even though, as in this instance, the reactions "were not apparent on the surface." If these data are applicable to humans, food additives with even minor allergenic qualities cannot be dismissed as "harmless."

Increased numbers of allergists have observed and reported adverse effects inflicted by a wide range of chemicals, including food additives, on susceptible individuals. Dr. Stephen D. Lockey, Sr., Dr. Eloise W. Kailin and Dr. Theron G. Randolph have attempted to make other allergists, as well as general practitioners, aware of the difficulties encountered in identifying these chemicals. Although the complaining, chronically ill patient's physician may suspect several chemical exposures, the patient may be reacting not only to these, but also to *other unsuspected but related ones.* The physician, not knowing the scope of the chemical allergens that might be involved, nor how to protect the patient from them, is at a loss in handling the case. Because the totality of the chemical environment and its full range of potential effects have not been described, the physician is apt to treat such a patient with *additional related substances* (such as drugs), thereby intensifying the problem.

Vegetable gums are among the food additives that are well-established allergens. Allergic reactions to vegetable gums were reported as early as 1932. But the FDA allows them to be used in many prepared foods and beverages, frequently without label declaration. Even when their presence is declared on the label, the vague term "vegetable gums" may be printed rather than the name of the specific gums.

The vegetable gums used in foods and beverages include acacia (gum arabic), agar, algin, bassora, chick, gelatin, ghatti, guar, Irish moss (carrageenan), karaya, locust bean (carob bean gum), mesquite, pectin, quince seed, and tragacanth. Allergic reactions to acacia and karaya are frequently caused by ingestion of food, inhalation, or surface or occupational contact. One woman, highly sensitive to karaya, chided a physician who wrote in his syndicated column that karaya gum was "harmless." The woman wrote, "I am seriously allergic to karaya gum. This was discovered in a routine allergy test. I assume that since allergists test everybody for this gum, they have found somebody allergic to it. It made my life miserable for several years, causing sharp gas pains and cramps in the colon."

Although avoidance of vegetable gums may be crucial for such an individual, it is nearly impossible. Vegetable gums may be included in the following:

breads
breakfast foods
cake icings
candy
charlotte russe
cheese spreads
chewing gum
chocolate milk
coffee substitutes
confectioneries
custards, frozen
diabetic preparations
French dressing
fruit juices, frozen & dehydrated
fruit, dehydrated
gelatin
gravies, commercial
"health" foods
ice cream
jellies
jels
junkets
kara jel
malted milk drinks

marshmallows
mayonnaise
meat, ground, preparations
meat, fish & poultry, canned
meringues
mustard, prepared
orange concentrates
pastries
pie fillings
potato salad, prepared
puddings
sherbets
specialty foods
starch-free desserts
syrups
toppings
tomato products: catsup, purée, consommé
wheat cakes
whipped cream, commercial
wines
yogurt
plus pharmaceuticals, as well as industrial and household products

Frequently, the public wrongly assumes that food additives from "natural" substances are innocuous. This is not necessarily true. In the past, three food flavorings derived from natural sources—coumarin from the tonka bean, safrole from sassafras, and oil of calamus from sweet flag—have been banned because they were harmful. In 1970, British officials granted only provisional acceptance to the use of guar gum in foods. They suggested that further information about this vegetable gum was needed and recommended that the additive should be reviewed within the next five years. Recently, the FDA requested reviews for two more vegetable gums, carob bean gum and carrageenan, after adverse findings had been reported.

An individual sensitive to any of these vegetable gums, but unaware of the cause, might wrongly assume that he is allergic to the food itself. For example, a person might believe that he was allergic to whipped cream, when actually he might be sensitive to the vegetable gum used in commercially prepared whipped cream. Similarly, he might react to other treated foods, all of which would produce a confusing pattern of allergic reactions. These are a few reported cases:

—A physician thought that he was allergic to dates. After avoiding them for many years, he discovered that if he washed the dates before eating them, he experienced no allergic reactions. He was not allergic to the dates, but to the substance used for polishing them.

—Papain, an enzyme from papaya, is used as a meat tenderizer in homes and at restaurants. Papain is a frequent cause of reactions to meat. Individuals sensitive to papaya may exhibit an intolerance to beef, ham, and luncheon meats treated with papain tenderizers. Occasionally, tenderizers are administered to cattle before slaughter. The resulting papain accumulation in the meat tissues can cause reactions in varying degrees with sensitive individuals.

—An individual may appear to be milk intolerant, a common condition frequently due to the absence or insufficiency of an enzyme to digest it properly. However, the individual may *not* be milk intolerant, but rather be reacting to traces of penicillin or sulfa which may be residues from drugs that had been administered to the cow.

—How wrong factors may be ascribed to an allergy is illustrated in the case of a middle-aged man who sought help for severe headaches that occurred only on Thanksgiving, Christmas, and New Year's Day. An allergist found three common factors involved in these holiday headaches. The patient always ate and drank more than usual, his mother-in-law was present on the holidays, and the main dish was always turkey. There were many hurt feelings and exchanges of unkind words with his mother-in-law, until it was established that her presence was *not* causing the headaches. The man was extremely sensitive to penicillin. The holiday turkeys always came from a state where fowl were fed on penicillin-treated mash, and the residues in the birds caused his violent headaches.

Cottonseed and its derivatives, such as cottonseed oil, frequently induce reactions in sensitive individuals. Such persons have difficulty in avoiding these commonly used food additives, which are also present in a large number of consumer goods. Cottonseed oil may be present in many candies (especially chocolate), mayonnaise and salad dressings, and canned sardines. It is used extensively in restaurant foods, especially in frying. It is commonly used in the production of potato chips, cheap bakery cakes, cookies, popcorn, and doughnuts and in the manufacture of gin and xylose (a sugar substitute which is often used in soft drinks and fig-filled cookies). Cottonseed-sensitive individuals also have difficulty tolerating milk from cows that have been fed on cottonseed mash; but it is virtually impossible to know whether cows have been fed with cottonseed mash. Many consumer goods also contain cottonseed or its derivatives. Sensitive individuals need to shun fluffy blankets, coverings, certain soaps, cosmetics, ointments, paints, and paper.

Sodium benzoate, a widely used preservative with many processed foods and beverages, has been reported by various investigators to cause acute urticaria (hives) in individuals. One physician reported several episodes of acute urticaria which he experienced within 25 minutes after ingesting foods or beverages containing sodium benzoate. Since the presence of sodium benzoate or other benzoic acid derivatives must be declared on food labels, the physician became a careful label reader. He switched from margarine, which usually contains sodium benzoate, to butter, in which this preservative is specifically forbidden. Nonetheless, the physician experienced acute hives after eating the butter. Although the dairy denied the presence of sodium benzoate in the butter, an independent laboratory confirmed the presence of the preservative in the samples submitted by the physician.

Sulfur compounds—frequently used as preservatives, bleaching agents, and antibrowning agents—are recognized as inducing reactions in susceptible individuals. One allergist noted that few of his patients were able to eat French fried potatoes in restaurants, although they could tolerate them when prepared at home. He attributed this intolerance to the almost universal restaurant practice of purchasing prepeeled and sliced potatoes for French frying, which are dipped in a solution of sulfur dioxide as an antibrowning measure. The same process may be used in the manufacture of potato chips and in handling freshly cut apples and peaches. Some fresh fruits and vegetables, especially asparagus and mushrooms, also may be treated with sulfur solutions. Corn kernels may be soaked in a sulfur dioxide solution during processing. This leaves sulfur residue on all manufactured corn products—including cornstarch, corn flour, corn sugar (dextrose and glucose), corn oil and corn-dried dextrins—so that they must be avoided by the sulfur dioxide-sensitive individual. Sulfur also is employed commonly in the manufacture of cane and beet sugar.

Randolph reported that several test subjects had strong adverse reactions to sulfured peaches. One individual who could tolerate uncontaminated peaches, reacted acutely to sulfured ones. Within 20 minutes after eating them, she complained of nervousness and tenseness, with alternating chilling and sweating sensations. After 30 minutes, she became nauseated. After 35 minutes, she vomited part of the peach. At 40 minutes, she remained cold, clammy, pale, and depressed. Even after her stomach contents were pumped, she continued to have severe abdominal cramps, residual aching, fatigue, and depression for the rest of the day.

Citric acid, a commonly used additive for many processing purposes, causes an allergic reaction in many people. A Washington, D.C., boy who was allergic to citric acid, usually ate only home-canned tomatoes. After eating commercially-canned tomatoes, he became ill. The tomatoes had been canned with citric acid, but this additive had not been listed on the label because the law presently does not require full ingredient disclosure.

A number of observed skin reactions have been attributed to cyclamates. These include photosensitivity (an abnormal sensitivity of the skin to sunlight) pruritus (itching), dermatographia (tracings made on skin that leave distinct reddish elevated marks), urticaria (hives), angio-edema (swelling of lymph or blood vessels), localized patches or patches of dermatitis, dermatitis herpetiformis (marked by skin lesions occurring in various combinations).

Saccharin has been reported to produce numerous adverse effects in individuals. While some of the effects may be allergic responses in sensitive individuals, others are considered as toxic reactions and interactions affecting the skin, cardiac rhythm and gastrointestinal tract. Reported reactions to saccharin include headache, tachycardia (relatively rapid heart beat), skipped pulse beat, breaking out in a cold sweat, nausea, pruritus (itching), fluttering in the ear, swelling and blistering of the tongue, and various skin reactions such as erythema (reddening), prickly sensations, photosensitivity and edematous papules (pimple-like swellings).

One allergist suggested that many people who suffer from migraine may be allergic to sodium propionate, a mold retarder. Although this compound occurs naturally in some forms of Swiss cheese, a synthetic form is used as an additive in bread.

Adverse reactions to BHA and BHT have been reported clinically by various allergists, and at least one controlled study, conducted with humans, demonstrated that these antioxidants induced adverse reactions in susceptible individuals. Patients chosen for this study were already known as chemically sensitive individuals. Some had symptoms of chronic vasomotor rhinitis (an allergic inflammation of the nose's mucous membrane) with or without nasal polyps, with or without associated asthma. Some suffered primarily from asthma. When BHA and BHT were given orally to these individuals, the rhinitis patients had a worsening of their symptoms within 5 to 75 minutes. A few severe asthmatics generally began to develop a marked flare-up of asthmatic symptoms within 5 to 60 minutes; at times, these individuals had to be given medication for relief.

The vascular reaction increased dramatically in two severe asthmatics. When BHA and BHT were administered to them, their vascular response increased by a factor of 100 to 200 percent within five minutes and required an hour to return to normal. A slower onset of vascular reaction took place in the rhinitis patients. Other marked symptoms experienced by the group included marked diaphoresis (profuse and artificially induced perspiration), sleepiness, headache, occasional pain high in the back of the sternal bone and radiating to the back, flushing, and suffusion of the conjunctiva in the eye.

Two clinical cases concerned individual sensitivity to BHA- and BHT-treated foods and food packaging (see pages 16–17). The allergist who reported these cases encountered another within his own community. A woman suffered such a severe reaction to BHT that the physician had to make an emergency house call and administer hormonal treatment.

Another allergist treated a woman for skin blisters and eye hemorrhaging, symptoms traced to BHT and BHA sensitivity. The woman had enjoyed excellent health and had been free of allergic reactions. Her meals were made largely from basic commodities that she had prepared in her own kitchen. After eating commercially processed instant mashed potatoes for the first time, she experienced the blistering and hemorrhaging in one eye. The mashed potatoes were the only newly introduced item in her diet. When she ate this processed food once again, and the symptoms recurred, both her physician and ophthalmologist suspected BHT and BHA, which were present in the product. They advised her to avoid foods containing these antioxidants. She did so, and the symptoms subsided.

At a later date, the woman had a flare-up of symptoms. This time they were traced to a breakfast cereal, never before used in her household, which contained BHT and BHA. After that incident, the woman became a concerned label reader, and she studiously avoided foods or packaging that contained either of these additives.

Again, the symptoms returned. This time, the problem was traced to a shortening that she had used for some time. Upon examining the label closely, she was astonished to find that the shortening was labeled "new and improved," with BHT and BHA.

Both the woman and her physicians tried to learn from government officials what foods contained the two additives. Letters and telephone calls were either ignored or answered unsatisfactorily. She was told repeatedly that all she had to do was *read the label.*

But reading labels gives no assurance that BHT and BHA will be avoided. Since BHT and BHA may be incorporated in food packaging and in animal feeds, as well as in foodstuffs, they can enter the end product *indirectly.* Today, it is nearly impossible to find any factory-processed food or food packaging material that does not contain one or both of these chemicals. BHT and BHA manufacturers suggest the use of these antioxidants in animal fats such as lard, beef tallow, bacon, chicken fat, butter, cream, shortenings, and grease; fried foods such as potato chips, doughnuts, and processed meats and fish; baked goods such as crackers, pastries, cakes, candies, and cookies; vegetable fats such as shortenings, margarine, peanut butter, and salad oils and dressing; ground grain meals and grain germs; a miscellany of other food items, including nutmeats, raisins, milk, candied fruit, whipped topping mixes, imitation fruit drinks, breakfast foods, extracts, essential oils, spices and pet foods; food-packaging paper and containers such as milk cartons, containers (cottage cheese, ice cream, potato chips, cereals, cookies and pastries), wrappers (breads, butter, and cheeses), rubber gaskets that seal food jars, and household wax paper. These antioxidants are also found in some beverages, chewing gum, cosmetics, drugs, and animal feeds.

Allergic reactions to monosodium glutamate have been reported from time to time. Three of the components of this flavor enhancer—namely wheat, corn, and sugarbeet by-products—are common food allergens. As early as 1955, *Consumers' Research Bulletin* published a report by a physician who had traced a serious allergy to the use of monosodium glutamate. Within a half hour after eating meals prepared at home, as well as at fine restaurants, a woman and her son developed acute distress symptoms that resembled gallbladder trouble. They experienced epigastric full-ness, belching, distention, and marked upper-abdominal discom-fort. The sensitivity was traced to monosodium glutamate.

In 1968, individual sensitivity to monosodium glutamate re-ceived notoriety, precipitated by a letter to the editor of a medical journal by Dr. Robert Ho Man Kwok, senior research investigator at the National Biomedical Research Foundation. Kwok described a strange syndrome that he personally experienced in restaurants serving Northern Chinese food. About 15 to 20 minutes after eating, he developed a "numbness at the back of the neck, gradually radiating to both arms and the back, general weakness and palpitation." Kwok added that some of his Chinese friends, both medical and nonmedical, also complained of similar symp-toms after eating Chinese food. He speculated that it might be caused by some ingredient in the soy sauce, by the high sodium content of the food, and/or by the generous use of monosodium glutamate in many Chinese restaurants.

Kwok's description elicited other reports of what came to be dubbed the "Chinese Restaurant Syndrome" as well as "Kwok's Quease." But for the individuals who were sensitive to this additive, it was no joking matter. Many physicians confirmed similar symptoms in patients, including "profuse, cold sweat," "tightness on both sides of the head . . . felt as though, at any second, the sides of my head would burst," and "pounding, throbbing sensa-tion in the head, viselike."

Interest in the subject continued, and medical researchers followed up Kwok's lead. A neurologist and a pharmacologist found that monosodium glutamate induced CRS. They acknowl-edged that the syndrome had been well-known to Chinese restaura-teurs and was familiar to some allergists. Additional experiments, conducted by pharmacology students, confirmed the allergenicity of monosodium glutamate.

At the same time, data were reported linking this additive to far more serious consequences. Dr. John W. Olney found monosodium glutamate capable of inducing brain damage in newly born animals (see page 101).

A baby girl, normal until the age of six months, began to have seizures. She was hospitalized and placed on anticonvulsant medication, but the seizures continued. The child was feverish, lost appetite and weight, and was not growing well. She was taken to an institute for nervous and mental disorders, where Dr. Marguerite Stemmermann reviewed the child's dietary intake. She discovered that the little girl had begun sharing the family's food at the dinner table at the age of six months. The seizures, resembling shuddering fits, had begun to appear and grew in frequency. By the time Stemmermann examined the child at one year of age, the child was experiencing more than a hundred daily seizures. Examination showed that the child did not lose consciousness. Repeated electroencephalogram tests revealed no cortical disturbances.

Stemmermann found that eliminating monosodium glutamate from the child's diet stopped the multiple petit mal seizures within three days. After the seizures stopped, the anticonvulsant medication gradually was withdrawn. Then, after a year without symptoms, the child was experimentally given half a frankfurter containing monosodium glutamate. Within three hours, she experienced a shuddering seizure. A week later, a bit of spaghetti sauce, also containing monosodium glutamate, induced a similar reaction.

Approximately three months later the child once again had seizures. She had been fed some fresh sausage meat from a hog raised by a member of the family. The child's mother called the slaughterhouse and inquired whether any monosodium glutamate had been added while the sausage meat had been prepared. The butcher assured the mother that no monosodium glutamate had been added to the meat. The child was fed some of the sausage meat again, and seizures followed. The child's mother gave some thought to the problem and wondered if any of the spices used with the sausage meat might contain monosodium glutamate. Again, she called the slaughterhouse. The butcher checked the label on the spice mixture, and indeed, monosodium glutamate was present!

According to the mother's report, her little girl enjoys good health as long as she remains on a monosodium-glutamate-free diet.

Stemmermann stressed that this is the only case of infant monosodium glutamate sensitivity she has found, although some ten such cases have been studied to date. Stemmermann suggested that her patient may have some enzyme defect, making her unable to handle either glutamine or glutamic acid. The child's seizures were not the usual, minor motor epileptogenic manifestations, reported Stemmermann, but rather most likely of hypothalamic origin, representing an infantile form of CRS. Such an infantile form would be rare mainly because few children are introduced to adult foods such as spaghetti sauce or frankfurters at six months of age.

More allergic responses to synthetic flavorings and food dyes have been reported than for any other group of food additives. In fact, flavoring agents comprise about 80 percent of all additives used. Because of the extremely widespread distribution of these substances, not only in foods and beverages, but also in pharmaceuticals, cosmetics, and other consumer goods, virtually everyone has some daily contact with them. A list of foods and beverages containing these chemicals, in various combinations, would be extensive. Although highly processed foods and beverages contain these additives in large numbers, even basic commodities are not free of them. For example, the dairy industry has long been allowed to add color to butter, cheeses, and ice cream *without any label declaration.*

Allergic responses to flavorings and food dyes have been reported in numerous individuals. These responses affect various tissues and organs. Feingold reported, "Many cases of obscure diagnosis are probably due to the additives and the cause is not generally recognized by either the profession or the public." Reported adverse responses to food dyes and flavorings include:

—*Respiratory:* allergic rhinitis, nasal polyps, severe and intractable asthma, coughing and throat swelling.

—*Dermal (skin):* itching, localized skin lesions, chronic and generalized urticaria, and angioedema (patches of circumscribed swellings of the skin, mucous membranes and sometimes viscera, believed to be induced by allergic response).

—*Gastrointestinal:* swollen tongue, canker sores, flatulence, heartburn, belching, constipation and internal bleeding.

—*Hematological (blood):* purpura (bleeding into skin, hemorrhaging into mucous membranes and other tissues) and eosinophilia (abnormal increased number of eosinophils in the blood, characteristic of allergic response).

—*Neurological:* emotional upsets, migraine and other headaches, and behavioral disturbances (including hyperkinesis, epileptiform seizures, and anphylactic shock).

—*Skeletal:* arthralgia with swellings and pains in the joints.

According to allergists, there is little difference between additives such as synthetic flavorings and food dyes, and many drugs. Recognizing this relationship, knowledge about adverse drug reactions can be useful in interpreting the reactions caused by synthetic flavors and food dyes.

Feingold reported that genetic studies have demonstrated that each person has a unique "biological individuality." Pharmacological reactions of drugs depend, to a great extent, upon proteins that have a high degree of specificity. The quality and quantity of these proteins can be altered through genetic mutations, which influence drug metabolism, their binding abilities, and drug receptor interactions. *A number of metabolic variations are actually not abnormalities, since the individuals show no disturbances under normal conditions.* In the presence of certain drugs, however, these metabolic variations express their potentially dangerous character.

Another important point is the possibility of cross reactivity among each group of chemicals, resulting in more than one dye or one flavoring being at fault in the same individual. Cross reactivity may occur since food dyes are derived from four basic groups that are *structurally related:*

—*Triphenylmethane:* FD&C Blue No. 1 (Brilliant Blue FCF), as well as FD&C Green No. 3 (Fast Green FCF).

—*Sulfonated indigo:* FD&C Blue No. 2 (Indigotine).

—*Azo:* FD&C Red No. 4 (Ponceau SX), Citrus Red No. 2, FD&C Yellow No. 5 (Tartrazine), FD&C Yellow No. 6 (Sunset Yellow FCF), and Orange B.

—*Xanthene:* FD&C Red No. 3 (Erythrosine).

Flavoring agents, numbering in the thousands, show a similarly *close structural relationship.*

In order to understand how these substances induce allergic response in an individual, it is necessary to be familiar with terms used in the allergy field:

—*Antigen:* usually a protein or carbohydrate substance (a toxin, enzyme, or certain constituents of blood corpuscles or of other cells) that, when introduced into the body, stimulates the production of an antibody.

—*Antibody:* any of various body globulins normally present or produced in response to infection or administration of suitable antigens or haptens that combine specifically with antigens (as bacteria to toxins or foreign red blood cells) and neutralize toxins, agglutinate bacteria or cells, and precipitate soluble antigens.

—*Hapten:* a substance not antigenic in itself that, in combination with a carrier antigen, confers specificity or antigenicity or both.

—*Covalent bonds:* a nonionic bond formed by shared electrons, usually a pair, each of which originally belonged to a different or the same atom.

Chemicals with low molecular weights, such as synthetic flavors and food dyes, produce body reactions (see page 32). Immunochemistry studies have shown that low molecular weight chemicals coat the cells and combine with body proteins to form complexes that are potential antigens. According to Dr. Lockey, these chemicals present problems, particularly those substances with low molecular structures, which "are causing an increase in the rate of undesired [allergic] reactions ranging from minor to fatal."

Food dyes that form covalent chemical bonds with food proteins are particularly suspect as haptens. Tartrazine has demonstrated this characteristic more frequently, perhaps, than any other food dye.

Tartrazine may produce symptoms in aspirin-sensitive individuals. As a result, an aspirin-sensitive individual may avoid substances containing salicylates and still have aspirinlike reactions when he ingests tartrazine-containing foods or beverages. Another common food additive, the preservative sodium benzoate, may also induce allergic reactions in an aspirin-sensitive individual.

In 1968, studies reported that aspirin-sensitive individuals showed symptoms of aspirin allergy after eating fresh pork, sweet corn, soft drinks, and cheese crackers. None of the patients who reported reactions after ingestion of food gave positive skin reactions to the foods under suspicion. Analysis of the suspected foods established the presence of multiple additives in all but two of the samples. Of the preservatives, sodium benzoate was used most commonly; of food dyes, tartrazine was a component of all but one of the "yellows" in the orange-colored foods. The ability of tartrazine to induce tissue swellings and respiratory symptoms in susceptible patients had been established earlier. These more recent studies demonstrated that reactions to tartrazine and aspirin might be present in the same patients.

In 1972, Swedish studies with eight aspirin-sensitive individuals reported a higher incidence of tartrazine sensitivity than earlier studies. Seven out of eight patients were highly sensitive to tartrazine. They reacted with symptoms of asthma, urticaria, or both. The researchers concluded that tartrazine should not be allowed in foods and drugs unless appropriate information was available to consumers. Probably as a result of this recommendation, the National Foods Administration of Sweden promptly required the presence of tartrazine to be declared on labels.

Several allergists have reported other adverse reactions to tartrazine in sensitive individuals. Lockey reported six cases of chronic and generalized urticaria due to tartrazine-treated foods and drugs. Feingold attributed allergic reactions such as urticaria and blood vessel swellings to tartrazine.

Drs. Elmer W. Fisherman and Gerald Cohen reported that aspirin-sensitive patients had allergic reactions, in varying degrees, to tartrazine and another food dye, erythrosine, as well as to the preservative sodium benzoate.

Drs. Francis H. Chafee and Guy A. Settipane reported a case of severe intractable asthma, accompanied by swelling of blood vessels and blood changes, induced by certain FD&C approved dyes (notably tartrazine and FD&C Blue No. 1), as well as by sodium benzoate. They also found that FD&C Blue No. 1 was the only dye in one drug that caused symptoms in the patient; in another instance with the same patient, FD&C Yellow No. 6 was the only dye in the drug that caused symptoms. Neither of these two dyes gave any response in double-blind oral tests. Consequently, Chafee and Settipane pointed out that using such tests might lead to an erroneous conclusion by researchers that these dyes are poor antibody stimulators, whereas they happen to be *strong stimulators.* By means of a skin-window procedure, Chafee and Settipane were able to induce positive results. This technique demonstrated that antibodies were present and confirmed the sensitizing property of these substances. Chafee and Settipane gave credit to the patient's cooperation in the solution of this case. "It can honestly be said that, if it were not for her objectivity and intelligence in observing, interpreting, and reporting . . . her symptoms, she probably would not be alive today."

Chafee and Settipane noted the structural relationship of tartrazine, Sunset Yellow FCF, sodium benzoate, aspirin, and certain drugs. All of these compounds are aromatic. Some include heterocyclic rings, such as are found in tartrazine. They all contain acidic carboxyl or sulfonic acid groups. Their patient, whose case was reported, apparently had no clinical reaction to FD&C Yellow No. 3 (now banned). Although this dye is aromatic, it is free of acidic groups. The patient's sensitivity to sodium benzoate, as well as aspirin and other drugs, may therefore be due to the presence of a carboxyl group on an aromatic ring. Chafee and Settipane concluded that the reactive acidic groups are somehow involved in a haptenic formation. Those dyes containing only sulfonic acid groups appeared to be less effective in producing a sensitive reaction in this patient, and no clinical reaction occurred when she ingested those chemicals that have basic, not acidic, groups.

Randolph reported extreme reactions in individuals sensitive to food dyes in imitation fruit drinks and alcoholic beverages. In one instance, a 15-year-old boy did not react adversely to chemically uncontaminated grapes, commercial grape juice, or various sugars. After the boy drank an artificially colored grape-flavored soft drink, however, he had epileptiform seizures. A trial ingestion of the suspected dye in a soft drink precipitated a typical attack.

Amaranth (FD&C Red No. 2) is yet another food dye that has induced allergic reactions in sensitive individuals. Randolph reported that acute respiratory symptoms, accompanied by headache and depression, were induced in some patients after they ingested a calculated amount of amaranth equal to that in a large serving of an amaranth-containing gelatin dessert. Several of Randolph's patients, tolerant of untreated white or sweet potatoes, reported unquestionable adverse reactions to eating red-dyed white or sweet potatoes.

Repeatedly, allergists have recommended that all additives—including dyes and flavoring agents—be listed on labels, and that these additives be listed specifically—not just by vague terms such as "artificial color" or "artificial flavor." Lockey reported that on two occasions, ice cream with artificial chocolate and artificial strawberry flavorings brought on anaphylactic shock reaction in a man who was not allergic either to real chocolate or real strawberries. "The fact that these substances are not listed by names on foods, beverages, cosmetics and medicines," said Lockey, "makes the task of physicians difficult, and in some cases fatalities have occurred."

Chafee and Settipane noted that the names of dyes used with drugs are regarded as trade secrets. Although these two physicians reported that they had cooperation from medical departments of companies after they explained the reason for their request, "even so, it has been a time-consuming procedure. It is difficult for the average physician and nigh impossible for the patient to obtain this information." Instead, Chafee and Settipane suggested:

It would be far easier for the physician, let alone patients sensitive to these chemicals, if FDA were to require listing of dyes on the package. The same comment is applicable to food. These dyes, such as tartrazine, are at times added without being listed on the label and some food manufacturers are loath to admit that chemicals other than those required to be listed are added to their products. Other companies, in contrast, have freely answered our requested information.

Future prospects indicate an *even greater* consumption of flavorings and food dyes as the trend toward more and more fabricated foods continues. New products, such as synthetic "chicken" and synthetic "beef" derived from soybean proteins, are flavored and colored with synthetics developed through the food technologists' ingenuity. Consequently, the need for adequate labeling becomes even more urgent.

A simple way to indicate which specific food dyes have been used in a particular consumer product—whether it be foods, beverages, drugs, cosmetics or other consumer goods—would be to assign each of the dyes a code letter or number. FD&C Red No. 3 (erythrosine) could be listed simply as R3 and FD&C Yellow No. 5 (tartrazine) as Y5. A similar coding could be formulated for flavoring agents, so that the presence of these allergenic substances could be readily identified by those individuals who need to avoid them. For years the FDA resisted various suggestions to make such label information available, by arguing that the agency lacked such power. In October 1974, in a sharp reversal, the FDA announced that its regulations would not prohibit the use of such codings on food labels, but manufacturers would not be allowed to claim that natural ingredients were safer than artificial ones.

9

The Agents of Irreversible Effects: Carcinogens

● . . . Consideration of these chemical agents of disease [carcinogens] stands about in the position of thought 50 to a hundred years ago on microbial agents of disease. It was long doubted that a few tiny microbes could propagate in the body and cause disease. Today, there is much incredulous inertia over the public health aspects of discoveries that a few tiny molecules can start a body cell propagating to form cancer. Yet it is upon this molecular-cellular level that the phenomenon of cancer causation takes place.

William E. Smith, M.D.

● We have produced no evidence there is a safe dose of a carcinogen. Exposure to cancer-producing agents . . . shows that the tissue which is exposed acquires *new* susceptibility. The tissue stores the damage, so to speak, so that even with low levels of a carcinogen, if the cells are exposed to additional insults, the damage can add up so you reach a level where a tumor develops. All of this gives us a situation in which we cannot assume that low-level exposure to carcinogens may be insignificant.

Umberto Saffiotti, M.D., Associate Scientific Director for Carcinogenesis, National Cancer Institute

● Substances with reversible toxicological actions must be judged differently from those with irreversible (e.g., carcinogenic) actions. . . . For substances producing irreversible summative toxic effects . . . there is no nontoxic threshold doses. For this reason, very small doses of such substances must be considered dangerous if they are taken continuously and possibly for the whole duration of life.

German Research Council

● The conference recommends that, as a basis for active cancer prevention, the proper authorities of various countries promulgate exact and adequate rules and regulations prohibiting the addition to food of substances having potential carcinogenicity.

International Union Against Cancer

● No one knows how much or how little of a substance that induces cancer in an animal when included in diet is necessary to induce cancer in man. Now some people take issue with that statement. . . . I think it is perfectly all right for scientists and people in the medical profession to argue about that question. But our point is that, while the argument is going on, the consumer should not, in effect, be asked to serve as a guinea pig.

Arthur S. Flemming, Secretary of Health, Education and Welfare

• It is one of the biggest deceptions propagated by public health officials to say that a compound . . . has been around for years and there is no problem. It takes 20 years of latency before you can see bladder cancer in humans.

Marvin S. Legator, Chief, Cell Biology Branch, FDA, and Professor of Microbial Genetics, George Washington University

• Cyclamates may be only the tip of the iceberg. What other chemicals are there which can produce cancer? Some strongly suspect that the synthetic estrogen which remains in the meat we consume may be a cancer-producing agent. Various food dyes and colorings are also being tested for cancer. So is saccharin. Of even greater concern is the growing evidence that a majority of human cancers come from the chemical pollutants in our environment. . . . Proving a relationship between a chemical and cancer, as we have with cigarettes, may take 20 years. The difficulty of establishing such proof is infinitely greater with food chemicals, where the entire population is exposed.

Senator Abraham S. Ribicoff

• It is preposterous . . . that [the administration] can recommend a $100 million program for the treatment and prevention of cancer when current FDA practice is deliberately allowing an increase in the total burden of carcinogenic elements in our human diet.

Samuel S. Epstein, M.D., Swetland Professor of Environmental Health and Human Ecology, School of Medicine, Department of Pharmacology, Case Western Reserve University

• Prevention of cancer in the year 2000 is the order of the day in 1974.

Irving J. Selikoff, M.D., Director, Environmental Sciences Laboratory, School of Medicine, Mount Sinai City University, and E. Cuyler Hammond, Sc.D., Vice President for Epidemiology and Statistics, American Cancer Society

• I don't think we should wait for absolute proof that some of these chemicals cause cancer before restricting their use. It may be years before we know what these chemicals will do. We should minimize their use now.

John R. Goldsmith, Environmental Cancer Specialist, California Health Department

The potential human hazards from carcinogenic food additives and contaminants such as pesticide residues were described by Dr. Wilhelm C. Hueper, then Chief of the Environmental Cancer Section of the National Cancer Institute:

Exposure to many of these agents is lifelong, even if we have become exposed to only relatively minute amounts. To give an illustration, the average consumption of synthetic dyes in food for the average American per year [1957] is only 4 grams. That is not very high. But we get exposure for practically our entire lifetime. Since the effect of carcinogens on the tissues are summation effects, one effect is superimposed upon the other. Because carcinogenic effects are irreversible, this aspect deserves serious consideration.

Then, . . . we have also to consider the fact that materials which may be carcinogens and added to our food supply are present in other products of human consumption, or encountered in occupational activities or are pollutants of our general environment like the air, the soil, or the water.

So if one is to determine the degree of hazard which may come from food additives, one has to determine it in the light of all of the additional opportunities and intensities of exposure to the same or similar carcinogens. . . . It would be a wise precautionary measure not to add any chemicals to our food supply which produce cancer either in man or in experimental animals.

When cancerologists learned how to induce cancer experimentally, they discovered basic principles about the development of carcinogenesis. The intracellular changes represent the culmination of a process that develops over a long period of time. Although the chronologic length of this induction period differs from species to species, a striking similarity exists in biologic time units. The latency period is more or less the same fraction of each species' natural life span. For example, inducing cancer with coal tar requires an average of 6 months in a mouse and 15 years in a human. Since the average life span is 2 years for a mouse and 70 years for a human, 6 months represent $\frac{1}{4}$ of the mouse's life span and 15 years represent nearly $\frac{1}{4}$ of the human's life span.

During this induction period, the tissue on which the carcinogen acts undergoes a series of pathological changes, involving, among other things, increased cell division. Eventually, a few cells within the altered tissue undergo an intracellular change that transforms them into malignant cells. When this happens, the scene changes from the exterior to the interior of the cell.

Once this irreversible intracellular change has occurred, it persists even if the carcinogenic agent is withdrawn. Since the development of cancer cells has its immediate origin in an intracellular change, this change may be called the cancer's proximate cause. But since this change occurs most frequently in a tissue which has undergone pathological changes as a result of exposure to a carcinogenic agent's action, a distinction must be made between proximate and remote causes. Studies of remote cancer causes have made it possible to interpret many features of cancer's origin that formerly were obscure.

The National Center for Health Statistics announced in 1971 that an average of 161.4 out of every 100,000 deaths were attributable to cancer. The cancer mortality rate had *tripled* since 1950. Epstein commented that such statistics should not be surprising, since they are "precisely consistent with what one would expect from the increasing load of carcinogens" in our environment.

Most cancerologists agree that about 80 percent of all human cancers would be prevented if all contact with known exogenous (i.e. having a cause external to the body) carcinogens could be avoided. Of two million known chemicals that humans may be exposed to in daily life, only about six thousand have been thoroughly tested, according to Dr. G. B. Gori of the National Cancer Institute. Gori recommended that testing should be more thorough and more stringent.

To date, the characteristics of physical and chemical agents identified as carcinogens differ greatly. The food additives included among the carcinogenic chemical agents form two distinctive groups. Agents that are foreign to the physiologic functions of the body and are not normally formed by it form one group, which includes synthetic flavors and food dyes. The other group consists of substances normally found within the body that possess definite physiologic functions, but which may be carcinogenic. Growth-promotant hormones used with livestock are in this group. In terms of human hazards, four factors about potentially carcinogenic food additives must be considered: *(1)* the carcinogenic nature of the substance, *(2)* the precancerous condition of the body, *(3)* individual susceptibility, and *(4)* a time factor.

Of the food additives that are exogenous carcinogens, Smith warned:

These agents are of widely varying molecular structure, but among them a recurring common denominator is that they tend to be biologically foreign substances that cells have not in the course of evolution learned to handle. This is a basic reason for concern over the growing custom of adding biologically foreign substances to food for various immediate technical purposes. It is simply not in the public interest to expose consumers to the unforeseeable risks of a host of biologically foreign food additives that may provide eye appeal or advertising values. . . .

Polycyclic aromatic hydrocarbons, their derivatives and analogs, are compounds that are highly suspected carcinogens. (The basic aromatic hydrocarbon is benzene, a chemical in which the carbon and hydrogen atoms are arranged in a ring. Other aromatic hydrocarbons are variations of that basic structure. Polycyclic has two or more rings.) Many food flavoring agents and food dyes, as well as some food additives, are polycyclic aromatic hydrocarbons.

The United States Public Health Service (USPHS) tested chemical compounds for the ability to induce tumors. Tumors may be benign or malignant, but oncologists acknowledge that benignancy may progress to malignancy. Consequently, any substance that produces tumors consistently is regarded as a potential carcinogen. By 1957, USPHS had demonstrated tumorigenicity in more than 450 compounds, of which *more than 200 were polycyclic aromatic hydrocarbons, their derivatives and analogs.*

An internal FDA memorandum, released in March 1973, disclosed that many animal drugs, suspected as carcinogens, may be present in meat, poultry, eggs, and milk. The memorandum, prepared in September 1972 by K. F. Johnson, Director of Veterinary Medical Research at the FDA, revealed that existing laboratory methods are inadequate to test meat and dairy products for illegal residues for 17 out of 19 suspected or proven carcinogenic drugs used in animal feeds or injected into livestock. "Unless the FDA resolves the drug residue problem," Johnson warned, "we will soon be in direct confrontation with Congress and the consumers defending an untenable position. For the FDA to ignore this problem would be disastrous."

The memorandum was made public by Senators Ribicoff and Magnuson. On the Senate floor Ribicoff warned that the FDA is allowing consumers to be subjected to "an intolerable risk." He called on the FDA to withdraw approval immediately for carcinogenic and other possibly hazardous drugs used in food animals. Adequate test procedures exist for only a handful of these drugs.

Ribicoff reported, "There are a total of 19 separate animal drugs that are suspected carcinogens; 23 separate animal drugs the residues of which could be a human health hazard because of possible hypersensitivity, acute toxicity, and the development of resistant strains of bacteria."

Defending the FDA's policy, Peter Hutt, the agency's general counsel, replied that "in most if not all instances cited" in the memorandum "we have already moved forward with requests that manufacturers in question develop more sensitive methods." Hutt told the Senate Commerce Environment Subcommittee that recent FDA proposals to withdraw approval for two of the carcinogenic animal drugs used in animal feeds demonstrated that the agency was acting effectively on these issues.

Consumer spokesmen disagreed and voiced their criticisms at a meeting held with FDA officials. Merely publishing a proposed withdrawal notice was insufficient. The FDA had published such proposed withdrawal notices for several other suspected cancer-inciting animal drugs *two years prior;* but it never took any final action, nor did it remove the substances from the market.

Consumer spokesmen also criticized testing procedures used with antibiotic drugs with livestock. The test protocols permitted by the FDA had contradicted the agency's own task force recommendations. The task force had warned that these drugs represent a serious potential health hazard, and should be *promptly* withdrawn from use. Instead, the FDA's new protocols allow manufacturers to market the drugs for years while they conduct further safety tests.

The hazards of food additives that have counterparts in the body and are already performing physiologic functions were described by endocrinologist Dr. Roy Hertz in his testimony regarding DES. Hertz warned that any disturbance of the body's hormonal system is fraught with danger. Any impingement on the normal hormonal balance of what is produced by the individual human, is a substantial hazard. In addition to the hormones produced in the body, we carry a certain estrogenic dietary load, since grains and vegetables contain natural estrogenic substances. Even under ideal conditions, hormonal balance is especially precarious for females. "Every woman has this hazard in her body at all times. One out of every 16 women who are born will ultimately during the course of her life develop breast cancer." Hertz emphatically opposed the addition of *any estrogen of any kind* to the food supply.

The long latent precancerous period for humans can be 10, 20, or at times, even 30 years. Within limits, the time of appearance of tumors after the original exposure to a carcinogenic agent depends on the dose and frequency of exposure. But small doses, and *even a single dose,* may induce tumors, especially after prolonged latent periods. With test animals, the hazard of repeated small doses was greater than that of infrequent large doses. *Food additives are substances that will be ingested repeatedly in small doses over a life span.*

Host susceptibility is an important factor in carcinogenesis. For both test animals and humans, exposure to carcinogens does not induce a uniform effect. In some, cancer will appear earlier than in others, and in some it may not appear at all. The factor of susceptibility may not extend to all organs in the body of an individual, but may be restricted to a particular one. Susceptibility may depend on the general health or resistance of an individual while subjected to the carcinogen, or on such factors as genetics or dietary patterns.

Time is yet another variable with carcinogenesis. A prolonged period, varying inversely with the strength of the carcinogenic stimulus and with the degree of susceptibility, may be necessary for a carcinogen to induce cancer even in a susceptible human. The time period will be briefest when a strong stimulus is applied to a highly susceptible individual and longest when the two variables have low values. Consequently, the appearance of cancer at an *early* age indicates either a strong carcinogenic stimulus, a high degree of susceptibility, or a combination of both. Food additives with known or suspected carcinogenic properties are generally not strong carcinogenic stimuli.

However, if the carcinogenic stimulus is of lesser strength, if exposure is intermittent, and/or if the degree of susceptibility is low, cancer is apt to develop at a *later* age. A carcinogen of lesser strength, acting on an individual with a low degree of susceptibility, may still be too weak a combination to induce cancer in early middle age, but it may induce cancer at a later age. This accounts for the rapid increase in the cancer incidence rate with *advancing* age. Basically, this is the hazard of food additives with known or suspected carcinogenic properties that are ingested in small quantities over a life span.

A carcinogen that is a strong stimulus may be readily identified by the very circumstances that aroused suspicion. However, there are numerous "weak" carcinogens, less strong in their power to stimulate, more difficult to detect, but possibly more important as promoters of human cancer. Weak carcinogens may require more time to induce cancer; have a lower incidence of cancer promotion in a given population; and require higher doses to induce cancer. Cyclamates are considered to be weak carcinogens.

"Cocarcinogens" also are of grave concern. Cocarcinogens, not carcinogenic themselves, may promote cancer by acting synergistically if they are present with one or more substances that *are* carcinogenic. Findings indicate that saccharin, most probably, is a cocarcinogen.

Kai Setälä, Paul Holsti and Sinikka Lundbom, Finnish pathologists from the University of Helsinki, urged that serious attention be devoted to food additives and other substances in the human environment that are possible cocarcinogens and/or tumor-promoting agents which are capable of enhancing the effects of *actual* carcinogens. These pathologists noted: "There are justified reasons to assume that, at least under certain circumstances, the tumor promoters and/or cocarcinogens are of greater significance in tumorigenesis than perhaps so far is realized." They offered examples of food additives that possessed strong tumor-promoting and/or cocarcinogenic properties, including emulsifiers and wetting agents. They observed, "The time of appearance of tumors, the incidence of tumors, as well as the number of tumors per tumor-bearing animals are directly related to the frequency with which these seemingly harmless tumor promoters are applied and to the concentration in which the promoters are employed."

Epstein warned that the effects of food additives, as well as of certain pesticides, that are cocarcinogens may easily escape detection by conventional biological tests. Although these substances may pose as great a hazard as the most obvious potent carcinogens, they are unlikely to be clearly implicated in epidemiological studies.

Testing for the carcinogenic properties of a food additive is distinctly different from testing for its toxicity. There is no necessary relationship between carcinogenesis and toxicity. Because the appearance of cancer usually requires the long precancerous preparatory period, standards of testing suitable for observing chronic toxicity are usually inadequate for observing carcinogenic properties. In fact, only occasionally have chronic toxicity tests in the screening of chemicals for toxic qualities revealed their carcinogenic qualities. As a rule, the minimal carcinogenic dose is *distinctly lower* than the minimal chronic toxic dose. For this reason, frequently *carcinogenic response may develop after exposure to carcinogenic chemicals without any preceding or simultaneous appearance of any toxic symptoms.*

The need for special carcinogenic testing was recognized by Dr. Alan T. Spiher, Jr. in an internal FDA memorandum to Dr. Albert C. Kolbye, Jr.:

There seems to be some confusion in assessment of the relative risk from carcinogens and from ordinary chemical toxicants in our food supply and in the environment. A no-effect level can be developed in animals for a chemical toxicant, and the relative risk of translating this information to man can be assessed. If an error occurs and the allowable dietary level produces toxicity in man, the offending agent can be removed and the deleterious effect is reversible and complete recovery is expected. In the case of carcinogens . . . we have a drastic difference in the result of any miscalculations. If cancer . . . changes are induced, these are irreversible —no recovery is possible; even if the offending agent is removed from the diet the damage is done. Malignant cancer will develop. . . .

Spiher's clarification, written in 1969, gave a glimpse of the dispute within the FDA that has been raging since the inception of the Delaney Clause more than a decade earlier.

When the Delaney Clause was proposed, George P. Larrick, then commissioner of the FDA, opposed any mandatory carcinogenic testing and refused to admit that cancer causation should receive any special mention. The proposed Delaney Clause was opposed vigorously by industry as well, since it placed the onus of costly testings on the food, drug, and cosmetic manufacturers. These groups recognized that vigorous enforcement of the Delaney Clause might result in the withdrawal of many consumer goods. In addition to the economic losses, public anxieties would be aroused. The FDA reluctantly agreed to include the Delaney Clause in the proposed 1958 Amendment to the Food, Drug, and Cosmetic Act only when Delaney threatened to block the FDA's own bill from coming to a vote.

The Delaney Clause was written into the amended 1958 law, as well as into the amended Color Additive Act in 1960, over strong industrial protests and misgivings by FDA officials. Industry spokesmen conducted vigorous campaigns to demonstrate that the Delaney Clause was "rigid," "unscientific," and "worked against the broad public interest"; imposed "limitations upon agricultural progress through research"; and allowed "no scientific judgment of the results of research." On the other hand, cancer experts contended that the Delaney Clause allows "much room for the exercise of scientific judgment," and that "no one at this time can tell how much or how little of a carcinogen will be required to produce cancer in any human being."

Arthur S. Flemming, then Secretary of Health, Education and Welfare, testified:

The rallying point against [the Delaney Clause] is the catch phrase that it takes away the scientist's right to exercise judgment. The issue thus made is a false one, because the clause allows the exercise of all the judgment that can safely be exercised on the basis of our present knowledge. . . . It allows the Department [FDA] and its scientific people full discretion and judgment in deciding whether a substance has been shown to produce cancer when added to the diet of test animals. But once this decision has been made, the limits of judgment have been reached and there is no reliable basis on which discretion could be exercised in determining a safe threshold for the established carcinogen.

Despite Flemming's forthright statement, the FDA invoked the Delaney Clause on rare occasions and only with great reluctance. Soon after the clause became law, the FDA was forced to ban the weedicide aminotriazole, which had been used after harvest in cranberry bogs, and the use of DES for pellet implants in poultry. In both cases, the substances were shown to be cancer-inciting. The agency, which had never given whole-hearted support to the Delaney Clause, found numerous ways to circumvent it. The rejection of certain testing routes as "inappropriate" was one means (see pages 63–65). Another was devised in 1962, when the FDA requested congress to modify the Delaney Clause by exempting drugs used in animal feeds. The new Drug Amendments of 1962 *permitted the use in animal feeds of drugs which had been found to promote cancer when ingested by animals or humans,* provided their use did not result in detectable residues of the drug in any edible animal tissues. In passing this law, members of congress were hoodwinked into believing that the consuming public was being protected adequately against carcinogens. As revealed in the congressional hearings on DES during the early 1970s, the Drug Amendments of 1962 officially permitted public exposure to carcinogens.

The FDA attempted to circumvent the Delaney Clause once again during the cyclamate affair. By legal legerdemain, the FDA reclassified cyclamates as "drugs" to avoid having to invoke the Delaney Clause with them as "foods." The reclassification backfired, thanks to astute questioning by Congressman L. H. Fountain, and the Delaney Clause *was* invoked.

To date, the FDA's most shocking disregard of the Delaney Clause has been with DES. Basic to the argument about the Delaney Clause has been the attempt to establish the concept of a "safe" dose for a carcinogen. The idea of a "toxicologically insignificant" level for a carcinogen has been argued since the inception of the Delaney Clause and has succeeded in polarizing individuals and groups (see page 38). During the congressional hearings on DES the behind-scenes controversy became public.

On one side was a committee formed by the U.S. Surgeon General, with four scientists from the National Institutes of Health (NIH) and four scientists from the academic community. Although this group submitted a report of major significance on cancer prevention in April 1970, the report had never been published in the scientific literature and was unknown to the general public for a year and a half. *The report gave unqualified support to the Delaney Clause,* and rejected the concept of a "safe" dose for a carcinogen.

On the other side was the Food Protection Committee of the NAS–NRC task force. Its report, "Guidelines for Estimating Toxicologically Insignificant Levels of Chemicals in Foods," *was* publicized. The Surgeon General's group repudiated the task force's concept of a "toxicologically insignificant" level for a carcinogen. It also criticized the qualifications of the task force's members: Of the nine members, five were employed by industry and one by a commercial laboratory, thus giving nonacademic scientists a staggering six to three majority. None of the scientists on the task force was primarily a cancer expert. Funds for the Food Protection Committee were from grants from the food, chemical, and packaging industries.

Regulations require the FDA to be "guided" by the "principles for establishing the safety of food additives in current publications by the NAS–NRC," rather than by the parent body of FDA, the Department of Health, Education and Welfare (HEW), or by the Surgeon General. The FDA chose to use the Food Protection Committee's "guidelines" to bolster its own position regarding DES, and thus, once more circumvented the Delaney Clause.

The Surgeon General's report remained unpublished. HEW chose neither to publish nor to suppress it. In March 1971, Dr. Saffiotti, one of the members who had drawn up the Surgeon General's report, testified before Senate Subcommittee Hearings on Agricultural Research and quietly submitted the report for publication in the printed hearings. In April 1971, making no mention of the report, he appended it to his testimony before the Senate Subcommittee Hearings on Executive Reorganization. Both Saffiotti and the Surgeon General, Jesse L. Steinfeld, made copies of the report freely available to those persons who knew of its existence and requested it. In addition, they used many of the significant portions in their appearances before scientific groups and at other congressional hearings, including hearings on DES.

The FDA chose to use the Food Protection Committee's guidelines and a distorted application of the Mantel–Bryan Model (see pages 38–39). The FDA's reluctance to ban DES from livestock feed was well-documented throughout the congressional hearings on this potential carcinogen. When this hormone finally was banned in 1972, there was little rejoicing either at the FDA or the USDA that a potential carcinogen had been removed from the food supply. On the contrary, Charles C. Edwards (then commissioner of the FDA) apologized that he had been left with no choice but to ban diethylstilbestrol under what he implied were unreasonable dictates, and Secretary of Agriculture Earl L. Butz expressed "regrets." By January 1974, however, a federal appeals court overturned the ban on a legal technicality, and the *FDA declined to invoke the Delaney Clause as legal sanction for its action.* The agency once again revealed its repudiation of the Delaney Clause, and once again public protection against carcinogens was weakened. By declining to invoke the Delaney Clause, the FDA was forced to rely on the weaker base of legislation that permitted the removal of unsafe food and feed additives. The agency already had weakened its position when the ban was imposed in 1972 by declaring that DES did not constitute an "imminent hazard" to public health. Obviously, *the phrase "imminent hazard" is totally inapplicable to any carcinogen,* since carcinogens have long periods of latency before they do demonstrable harm.

The FDA's handling of the DES case prompted a long-time FDA critic, Gilbert Goldhammer, consultant to the congressional committee that held the DES hearings, to comment that "if the FDA wanted to get the court to overturn the ban, it could not have done a better job." As a result of the FDA's failure to invoke the Delaney Clause, a long and complicated series of legal actions, which will ultimately culminate in a hearing, were instituted. Both FDA officials and industry representatives admit that these actions will require a *minimum* of one to two years before a final decision can be reached. Meanwhile, consumers are exposed once again to the potential carcinogen DES in their meat supply.

The Delaney Clause has been crucial also in the ban on cyclamates in 1970. It is possible that cyclamates, like DES, may be returned to the food supply via the courts rather than the laboratories. Three years after cyclamates had been banned, a cyclamates producer submitted new data and petitioned that the ban be lifted. The FDA found the new data "inconclusive" in regard to the cancer-causing potential of cyclamates. The FDA requested that the original rat studies that led to the ban be repeated, and requested additional data on the effects, if any, on the reproductive organs and cardiovascular system. The FDA rejected newly submitted data and stated that "none of the data have adequately demonstrated or denied the findings of carcinogenesis of calcium cyclamate." The petitioner then announced its plans, if necessary, to take the issue to court in order to have the ban lifted. The FDA, which has been under strong attacks concerning its role in downplaying negative findings on additives and drugs, is expected to act cautiously before announcing a final decision on cyclamates. The issue is further complicated by the fact that the safety of two possible alternatives to cyclamates, saccharin and Aspartame, has also been questioned.

As the Delaney Clause continued to come under repeated attacks, a movement appeared to grow, spearheaded by industry and supported tacitly by the FDA, to weaken the clause by "modifying" it. As a counterattack, a two-day workshop was hastily called in 1973, titled "The Scientific Basis for the Delaney Amendment," sponsored by the New York Academy of Sciences. Participants included more than a hundred scientists and lawyers from industry, government, and academia. Significantly, although Dr. Edwards, then commissioner of the FDA, had repeatedly received invitations to attend, he declined to be present and sent no surrogate. Surprisingly, even some representatives from affected industries supported the Delaney Clause. Dr. A. H. Conney, a scientist employed by the drug and food-chemical firm of Hoffmann–La Roche, praised the clause as "justifiable" and said that its benefits go "to the public rather than to a small interest group." Earl I. Lambert, attorney with Covington and Burling (a prominent Washington, D.C., law firm that represents major food companies and food industry associations among its clients) concluded, "On the basis of the evidence presented, I don't see any practical basis for a change in the Delaney Clause at this time."

Possibly, this workshop succeeded in forestalling any plans to modify the Delaney Clause. But the FDA, by consistently choosing to undercut, circumvent, or ignore the Delaney Clause, has learned to live with this piece of legislation by rendering it ineffective.

Related to the Delaney Clause, a pivotal point has developed regarding the definition of a carcinogen. The public wrongly assumes that there is universal agreement in defining a carcinogen. While cancer experts are in general agreement, the FDA has narrowed the term.

The Surgeon General's report on DES stated, "Any substance which is shown conclusively to cause tumors in animals should be considered carcinogenic and, therefore, a potential cancer hazard for man."

Ignoring this definition, the FDA selected one offered by the Food Protection Committee's report: "For practical purposes a carcinogen is a substance that when administered by an appropriate route, causes an increased incidence of malignant tumors in experimental animals as compared with a control series of untreated animals."

The essential—and significant—difference in the two definitions is the FDA's insistence that the word "malignant" be prefixed to tumors, a qualifying term absent in the Surgeon General's report. *By narrowing the term, the FDA succeeded in making it more difficult to label substances, such as cyclamates, as carcinogens.*

A difference of opinion exists among experts in the field of carcinogenesis regarding the precise meaning of the term "malignant." Some require a showing of *metastasis* (the spread of cancer through the bloodstream to organs remote from the site of the original tumor), as well as a capacity for implantation into other individual test animals of the same species. But other experts regard as a malignancy any tumor which, if left untreated, would kill the host. In the practice of human medicine, for example, it is unnecessary to show metastasis or capability of successful implantation in order to make a cancer diagnosis. Microscopic tissue examination suffices.

Expert testimony presented at congressional hearings on DES also made it clear that pathologists disagree as to whether a tumor produced by a suspected carcinogen should be classified as malignant or benign. Since the Delaney Clause prohibits the use of carcinogens, the definition of a carcinogen should be formulated to give the *maximum* protection to the public. But the FDA's definition of a carcinogen offers the *least* protection.

10

The Agents of Irreversible Effects: Teratogens

• . . . the fetus has a unique position legally and medically. It does not choose many of the things that are imposed upon him. Hence, he deserves more protection by some public spokesmen than his mother can provide for him.
> Karlis Adamsons, M.D., Professor of Obstetrics and Gynecology, School of Medicine, Mount Sinai, City University

• Man has not evolved means of protecting the embryo against the discoveries of his own laboratories.
> Dr. James D. Ebert, Carnegie Institution

• . . . more than 1,000 chemicals regularly added to our foods have never been tested for their potential to cause . . . birth defects . . . today there is only one limited testing for birth defects. Thus a gaping hole presently exists in the law which may permit the most harmful chemicals to slip untested into the marketplace.
> Senator Abraham S. Ribicoff

• The magnitude of the problems of congenital malformations hardly needs further emphasis in view of the often repeated reference to the fact that one-third of the beds in children's hospitals today are occupied by congenitally defective individuals, and that congenital disease is the third most common cause of death in the newborn, which accounts for 14 percent of all infant deaths. One of the more reliable prospective surveys of recent years indicates that from 4 to 7.5 percent of human deliveries yield individuals that have developmental defects that will interfere with survival or result in clinical disease before the end of the first year of life.
> Food and Drug Administration Advisory Committee on Protocols for Safety Evaluations: Panel on Reproduction Report on Reproduction Studies in the Safety Evaluation of Food Additives and Pesticide Residues

• . . . it has been recently estimated that the costs to society of one severely malformed child, in terms of medical and other care and deprivation of potential earnings, amount to several hundred thousand dollars.
> Report of the Secretary's Commission on Pesticides and Their Relationship to Environmental Health, U.S. Department of Health, Education and Welfare

● Under what conditions will it be possible to say that there is an additive which is so needed in our food supply that *any* risk of one of these effects [carcinogenicity, teratogenicity, mutagenicity] is acceptable? My children would have to be in more than highly theoretical danger of starving before I would want *any* risk.

Dr. Alan T. Spiher, Jr., Assistant to the Director, Office of Compliance, FDA

Currently, in the United States, some three to five percent of all humans are born with birth defects. These congenital malformations, called *terata*, may be extreme structural abnormalities of prenatal origin, obvious at birth or shortly thereafter, which either kill or disable. Or, they may be less obvious defects—producing microscopic, biochemical, or functional abnormalities—which, nevertheless, handicap the individual to some degree.

Presently, the major causes of *teratogenesis* (the production of defects) are unknown. A relatively small minority, some 20 percent, are thought to be from chromosome aberrations, as well as from infections, drugs, environmental contaminants, maternal metabolic imbalance, and radiation exposure. The remaining 80 percent has not yet been attributed to any specific cause, but chemical compounds such as food additives, pesticide residues, or other environmental contaminants are being suspected more all the time.

Any change in the normal environment of the developing human embryo may lead to birth defects. Malnutrition, insufficient oxygen for embryonic tissue, and exposure to toxic substances may all induce congenital abnormalities. Some chemicals act upon the tissues' molecular components and interact with the cells' chemical constituents. Any interference with the embryonic cells' chemical processes may lead to defective developmental forms. Defects produced by chemical assault may closely resemble abnormalities that occur under abnormal hereditary conditions. Consequently, it may be difficult to attribute a birth defect to a genetic cause or to a chemical assault.

For some time, scientists have recognized that a pregnant woman, exposed to certain substances, is unable to shield an embryo from the harmful effects of known teratogens. Nitrogen mustard, sex hormones, German measles virus (rubella) and methyl mercury (Minamata disease) have become recognized teratogens with human infants. Some chemicals and drugs were known to interfere with the growth of the rapidly proliferating cells of a developing human embryo. However, a widespread and false assumption had persisted that somehow the pregnant woman has a natural ability to protect her embryo from harmful effects of the external environment.

The thalidomide tragedy, in the early 1960s, with the birth of several thousand grossly deformed infants, brought a shocking awareness of a hazard that had already existed, but which had been unappreciated: An early human embryo may be extremely vulnerable to chemical substances that may be well-tolerated, or even therapeutic, to a pregnant woman. If the birth defects had not been so obvious in the thalidomide-affected infants, the teratogenic nature of the substance might easily have escaped notice.

After the thalidomide experience, regulatory agencies began to *request* that teratogenic studies be included in the battery of toxicological tests made on food additives, pesticides, and drugs. Scientists and congressmen who recognized the importance of excluding as many teratogenic exposures as possible from the human environment, urged that such studies be made *mandatory*.

During congressional hearings on Chemicals and the Future of Man, Senator Ribicoff asked Dr. Epstein if the FDA's policy of "discretionary" teratogenic testing adequately protected the public. Epstein replied:

. . . I am very unhappy that this requirement is discretionary. I think it should be mandatory. The possibility exists that this discretion is well exercised. But this imposes a constraint on the petitioner of the Bureau [FDA]. If he has to try to make up his mind whether he should impose teratogenic testing, he is subject to pressures and lobbying. There should be clearly stated requirements for this and protocols should be promulgated. . . .

An official report dealing, in part, with teratogens, concluded:

"The reproductive process brings into focus an entire physiology not considered in other safety evaluation protocols, and . . . hazards which exist during reproduction will not be manifest in any other type of study." Nonetheless, a current information gap exists, and scientists admit that many aspects of the reproductive processes are poorly understood. The teratogenic hazards of relatively few substances are known with any degree of certainty, and these few substances are mainly drugs. Far less is known about the teratogenic potentials for food additives, pesticide residues, and environmental contaminants.

At present, it is not known with any precision how soon the human embryo becomes susceptible to outside influences that are capable of altering its development. Sensitivity to the outside environment may actually be important even *before* conception. In test-tube studies, food additives such as sulfites were demonstrated to inhibit nucleic acid synthesis. This can exert teratogenic effects even prior to pregnancy. Would-be fathers also have been cautioned to avoid unnecessary drugs since such substances can damage the genes carried by the sperm cells.

Medications such as triparanol (a drug now withdrawn from use), as well as some antisera, are known to exert teratogenic effects prior to the period of fetal growth. Antibiotic therapy early in pregnancy appears to be connected with congenital defects in the newborn. (Antibiotic residues may be present in many foods, since they are permitted in animal feed.) The combination of an antibiotic and aspirin may produce a teratogenic effect.

If parallels can be drawn from animal studies, the period of *maximum sensitivity* to teratogenic effects is *very early after conception* (6 to 15 days in the mouse or rat, 6 to 18 days in the rabbit, 4 to 14 days in the hamster, 6 to 20 days in the guinea pig, 7 to 35 days in the pig, and 9 to 40 days in the monkey). The human embryo also is likely to be highly sensitive to agents interfering with its development shortly after conception. Unfortunately, during these early critical days a woman may be unaware or uncertain of her pregnancy.

During this early pregnancy period, the prospective mother will probably continue her customary life habits, which may include self-medication with drugs. She may also eat convenience foods containing a number of additives. In recent years, many medical warnings have advised pregnant women to avoid or drastically reduce their use of drugs, alcohol, and cigarettes. Offspring abnormalities associated with such a commonly used drug as aspirin include congenital heart disease and mongolism; while the use of barbiturates has been related to heart disease, limb deformities, and cleft palate. Perhaps the only reason that food additives have not been included in these warnings is that they have not been studied for teratogenicity.

Numerous animal studies have implicated antinausea drugs (such as phenobarbital) and tranquilizers (such as chlorpromazine) as teratogens. Suspected drugs include antimalarials, anticoagulants, central nervous system drugs (including salicylates and analgesics), metabolic drugs (such as DES), excessive amounts of vitamins A and D, steroids, insulin and iodine. "Social" toxicants —narcotics, hallucinogens, tobacco, and alcohol—have also been implicated. Of an estimated two million alcoholic women in the United States, at least half are of childbearing age. A pattern of serious birth defects is found among children born to women who are chronic alcoholics. An FDA advisory committee cautioned that it is difficult:

. . . to identify all of the potentially toxic substances to which the early embryo may be exposed. Contamination of air and water; presence of preservatives, colorants, pesticide residues, and other agents in food; and the increasing drug usage by all segments of the population all add up to a disquieting array of possibilities. It is not easy to rule out in advance, or even to recognize after the fact, harmful effects that may result from these unnatural substances. The problem is sufficiently difficult even when the effects of individual compounds are sought. Scientists have increasingly recognized that two or more chemical substances can interact in the living organism to produce totally unexpected types and degrees of response. As an example, a usually safe drug and an unknown chemical contaminant from the environment can, by such interaction, produce a potentiating effect which is an effect that may be much greater than the sum of the separate effects, and there is experimental evidence that the embryo probably is more susceptible to this interaction than the mother.

Since food additives are likely to be ingested in combinations, those suspected as teratogens may possibly have synergistic effects. Animal studies have demonstrated that certain combinations of chemical teratogens can induce malformations at a higher rate than when only one agent is used. Such synergisms may explain some of the unaccounted-for human malformations.

Presently, scientists lack information about the biochemical and metabolic processes in early human embryo development. Such information is vital for determining embryo sensitivity to toxic agents. Although, in general, the basic life processes are similar during the embryotic and postnatal periods, some details differ markedly. There are different metabolic pathways, and during an early developmental stage, the detoxication mechanisms are under-developed (see pages 56–57). These differences may explain the embryo's extreme sensitivity to many chemical toxins.

The study of *embryonic pharmacology* (how foreign substances, or abnormal amounts of natural ones, can affect metabolism at early stages of development) is also important. Even the *slightest* interference with the precisely timed growth schedule of the embryo can affect the entire embryonic developmental process, resulting in either embryonic fatality or the birth of a defective child. Yet much information about embryonic pharmacology remains unknown.

Possibly the most significant information gap concerns the levels of toxic substances, taken into the pregnant woman's body, that reach the embryo. The mother's own protective mechanisms, primarily her liver and kidneys, may protect the embryo significantly by detoxifying and excreting toxic substances. The rate at which her organs are able to reduce the concentration of the toxin in the maternal blood will affect the amount reaching and crossing into the placenta. The ratio between the concentration of a toxic substance in the mother's blood with that in the embryo's blood appears to be of utmost importance in determining teratogenesis. For years, there was a widespread, mistaken belief that the placenta formed a barrier to toxins. We now realize that *the placenta actually excludes very little.* Only very large chemical molecules or those bearing very high electrical charges are excluded. Since many food additives have low molecular weights (see pages 32–34), it comes as no surprise that many of them pass readily through the placenta. Cyclamate and its toxic breakdown product (cyclohexylamine), saccharin, sodium nitrite, DES, synthetic flavorings, food dyes, caffeine, salicylates, and other food additives have the capacity to pass through the human placenta. So do dioxins (which contaminate herbicides and have been found in margarine, food emulsifiers, glyceryl mono-oleate, oleic acid, chick livers, animal food stocks, and animal tallows). Most drugs (including antibiotics, steroids, alcohol, and nicotine) and environmental contaminants (such as PCBs, lead, mercury, cadmium, pesticides, and their breakdown products) pass readily through the placenta.

Although the placenta excludes few substances, it does regulate the transfer rate and controls the concentration ratio of a substance between the embryo and mother. But the concentration of a toxin or other substances in the fetus may be *higher* than in the mother:

—In studies with alcohol-treated pregnant monkeys, the alcoholic levels in fetal tissues were ten times higher than those in the mother's tissues.

—In studies with lead-exposed pregnant golden hamsters, even at relatively low dosage levels, the lead passed rapidly through the placenta and accumulated in substantial amounts in the embryos.

—In pregnant women who had eaten mercury-contaminated tuna fish, the mercury concentration in the fetal tissues was up to 30 times greater than in the mother's tissues.

Furthermore, substances may be *transplacental carcinogens.* Nitrosamines, highly carcinogenic compounds formed from sodium nitrite combined with amines, given to rats near the end of pregnancy, induced kidney, lower brain, and spinal cord cancers in the offspring. *Although the nitrosamines did not affect the pregnant animals, the cancers were passed along to the offspring via the placenta.*

It is believed that the placenta may be the site of teratogenic action. The embryo can be affected adversely, for example, if the placenta excludes materials essential for growth, admits substances not admitted under ordinary circumstances, fails to perform usual excretory or endocrine functions, or provides a site for infections.

The pregnant woman, as well as the embryo, is particularly vulnerable to toxins. The woman's detoxification mechanisms are altered during pregnancy. She is particularly susceptible to abnormal metabolic pathways. She may function at a borderline state of pyridoxine deficiency. Protein, carbohydrate, and lipid metabolisms are all altered during pregnancy.

Another hazard for the pregnant woman relates to the maintenance of pregnancy. Certain substances can interfere with the endocrine support of the pregnancy, causing either abortion or premature delivery. Although the cause of spontaneous labor is unknown, a group of substances (oxytocin or ergot derivatives) can stimulate, while others (epinephrine) can retard the progress of labor. *It is conceivable that such substances may exist among the large number of food additives.*

During early pregnancy, the embryo is particularly susceptible to teratogens that induce familiar anatomical defects. However, this early period is not the only developmental stage that can be adversely affected from outside influences. The period of fetal development, during the last two-thirds of human pregnancy, is the time when major growth and functional maturation occurs. During this time, the fetus may be susceptible to interference resulting from the mother's food and drug intake, as well as exposure to other chemicals or radiation.

About 120,000 fetally malnourished babies are born annually in the United States. Although such babies are not born prematurely, they are intrauterine growth-retarded or fetally malnourished, and are underweight at birth. Fetal nalnourishment results from defective cell nutrition and may not be recognized as a gross functional abnormality. Any chemical compound that interferes with normal cell nutrition needs to be carefully examined. Studies indicate that human fetal malnutrition impairs cell reproduction.

Malnutrition in a pregnant woman may cause long-term damage to the unborn child. Malnourished mothers have placentas that are as much as 15 percent smaller than those of well-nourished mothers. Babies born to such mothers have a high mortality rate, and those that survive have an increased incidence of sickness and other health problems.

"None of the presently available methods of screening in animals can provide an absolute assurance against the occurrence of a teratologic reaction in human beings. Therefore, the tendency is to err on the side of caution," stated some Canadian officials, who had recommended testing protocols for teratogenicity of chemicals.

Present teratogenic studies with animals are limited. Suitable techniques to recognize functional abnormalities in a fetus are not generally available. Even if the maternal experimental animal and the pregnant human female have similar metabolic patterns for the test compound, the animal and human fetal metabolism may not be the same. Also, the susceptibility to teratogenic activity may be quite different for different species or strains.

The placentas of test animals differ in several respects from human placentas. Rodents (and rabbits) have a yolk-sac placenta, as well as one similar to the human's. In humans, most foreign substances reach the fetus via the placenta; in rodents, the presence of two placentas allows the substance to reach the embryo in two different ways. In the earliest, most vulnerable stage, foreign substances probably enter the rodent embryo via the yolk-sac placenta. Some substances that may be broken down and stored by the yolk-sac placenta may pass easily through the human placenta. Consequently, it is difficult to extrapolate to humans studies of teratogenicity using animal placentae.

Many of the problems with teratogenic studies are similar to those of chronic toxicity tests (see pages 30–32). False data may result if the animals' diet is not carefully controlled. Nutritional stress or imbalance may exert marked teratogenic effects or modify them. Excesses or deficiencies of vitamins, minerals, proteins, carbohydrates, or fats can produce teratogenic effects. Although humans may be exposed to many teratogenic compounds in daily life, testing combinations of these substances is impracticable. The limited studies of multiple exposures, however, indicate that problems of synergism exist for teratogens, as well as for substances that are solely toxic. Weak teratogens can be strengthened when combined with other substances.

Scientists use the term *proteratogen* to describe substances that may not be teratogenic by themselves but may be capable of increasing the activity of a teratogen. The term also describes known teratogens below a threshold dose. Scientists believe that a combination of two or more nonteratogenic proteratogens might result in teratogenic activity. If such a mechanism exists, it would explain many presently unaccountable human malformations.

To date, relatively few reports directly implicate specific food additives with congenital malformations. This does not mean that a relationship does not exist; instead, it shows a shocking lack of data. The teratological quality of chemical compounds such as certain fungicides, herbicides, the detergent nitrilotriacetic acid (NTA), dioxin, salicylates, azo dyes, and other substances proposed, or introduced into the environment, emphasizes the need for teratological testing of food additives.

Cyclamates are suspected teratogens:

—In controlled tests with pigs, cyclohexylamine affected the animals' reproductive system and caused some loss of fetuses by resorption.

—Teratogenic effects of cyclamates have been observed with the chick embryo technique.

—A letter to the editor, published in a medical journal, suggested that limb malformation and cleft palate in two human infants may have resulted from ingestion of cyclamate-containing foods by their mothers.

—Arthur H. Wolff, Assistant Surgeon General, reported that diabetic women appeared to have six to ten times as many grossly deformed offspring after cyclamate ingestion as the normal population.

Maleic hydrazide, a chemical compound used to inhibit root and tuberous vegetables from sprouting, induced birth defects (and cancer) in test animals.

The food dye, FD&C Red No. 2 (amaranth) is both a highly suspect teratogen and carcinogen. The way in which the FDA has handled the problem of this dye underscores the agency's failure to act promptly and effectively to protect the public from hazardous additives.

In 1971 Soviet scientists reported test results that showed, among other adverse effects, that this dye diminished fertility in rats and caused some stillbirths. The FDA then conducted tests which confirmed the dye's teratogenic quality, including malformed and macerated (discolored and softened) animal fetuses and a decrease in litter size. Dr. Thomas Collins, of the FDA, demonstrated that FD&C Red No. 2 caused rat fetuses to die.

Some scientists within FDA expressed concern. The late Dr. Leo Friedman, then director of FDA's Division of Toxicology, was quoted as saying "There is no question that [FD&C] Red No. 2 is toxic in unborn children . . . In beverages the question of a fetal toxic effect is beyond doubt." In the autumn of 1971, a group of eight FDA scientists who had been investigating the dye, in an internal memorandum to the agency's top official, recommended that the dye be banned from food. In a subsequent memorandum they warned that the average American daily intake of the dye was nearly five times more than the estimated no-effect level.

As a result of data and these memoranda, in September 1971 the FDA announced its intention to drastically limit the use of the dye. However, this plan was never implemented. Instead, the agency ordered food manufacturers to conduct animal reproduction tests with food dyes. Such tests, not required in the past, generally had not been performed.

The food interests, especially the dye manufacturers, launched a concentrated drive to block implementation of the proposal. Industry strategy was described as forcing "delay after delay on a determination—in this case, restrictions of the dye—in hopes that it finally fizzles out." A major concern of the dye manufacturers was that a ban on FD&C Red No. 2 could lead to grave problems in the entire industry and threaten the use of *all* food dyes.

In December 1971, the FDA acquiesced to an industry request to submit the findings on FD&C Red No. 2 for review by a panel of the Food Protection Committee, NAS. The Committee, frequently criticized for being overly susceptible to industry's viewpoint, was attacked for its bias on FD&C Red No. 2. At the time of the review, the Committee received about 40 percent of its operating funds from the food industry. Although some panel members were chosen from colleges and universities, they were also receiving research and consulting grants from industry. Another charge was that despite the nature of the dye's possible hazards, no panel member was a geneticist nor expert on birth defects.

In its review, the panel discounted any hazards of the dye, but reported that it found no reason to curb its use. These conclusions were disputed by the Academy's own review committee. Eventually, the report, sent to the FDA, was accompanied by a "covering letter" stating that the report should be considered as the opinion of one group of scientists, but not a definite answer to FD&C Red No. 2's safety. The review, issued in June 1972, was challenged by the FDA scientists who had recommended that the dye be banned in food. As a result, the FDA appointed an ad hoc committee to review the controversy and to consider industry's complaints against interpretations of the fetal toxicity tests.

In May 1973, the ad hoc committee requested additional and newly designed tests. Collins was requested to repeat his tests. Both FDA's laboratory and an industry-sponsored laboratory was to repeat tests.

In June 1973—nearly three years after the FDA's initial tests on the dye—the ad hoc committee met and reviewed results of the new sets of tests. Although the final report has not yet been issued, the FDA concluded that the new tests indicated that the dye did not cause fetal toxicity.

This conclusion was challenged. Collins reported that the new tests had omitted some features, and failed to prove that the dye was not a carcinogen. Dr. David Gaynor, chief statistician at FDA's Center for Toxicological Research, concurred. Gaynor, who had reviewed the FDA's earlier tests, found them inconclusive. He sent an internal memorandum, warning that the dye could be cancer-causing. Gaynor recommended immediate additional testing. Other FDA scientists claimed that the newly conducted tests—described as the most definitive cancer tests ever conducted with the dye—were "in a mess." They charged that for a year the new study was virtually unmonitored, that mixups occurred with test animals, and that no examinations were made of many animals that had died. Only about ten percent of the original rats in the experiment survived, a percentage too low to draw meaningful conclusions. In addition, in a preliminary experiment, FD&C Red No. 2 caused swellings of the uterus in female mice, a sign of hormonal changes. Although the FDA claimed that this experiment was discontinued for lack of manpower, a leading FDA research scientist charged that this experiment was "more or less squelched."

A consumer group analyzed the data from the three early FDA cancer tests and the new FDA fetal toxicity tests with FD&C Red No. 2, and disputed the FDA's "clean findings" with both sets of tests. The group contended that rather than absolving the dye, the cancer test data strongly indicated that the dye causes cancer, and that one of the fetal toxicity tests indicated that, in fact, the dye may cause fetal death.

Despite these criticisms, in December 1974 the FDA announced plans for *its approval of the permanent use of FD&C Red No. 2.* Promptly, a storm of protests followed from congressmen and the public. The National Foundation-March of Dimes, an organization concerned with birth defects, urged a ban of the dye, and meanwhile advised pregnant women, especially, to avoid ingesting the dye whenever possible.

Meanwhile, an advisory committee consisting of five consulting scientists outside of the FDA had been formed at the agency's request in May 1973 to study the possible harmful effects of FD&C Red No. 2. Less than two months after the FDA announced its plans to approve permanent use of the dye this advisory committee recommended to the agency that the use of the dye be limited, and "strongly urged" the agency to conduct further tests. The committee's report also implied that the presence of the dye should be indicated on food labels so that the consumer would be warned. Richard Ronk, head of the Department of Color Additives, FDA, reported that the advisory committee's recommendations "opened it all up again and we'll have to take a fresh look. I think there will be some limitations on the dye. There is a possibility that we might ban it. We will study it, and there should be a decision by the spring [1975]."

Dr. J. H. Edwards, a British physician, was alarmed by the very high incidence of central nervous system congenital malformations in infants in Scotland. He compared the incidence of this birth defect in Great Britain to that in Rhode Island and in continental Europe. Whereas the incidence was high both in Great Britain and Rhode Island, it was low in continental Europe. As early as 1958, Edwards recommended that food additives be seriously considered as a possible cause of birth defects:

. . . particularly in view of the increasing number of preservatives, dyes, and bleaches in common use, and the increasing contamination of foodstuffs with antibiotics, weedkillers, insecticides, and synthetic estrogens. . . . Preservatives, dyes, and improvers in foodstuffs, which are commonly used with no recommendation other than that of being toxic to bacteria or colorful or producing a white frothy bread, *are so widespread that, if any were to cause embryonic damage, it would be extremely difficult to detect.* . . . Among factory-produced foodstuffs with a class gradient in intake, may be mentioned the coloring matter in margarine, the large number of mixtures which are supplied as dehydrated cakes and pastries, and ice cream. An aversion to foods processed on an industrial scale and a relative conservatism toward some modern farming techniques are possible reasons for the relatively low incidence of anencephalus [a fetus characterized by a congenital absence of all, or part, of the brain] on the European continent compared to that in such relatively well-fed regions as Great Britain and Rhode Island. [emphasis added]

11

The Agents of Irreversible Effects: Mutagens

• Potentially irrevocable [genetic] damage might be done without immediate warning by some of the more than 10,000 natural and synthetic chemical agents now produced commercially or by the million or more additional agents that have been isolated or synthesized by man, most in recent decades. Fewer than 200 of these suspected mutagens have been systematically assayed.

> Dr. James F. Crow, Chairman, Genetic Study Section,
> National Institutes of Health

• By far the most mutagenic agents known to man are chemicals, not radiation. And in this regard, food additives rather than fallout at present levels may present a greater danger.

> Dr. Richard Caldecott, Geneticist, Atomic Energy Commission

• The threat of genetic damage is our number one health problem.

> Dr. Marvin S. Legator, Chief, Cell Biology Branch, FDA;
> Professor of Microbial Genetics, George Washington University

• Given the problem of the number of new, suspicious compounds now pervading our environment, we face a formidable task in putting our genetic house in order.

> Dr. Joshua Lederberg, Nobel Prize Winner; Professor of Genetics,
> Stanford University

• There is reason to fear that some chemicals may constitute as important a risk as radiation, possibly a more serious one. Although knowledge of chemical mutagenesis in man is much less certain than that of radiation, a number of chemicals—some with widespread use—are known to induce genetic damage in some organisms. To consider only radiation hazards is to ignore what may be the submerged part of the iceberg. . . . Recent investigations have revealed chemical compounds that are highly mutagenic in experimental organisms, in concentrations which are not toxic and that have no overt effect on fertility.

> Dr. James F. Crow

• We must remember . . . that genetic damage is irreversible by any process known to us now. The risk to future generations, though difficult to assess in precise terms, is nevertheless very real. The prevention of any unnecessary mutational damage in the future is one of our most important and critical responsibilities today.

> Samuel S. Epstein, M.D., Chief, Laboratories of Environmental Carcinogenesis and Toxicology, Children's Cancer Research Foundation, Inc.; Research Associate in Pathology, Harvard Medical School, and Dr. Marvin S. Legator

● In the final analysis our genes are our most important legacy . . . if our gene pools become overloaded and overburdened by deleterious mutations, our future as a species is indeed bleak.

> W. Gary Flamm, Ph.D., Research Scientist, National Institute of Environmental Health Sciences

● The chemicals we ingest may affect more than our own health. They affect the health and vitality of future generations. The danger is that many of these chemicals may not harm us, but will later do silent violence to our children.

> Senator Abraham S. Ribicoff

● I like people. I like animals, too—whales and quails, dinosaurs and dodos. But I like human beings especially. And I am unhappy that the pool of human germ plasm, which determines the nature of the human race, is deteriorating.

> Dr. Linus Pauling, Nobel Prize Winner; Professor of Chemistry, Stanford University

● The genetic pattern we inherit determines our entire makeup. . . .

> Dr. Albert Szent-Györgyi, Nobel Prize Winner; Laboratory of the Institute for Muscle Research, Marine Biological Laboratory, Woods Hole

● It has been known to geneticists for decades that the vast majority of mutations are detrimental, in that nearly every one of them occasions, at least to some small degree, one or more of the many thousands of possible impairments, bodily, intellectual, or in the genetic basis of the emotional organization or moral fiber, that our organism is subject to. . . . [in] arriving at . . . [a] tally of at least one in five persons having a new mutant gene, we are leaving out of the reckoning any newly arisen mutations that may have been induced by one of the many novel practices of our day, such as exposure to radiation and to possibly mutagenic drugs, cosmetics, contraceptives, food additives, and industrial wastes that are thrown out into the air or water. None of these suspect chemicals has been adequately tested in this regard, that is, as to whether it is mutagenic. . . .

> Professor Hermann J. Muller, Nobel Prize Winner; Distinguished Service Professor of Zoology, Indiana University

● . . . visiting the iniquity of the fathers upon the children unto the third and fourth generation . . .

> Exodus 20:5

● If the public flatly refuses to take decisive action on the basis of the massive volumes of data linking cigarette smoking to lung cancer, how can you expect people to act vigorously on the more hazy and abstruse things like a chemical that may or may not

be mutagenic in man and may or may not produce its damaging effects for another hundred years or more?

Dr. James F. Crow

While carcinogens and teratogens inflict damage on separate individuals, mutagens may adversely affect generations of unborn humans. Mutagens can damage the human gene pool, and the magnitude of this effect is unknown.

The nature of mutation was clarified in the early 1920s with the discovery that high-energy radiation induced mutations. The first convincing evidence that man-made environmental agents could be mutagenic came in 1927 with the publication of Muller's paper, "Artificial Transmutation of the Gene," which demonstrated potential health hazards associated with indiscriminate radiation usage. The increased use of nuclear energy added a new dimension to the problem and greatly increased public awareness of genetic hazards.

After radiation-induced mutagenesis had been established, suspicions arose that many chemicals have the same effects. Proof of chemical-induced mutagenesis was demonstrated during World War II, when mustard gas was found to induce mutations in fruit flies. Since then, numerous chemicals, greatly diverse in structure and activity, have been found to be mutagenic agents. Mutagenic chemicals are potential health hazards when introduced into the human environment, and indeed, many may already be in widespread use.

Such chemicals may include food additives, pesticides, drugs, cosmetics, and other consumer goods, either purposely or accidentally introduced into the human environment. Food additives are of particular concern because they are used so widely over the entire population's life span. Some—such as sodium nitrite, sodium bisulfite, cyclamates, and maleic hydrazide—are biologically potent. The same mechanism that causes a chemical preservative such as sodium bisulfite to kill or inhibit the growth of microorganisms in food, may also cause damage in human cells. The fundamental cellular processes of *all* living organisms are similar. As the genetic foundations are examined more closely, the similarity of life patterns is readily observed. The DNA of bacteria, insects, weeds, rodents, and humans has exactly the same architecture. For this reason, the most suspicious chemical compounds are those that act directly on cells.

A new dimension in genetic study, developed almost entirely within the 1960s, deals with human *cytogenetics* (the study of human chromosomes). Considerable data have been collected in a brief time; but geneticists admit that despite accomplishments, they are far more impressed by the vistas of *as yet undiscovered* important facts for human states of health or disease.

The chromosomes carry all of the genes that instruct a fertilized ovum to become a human. There are 46 chromosomes in every human cell, 23 from each parent. The specific genetic information carried by each of the chromosomes is presently unknown. Neither do researchers know the effects of chemicals and radiation on chromosomes and fertility or the significance of small chromosome breaks (with the resulting losses of chromosome pieces). Will such chemicals cause defects in future generations? How many broken chromosomes are consistent with producing new generations of humans at all?

A mutation is any inherited change in the genetic material DNA, which is composed basically of four nucleotides. Genes are formed by various combinations of these nucleotides. A typical gene is approximately one thousand nucleotides in length. These nucleotides are arranged in a sequence that is specific for each gene. Every human cell has thousands of genes, but only the germinal cells transmit the genes from cell to cell, or from parents to progeny. The DNA must replicate *precisely*. Genetic information passes from DNA to RNA, which synthesizes protein. The structure of these proteins, encoded in DNA, gives form, shape, and function to the organism. DNA is also responsible for repairs. If DNA is damaged by any environmental agents it attempts restoration.

A mutation may be caused by a chemical change in an

individual gene. Individual gene changes are called *point mutations*. A mutation may also be caused by the rearrangement of a chromosome so that it gains or loses some parts. Such changes are often seen under an ordinary microscope. Changes involving the larger chromosomal units are called *chromosome aberrations*. Point mutations and chromosome aberrations are easily distinguished from each other. But it is difficult to determine the cause of a mutation-induced human defect.

Mutations may occur anywhere in the body. Frequently, the cell in which the mutation occurs is damaged. However, if the alteration does not stop the cell from dividing, the mutation may be transmitted to descendant cells. The effect may be carcinogenic or teratogenic, especially if the change takes place during embryonic development.

Of special concern are mutations occurring in the germ cells. Any mutation or chromosome change that is transmitted via the sperm or egg to the next generation can affect every cell of the descendant's body.

The range of effects produced by any genetic alteration in the germ cells includes all structures and metabolic processes. Some germ cell mutations have effects so mild they are difficult to perceive. At the other extreme, some are so severe that the individual cannot survive. If death occurs very early in the embryo's development, such lethal mutagenic effects may never be detected. If the death occurs at a later stage, it may lead to a miscarriage. An appreciable fraction, roughly one-fourth, of all "spontaneous" abortions, shows a detectable chromosome aberration. At present, we cannot tell how many of the remaining miscarriages may be caused by gene mutations or by chromosome aberrations too small for microscopic detection.

As many as one-third of all hospitalized children are treated for conditions caused by mutant genes.

Spontaneous mutations occur all the time. Environmental mutagens only add to this number. The problem is further complicated by the time-distribution of mutational effects. Some mutant genes are dominant, in which case, the abnormality of disease will appear in the generation after the mutation occurs. However, if the mutant gene is recessive, the abnormal genes must be in the chromosomes of both parents to produce the effect. In such cases, the abnormality or disease may not be recognized for many generations, until some child inherits a mutant gene simultaneously from both parents. *The overall effect of such mutations is spread over many generations. The effect in the first generation represents only a fraction of the total impact of the mutation process.*

A mutation causing a lethal effect will persist for only one generation and affects only one human. However, a mutation causing only a slight impairment survives, and its abnormalities will be transmitted from one generation to another, thereby affecting many people.

Hundreds of inherited diseases (including diabetes, phenylketonuria, albinism, and hemophilia) were initially caused by mutations. Collectively, such diseases account for a substantial fraction of human misery. Genetic factors also play a role in mental deficiencies and an assortment of human frailties. Consequently, the effects of mild mutations cannot be considered unimportant.

Experiments with fruit flies demonstrated that mildly adverse mutations occurred at least ten times as frequently as more severe mutations. It is likely that the main impact of mutations on the human population results from mild mutational effects that make the population weaker, more disease prone, and more apt to succumb to effects that otherwise might be resisted.

Any increased mutation rate, as well as their time-distribution, makes it impossible to predict in detail the kinds of effects that will occur from human exposure to numerous mutagens. Nor can an accurate quantitative assessment be made of the total harmful mutagenic impact on the population compared with other hazards.

In recent years, three expert committees have unanimously recommended that mutagenic testing be made mandatory for food additives. To date, no regulatory action has been taken. After the thalidomide tragedy, three-generation reproductive tests were made mandatory for drugs and pesticides, but the need to conduct teratogenic tests on food additives is at the discretion of the petition reviewers. Most scientists believe that mutagenic testing should be a *mandatory* part of the entire battery of chronic toxicity tests.

Testing chemicals for mutagenesis in humans is, to a large extent, difficult and impractical. Too much time is required to obtain results. Genetic disorders produced by mutations may occur in only one out of every 10,000 or 100,000 births. In order to obtain meaningful data, scientists would have to test millions of people. For example, it has been estimated that an adequate test to determine whether sodium nitrite is mutagenic in humans would require a carefully controlled study of at least 20 million people; other tests might require the entire population.

Mutagenic testing on lower organisms—such as bacteria, fungi, and viruses—is simple and inexpensive. Bacteria divide as rapidly as every 20 minutes. Subsequently, new generations can be studied, and large populations can be maintained in a small laboratory space. But such tests, by themselves, are unreliable for determining chemical mutagenicity for humans.

Tests on green plants and fruit flies are better for human extrapolation. But although humans, plants, and fruit flies share the same basic genetic material, the human metabolic processes may differ from those of the other organisms. For example, the human has liver enzymes which may be capable of detoxifying many chemicals poisonous to the plants and flies.

Cell cultures used to detect mutagens differ from cultures of bacteria, single-cell plants (such as algae) or single-cell animals (such as protozoa). Single-cell living things conduct all of their functions (such as respiration and digestion) within one cell. They do not interact with other cells. A cell culture is started by isolating cells from a particular tissue in a higher organism and nurturing it in nutrients prepared in the laboratory. While not as reliable as using whole, live animals, cell cultures are inexpensive to maintain and easy to grow. They have the advantages of tests with lower organisms, but are much closer to humans on the evolutionary scale. Cell culture tissues can serve as a bridge between mutation studies of nonmammalian and mammalian systems.

Mutagenic tests with whole, live mammals are more reliable than cell cultures, but they are also more expensive and time consuming. Rodents, especially mice, are used in "dominant lethal assay" tests. Males are treated with a potential mutagen and then are mated at various times to untreated females. About two weeks after conception, the females are sacrificed, and the number of live and dead embryos is noted. These studies show whether the chemical compound caused a mutation on a dominant male gene which is lethal to the embryo.

Another type of mutagenic test with mammals was developed originally to study genetic hazards of radiation. These tests are called *specific locus* tests. The chemical compound being tested is given to strains of male or female animals that have certain well-defined genetic characteristics bred into them. Any change in the expected number of offspring with the characteristic trait (for example, a coat color) signifies that the parental genes were affected.

A more recent type of mutagenic test combined the advantages of both nonmammalian and mammalian systems. This test was devised by the Cell Biology Branch of the FDA, as a result of the pioneering work of an outsider, Professor Hermann J. Muller. Muller had distinguished himself in the field of mutation research and radiation biology. In 1962, Muller presented a seminar on chemical mutagenesis to the FDA that detailed the potential public health hazards of chemically induced mutagens. At the same time, Muller discussed the possible use of cytogenetic procedures, being developed at that time, for evaluating genetically active chemicals.

Dr. Marvin S. Legator, who had joined the FDA shortly before Muller's seminar, was convinced by the thalidomide tragedy that mutagenicity testing should be routinely included in all testing programs. Legator was impressed by Muller's work. When the FDA established a Cell Biology Branch, Legator, who headed this research unit, incorporated Muller's original suggestions and further refined them. During 1968–69, he developed the *host-mediated assay test*.

In the host-mediated assay test, a mouse or rat (the host) is first injected with a potential mutagen. A bacterium or fungus (an indicator organism) is then injected into the host. After a given time period, the bacteria or fungi are checked for possible mutations. Microorganisms are easy to handle, and a large number can be checked for mutation. The fact that mutations have or have not occurred in the indicator organism reflects any changes the metabolism of the host organism has exerted on the suspected chemical.

Since no single method can detect all possible types of mutations, a combination of methods must be used. A positive result in *any* of the mammalian tests is evidence of a potential mutagenic hazard. Dr. Joshua Lederberg noted that most of the assays are so *insensitive* that any compound that scores positively as a mutagen "must have a portentous effect in any but the most peculiar circumstances. . . . When there are murky doubts about an issue as important as mutational damage, they must be resolved in favor of the species."

Several recommendations made to the FDA by an expert committee evaluating mutagenic chemicals are especially noteworthy:

The Committee recommends that the FDA encourage and support research for the development of mutagenesis tests which will be more sensitive, more economical, and of greater predictive value than current procedures; . . . that the FDA in concert with other appropriate federal agencies continues to develop and expand an orderly surveillance of the food supply with respect to possible unexpected adverse effects on the human population from the use of "approved" substances added to food; . . . that the FDA develop and maintain an up-to-date registry of chemicals with mutagenic and teratogenic potential and make this information generally available.

During the Congressional Hearings on Chemicals and the Future of Man, Dr. Lawrence Fishbein of the National Institute for Environmental Health Sciences displayed a chart listing more than one hundred separate chemicals as potential mutagens. The chemicals had been shown to induce point mutations, chromosome aberrations, or both in one or more test systems. The chemicals came from four major areas: food additives and feed additives, pesticides, drugs, and industrial chemicals. The food additive category included caffeine (a natural constituent of coffee, tea, and cocoa that also is used as a food additive in cola beverages); cyclamates (the artificial sweeteners); cyclohexylamine (a breakdown product of cyclamates); sodium bisulfite (a preservative in dried fruits); EDTA (a sequestering agent used in processed foods); allyl isothiocyanate (a mustard flavoring used as a "modifier" of hot sauces, relish flavors, salad dressings and synthetic mustard); and sodium nitrite, or nitrous acid (used as a preservative in meat, fish, and cheese). The feed additives included drugs used to prevent poultry disease and pesticides such as the fumigant, ethylene oxide; the anti-sprouting agent, maleic hydrazide; and numerous herbicides, fungicides, insecticides, chemosterilants, and seed sterilants.

Since caffeine is known to be present in the gonads and fetuses of humans who consume caffeine-containing beverages, the mutagenic effects caused by caffeine may be particularly damaging. It has been demonstrated that caffeine causes point mutations in phage (a bacteria-destroying agent used by geneticists in one system for mutagenicity testing, abbreviation for bacteriophage), other microorganisms, and some insects. Studies in 1949 showed that caffeine produced chromosome aberrations in plants. More recent studies, in 1966, showed that caffeine induced chromosome aberrations in human tissue cultures and onion root tips and produced mutations in bacteria, fungi, and fruit flies.

The killing of tissue culture cells can be increased by irradiating them with ultraviolet before placing them on a medium containing caffeine. Ultraviolet and caffeine also have a synergistic effect on mammalian cells. On the other hand, caffeine's mutagenicity for mammals is unclear. Some scientists have found a positive effect, but their tests were criticized by others as being poorly controlled. In other experiments, using dominant lethal assay tests with mice, findings were negative.

Caffeine is known to inhibit DNA repair enzymes in bacteria. But scientists are divided as to whether or not caffeine inhibits the natural repair of DNA damaged by other mutagenic agents, such as chemicals or radiation. As a result of test-tube studies of cultured human embryonic lung cells, some believe that caffeine may inhibit the enzymes normally involved in repairing damaged DNA. But studies with live mice failed to demonstrate any caffeine interference with DNA repair.

The mutagenicity of cyclamates has been the center of a controversy. When the Food Protection Committee was asked to review cyclamates for the FDA in 1969, a nine-member task force was created (see pages 208–9). Five members of the task force were directly employed by food or chemical interests, and another headed a commercial laboratory which serves these two industries. The sole genetics expert on the committee was Dr. James F. Crow, Professor of Medical Genetics at the University of Wisconsin. After evaluating the cyclamate data, Crow concluded that the evidence added up to "a fairly strong case that cyclamates represent a mutagenic hazard to man." When the committee reaffirmed the "safety" of cyclamates, Crow requested that his name be omitted from the report.

In 1973, Philip M. Boffey, of the Center for the Study of Responsive Law (a Ralph Nader affiliate), charged that the Food Protection Committee had suppressed Crow's minority viewpoint. Boffey continued:

No hint of Crow's thinking appears in the report. His views were suppressed and the Academy [National Academy of Sciences, the parent body of the Food Protection Committee] has never even acknowledged that he dissented. Crow was simply listed as "consultant" on the report, a designation which conveniently allowed the committee to imply that he had contributed to the report without in fact requiring that he sign it. . . . The episode provided further evidence of how the toxicologists on the

Academy's food protection panels tend to ignore the views of the underrepresented cancer and genetic experts.

Cyclamates induced chromosome aberrations in tests on plants and mammalian cells; chick embryo tests also indicated that cyclamates had mutagenic qualities.

In tissue culture tests, cyclohexylamine (the breakdown product of cyclamate), induced chromosome breakage. These tests, noted Dr. Joshua Lederberg, were the "forerunner of the eventual inculpation of the parent compound, cyclamate, as a cancer hazard." Lederberg suggested that experimental evidence of a mutagenic quality of a substance should be recognized as a danger sign. Such a compound may also be capable of hazards through its action on DNA and other cell constituents.

In dominant lethal assay tests using mice, cyclohexylamine showed significant mutagenesis. The results suggested possible mutagenesis for humans.

Sodium bisulfite also causes genetic alterations. Test-tube studies showed that sodium bisulfite destroys RNA's ability to carry genetic messages. The researchers concluded that sodium bisulfite "may constitute a genetic hazard to living organisms." Other tests with sodium bisulfite showed that it caused point mutations in phage and other microorganisms.

The sequestrant EDTA has a variety of uses in numerous processed foods:

—to promote color retention in dried bananas used as a component in packaged dry cereals; in canned kidney beans, processed dried pinto beans, and cooked canned chick peas; in cooked canned clams, crabmeat, and shrimp; in pecan pie filling; in frozen white potatoes; and in spice extractive in soluble carriers.

—to improve flavor retention in canned carbonated beverages; in the spice flavor of nonstandardized dressings; in standardized dressings such as French dressing, mayonnaise, and salad dressing; in sandwich spreads; in sauces; in margarine; and in spice extractive in soluble carriers.

—to retard can corrosion and increase stability of some FD&C colors in canned carbonated beverages.

—to retard struvite (crystal) formation in cooked canned crabmeat and shrimp.

—to protect against rancidity in nonstandardized dressings, in standardized dressings such as French dressing, mayonnaise, and salad dressings; in sandwich spread; and in sauces.

—to prevent gushing or wildness in fermented malt beverages.

—to prevent gumming ring formation on glass containers of French dressing.

—to improve keeping qualities of commercially prepared potato salad.

—to keep vegetables crisp in sandwich spread.

—to stabilize vitamin B_{12} in vitamin solutions.

In studies, EDTA induced chromosome aberrations and breakage in test plants, mitotic abnormalities (abnormalities in cell division) in onion roots, and chromosomal changes in fruit flies, as well as in two plant systems. Synergistic effects were shown in the chromosome aberrations of one plant system.

The very first compound reported to be mutagenic in published literature was allyl isothiocyanate, or mustard oil. This volatile oil is a well-known natural constituent of horseradish and other widely used condiments. Synthetic mustard oil is used as a flavoring agent with many foods.

Whether allyl isothiocyanate is mutagenic in mammals is unknown. Further study may either allay or confirm suspicions. If confirmed, it would not be the first time that a common dietary constituent was found to be harmful after centuries of use.

The FDA's approval of mustard oil as a "safe" food additive may be unwarranted. As early as 1955, it was reported that mice, painted with mustard oil, developed skin tumors. More recent studies showed that allyl isothiocyanate was cytotoxic (caused cell death) and mutagenic for fruit flies and *Ophiostoma* fungus. It also induced chromosome aberrations in onion root tips and point mutations in microorganisms and insects.

The potential mutagenicity of sodium nitrite is due to its conversion to nitrous acid in the human stomach. Numerous studies have demonstrated that nitrous acid attacks DNA and is a potent mutagen in bacteria, viruses, molds, and other organisms.

Dr. Ernst Freese, chief of the Laboratory of Molecular Biology at the NIH's National Institute of Neurological Diseases and Strokes, believes that the mutagenic effects of nitrous acid in lower organisms are sufficiently ominous to suggest that the use of sodium nitrite in foods should be severely limited, if not banned outright.

In addition, sodium nitrite or nitrous acid may react with amines in various foods, as well as within the body, to form nitrosamines (see pages 89–91). Some nitrosamines may cause genetic disorders, as well as cancer.

Ethylene oxide has been shown to induce point mutations in microorganisms and chromosome aberrations in plants (corn, barley, and *Vicia*). Ethylene oxide induced mutations in fruit flies, *Neurospora* fungus and barley plants. The use of ethylene oxide as a food fumigant has raised a number of significant questions. A possibility exists that ethylene oxide may interact with plastics, pharmaceuticals, or foods, which may exert a toxic effect when placed in contact with living tissue. Or, sorbed ethylene oxide may possibly change the physical and chemical properties of plastic wrappers. Also ethylene oxide may combine with natural inorganic chloride present in foodstuffs to form toxic chlorohydrin. Concentrations of ethylene chlorohydrin up to about 1,000 ppm have been found in whole spices fumigated with ethylene oxide. These chlorohydrins are relatively involatile, and they remain in foods even after processing. Foods fumigated with ethylene oxide had residue levels of ethylene chlorohydrin ranging from 4 ppm for paprika all the way up to 110 ppm for pepper. Other studies showed that ethylene chlorohydrin was formed and remained in fumigated wheat and flour.

Maleic hydrazide is an antisprouting agent used to treat potatoes, onions, and stored root crops; to protect citrus seedlings from frost damage; to prevent sucker production in tobacco plants; and to control weed growth and grass foliage. Maleic hydrazide induced point mutations in fruit flies and chromosome aberrations in plants (*Vicia faba*, onion root tips, barley, and maize). The action of maleic hydrazide is similar to that of X rays. Its activity is directed specifically to growing tissue, and therefore, it interferes with normal cell division. Studies showed that maleic hydrazide inhibited normal cell division in oats, corn, and soybeans, as well as in dry *Crepiscapullaris* seeds. Studies using intact cells suggested that maleic hydrazide affected certain enzyme systems within the cells. Maleic hydrazide produced chromosome breaks in almost every plant tested, as well as in cultured mouse cells.

Possible mutagenicity has been reported for other food additives not listed on Fishbein's chart.

In 1964, tests in Japan showed that both saccharin and sodium cyclamate were suspect as mutagens and teratogens. Saccharin given to pregnant mice on the critical four or five days after conception induced abortions. Researchers attempted to estimate from these studies what the potential hazards might be for humans, assuming that these substances were as potent in humans as in mice. The estimate was that 3.4 grams of cyclamate, given during a critical stage of human pregnancy to women averaging 120 pounds, would be fatal to 50 percent of the human embryos.

Dominant lethal assay tests were also conducted on saccharin. The results, reported in 1973, indicated that sodium saccharin may be mutagenic.

BHT and BHA have also been shown to induce chromosome aberrations. Both of these antioxidants induced amitotic divisions (cell divisions in which there is a simple cleavage of the nucleus without differentiation, followed by a division of the cytoplasm; amitotic division differs from the normal mitotic division). Such divisions result in changes in chromosome numbers or arrangements within the cells.

The FDA classifies gamma radiation preservation of foods as a food additive. X rays, gamma rays or electrons are used to effect changes on foods similar to the changes caused by heat. Bacteria may be killed, enzymes may be inactivated, and insects may be either killed or made incapable of reproduction.

Under the requirements of the Federal Food, Drug, and Cosmetic Act, any food treated by irradiation must be proved safe before it can be marketed. The irradiation must not leave a harmful residue of any kind on the food, nor may it significantly affect the food's nutritive value.

At present, food preserved by radiation is limited to wheat, wheat flour from nonirradiated wheat, and white potatoes. Packages of radiation-treated foods must be labeled appropriately: "treated with ionizing radiation" or "treated with gamma radiation" must appear on retail packages and "treated with ionizing radiation—do not radiate again" or "treated with gamma radiation—do not irradiate again" must appear on wholesale packages and on invoices or bills of lading for bulk shipments.

Federally sponsored food irradiation trials, launched in the early 1960s, involved nine agencies. From the beginning, the two most ardent supporters have been the United States Army and the Atomic Energy Commission.

Army officials hoped that radiation would achieve *permanent* preservation, so that foods could be shipped to front-line troops. Permanent food preservation required such high radiation levels that the program was not feasible. At high levels of radiation, vital food nutrients were destroyed, and new chemical compounds—suspected of being either acutely or chronically toxic, as well as carcinogenic—were formed. Such treated foods caused extensive damage in test animals.

Dr. Walter J. Nungester, a physician attached to the army's scientific advisory board, examined the early data on radiation food preservation and urged caution. Nungester said that data about food preservation was inconclusive, but what was known raised serious problems. He recommended that the army proceed slowly before launching any program of feeding irradiated foods to troops.

At least two types of cellular chemical changes were noted in the irradiated foods. These changes, which were in the carbon chains and the steroids, were termed "potentialities for biological activity which are, as yet, only a field for speculation." Ionizing energy, even at very low levels, is a potential carcinogen with living organisms.

In 1963, the FDA approved a petition by the army to feed troops with treated canned bacon and white potatoes. Later, during the same year, the FDA sanctioned the irradiation of wheat, wheat products, and flour for insect control in overseas shipments.

By 1968, the FDA had reversed its position. It denied two United States Army–Atomic Energy Commission petitions to irradiate strawberries and canned ham. The agency revoked its earlier approval of treated canned bacon, which had been in use for two years on a dozen military bases.

The FDA's reversal was based on new data. Studies at Cornell University showed that sugar exposed to a certain radiation level broke down. Lethal radiation effects could be transmitted to living plant cells and possibly to other living organisms. Although it had been known already that radiation affects living cells *directly*, this new study demonstrated that the newly formed chemical compound could affect plant cells *indirectly*. The effects were produced by stable substances, capable of acting long after radiation exposure had ceased. The studies also showed that, at *low* radiation levels, cell growth was not stopped but was stimulated.

The Cornell studies were extended to fruit flies. Radiation demonstrated adverse effects on cells. Growth was stunted, and chromosomes were damaged. The researchers noted that since all living cells contain sugar, "humans may suffer similar consequences from long-term consumption of irradiated foods."

Irradiated sugar was also studied at the University of Michigan Medical School. A sucrose solution, treated with cobalt 60, was tested on samples of human white blood corpuscles. The treated sugar solution was so toxic that the extent of the damage inflicted on individual chromosomes could not be assessed. Only a few of the cells divided normally. Although the scientists stated that the test results did not prove that eating irradiated food would damage human cells, they cautioned that this possibility "must not be lightly brushed aside now that mass consumption of irradiated foods is being seriously considered."

Despite these findings, plans to irradiate foods continued. In 1971, irradiated mushrooms and strawberries were test-marketed in Holland, and irradiated potatoes and onions were commercially available in Israel. Although the FDA presently limits food radiation preservation to wheat, wheat flour from nonirradiated wheat, and white potatoes, the Atomic Energy Commission continues an aggressive campaign to extend this process to other foods. This agency has petitioned the FDA to approve irradiated papayas, strawberries, and fish. It predicts that by the end of the 1970s, a number of irradiated food items—notably fruits and vegetables such as bananas, onions, and tomatoes—will be approved for United States markets.

In 1966, a World Health Organization report on irradiated foods urged extreme caution. The British Ministry of Health drafted regulations to ban completely the sale of irradiated foods and food products intended for human consumption.

Geneticists increasingly acknowledge that the human population's exposure to potentially mutagenic chemical compounds may be a greater hazard than exposure to present levels of radiation. Monitoring numerous chemicals is infinitely more difficult than monitoring radiation. Precise methods of measuring genetic risks from chemicals are lacking, while radiation hazards can be estimated.

Critics of mutagenic testing charge that any substance given to test animals at a high enough level will cause mutations. This notion is untrue. Dr. Cecil Jacobson of George Washington University demonstrated that only 7 out of 275 substances tested for mutagenicity proved to be mutagenic. Another test has confirmed Jacobson's studies: only 6 out of 100 substances tested were mutagenic.

No correlation exists between toxic and mutagenic effects. Some highly toxic compounds, such as cyanide, are hardly mutagenic; some highly mutagenic compounds, such as certain base analogs, are barely toxic.

But substances known to be teratogenic or carcinogenic are frequently also mutagenic. Aflatoxin molds, for example, may be teratogenic, carcinogenic, and mutagenic. Cyclamate has been shown to induce bladder tumors, in addition to having cytogenic effects. Although a chemical compound producing one response does not necessarily produce the others, the agents that produce alterations do have similarities. The type of damage inflicted by DNA interference depends on the organism's development stage, the types of cells affected, and the type of genetic interference inflicted. The final expression may be mutagenic, teratogenic, or carcinogenic.

If genetic interference results in abnormal differentiation at the time when the embryo's organs are developing, resulting in cell death, the damage may be teratogenic. If genetic interference involves mutations in germ cells, the damage may be hereditary changes that are mutagenic. If genetic interference involves mutations that take place in a mature organism's body cells when the cells are duplicating, the damage may be carcinogenic.

Just as there are weak carcinogens and weak teratogens, there are weak mutagens. Many weak mutagenic substances may only inflict damage after repeated exposures over a long time span.

Nonmutagenic compounds may be converted, either outside or within the body, to mutagenic ones. Consequently, any program to test the mutagenicity of compounds individually is inadequate. Compounds must be tested in combinations. Also, since mutagens often act at very low levels, the notion of "permissible" levels for mutagens has a frightening significance.

Some scientists have commented:

Surely one of the greatest responsibilities of our generation is our temporary custody of the genetic heritage received from our ancestors. We must make every reasonable effort to insure that this heritage is passed on to future generations undamaged. To do less, we believe, is grossly irresponsible.

12

The Regulators and the Regulated

• There is a distinct tendency to put regulations and rules for the enforcement of the law into the hands of industries engaged in food and drug activities. I consider this one of the most pernicious threats to pure food and drugs. Business is making rapid strides in the control of all our affairs. When we permit business in general to regulate the quality and character of our food and drug supplies, we are treading upon very dangerous ground. It is always advisable to consult business men and take such advice as they give that is unbiased, because of the intimate knowledge they have of the processes involved. It is never advisable to surrender entirely food and drug control to business interests.

Dr. Harvey W. Wiley, Commissioner of the FDA

• . . . no new chemical or no chemical that is subject to any question as to safety should be employed until its possible injurious effect, both on an acute and on a long-time chronic basis, has been shown to be nonexistent. In other words, any chemical that is proposed for use ought to be proved in advance of distribution in a food product to be utterly and completely without the possibility of human injury.

Dr. Paul B. Dunbar, Commissioner of the FDA

• We have had some very narrow escapes because of the use of additives that had no place in food. It is inconceivable that this country should continue to expose itself indefinitely to the risks inherent in the present scheme of food control.

George P. Larrick, Commissioner of the FDA

• In a number of cases the additives proposed have only an economic benefit to the food producer and no benefit at all to the person who eats the final product.

Dr. James L. Goddard, Commissioner of the FDA

• The thing that bugs me is that the people think the FDA is protecting them—it isn't. What the FDA is doing and what the public thinks it's doing are as different as night and day.

Dr. Herbert L. Ley, Commissioner of the FDA

• The public health cannot be endangered for months or for years while we attempt to accumulate all of the scientific data needed for an absolute determination of safety or danger. Therefore, we will sometimes make decisions to regulate out of commerce suspect products, on the basis of demonstrated doubt, and we will not regulate them back into society until science has allayed those doubts.

Dr. Charles C. Edwards, Commissioner of the FDA

• I accept as a basic premise the idea that while responsibility for safe food begins with industry and is principally the concern of industry, it does not end there. The FDA has been assigned by law as industry's chief auditor and as the consumer's special representative in matters of food safety. In terms of responsibility to the consumer, you might say that we're in the same boat. Please note I distinctly said "boat," not "bed"—there's a big difference; the difference in fact between a necessary working association and an intimate relationship.

Dr. Alexander M. Schmidt, Commissioner of the FDA

• The consumer until recently has had implicit faith in the regulatory agencies and in the legislative control over the regulatory [agencies] and the consumer is . . . beginning now to question the role both the legislative and regulatory agencies are playing in protecting him from hazards which we are now suddenly realizing are very real.

Samuel S. Epstein, M.D.

• . . . 210 million Americans have relied upon governmental agencies for protection, and the governmental agencies have not been giving the public the protection that it is entitled to, because if the Food and Drug Administration, the Department of Agriculture . . . and all the other various agencies [that] have a responsibility in [food additive safety testing] have not acted and have not moved into fields which are far beyond the capacity of the overwhelming majority of people to understand . . . we have been making suckers out of the American people.

Senator Abraham S. Ribicoff

At Dr. Alexander Schmidt's first press conference after assuming office as commissioner of the FDA in July 1973, he emphasized that "we must be as certain as possible that all food ingredients . . . are judged for safety by the best scientific methods at our command. I can assure you that I am placing this task at the top of my personal priority list."

Schmidt was referring to the review of the GRAS list launched three years earlier. The review had gotten off to a shaky start. At the time, considerable dissension had existed both within the FDA and its parent body, HEW, as to the best manner of publicly announcing the review. The review had begun while the cyclamate ban was still fresh in the public's mind. Studies about saccharin,

monosodium glutamate, NDGA, brominated vegetable oils, modified food starches, salt, carrageenan, and other food additives had
been receiving publicity. There was talk about removing certain
additives from the GRAS list, and the public was expressing
uneasiness and concern about food additives in general.

Congressional hearings had uncovered the surprising fact that
the so-called GRAS list was not actually a specific list at all. On
different occasions, various FDA officials quoted approximate
numbers of GRAS additives, but there was no universal agreement.
As the congressional hearings progressed, it became clear that the
GRAS list was a loose arrangement whereby the FDA permitted
food processors to decide for themselves whether specific food
additives were, in fact, generally recognized as safe. The processors
were not required to petition the FDA to have the additive placed
on the list. If a processor decided that an additive was safe, he
simply used it. If he had any doubt, the processor could request
that the FDA make a determination, but the processor was not
required to do so. This lax management was described by the
congressional investigators as "the never-never land of nonregulation."

In order for the FDA to remove an additive from the GRAS list,
the agency had to demonstrate its harmfulness. This reverse state
of affairs was due to the FDA's previous failure to enforce food
additive safety regulations and its voluntary relinquishment of
controls.

The Federal Food Additives Amendment of 1958 required food
additive manufacturers to prove the safety of their products.
Additives used prior to 1958 could be granted GRAS status in one
of two ways. The additive could be evaluated "by experience based
on common use in food" or by being "generally recognized, among
experts qualified by scientific training and experience to evaluate
safety, as having been adequately shown through scientific procedures . . . to be safe." Long-time common usage has been shown,
repeatedly, to be an unreliable method of determining safety. The
review of scientific data also proved to be inadequate.

In order to draw up the original GRAS list the FDA sent out the names of 189 food additives to some 900 scientific experts chosen by the agency. The experts were asked to comment on the safety of the additives, but they were *not* asked whether or not the additives had been tested. The 1958 law stated that GRAS additives were those *"having been adequately shown through scientific procedures . . . to be safe."* [emphasis added] Thus, the intention of the 1958 law was disregarded.

Of the 900 experts polled, only about 355 replied. Of these, only 194 (about one-fifth of all the scientists contacted) responded favorably, or without comment, about additives on the list. The remainder criticized parts of the list. But the FDA chose to brush aside the criticisms:

—A critical comment about cyclamates was dismissed by the agency.

—The safety of ammonium carbonate was questioned by Henry M. Burlage of the University of Texas. The FDA ignored his comment, and then stated that he was unqualified to discuss this additive's safety, although the FDA itself had selected him as a qualified expert to review the list!

—The safety of benzoic acid was questioned by Henry Scott, chairman of Wisconsin's Food Standards Advisory Committee. Scott pointed out that benzoates and benzoic acid were considered illegal in foods such as sauerkraut and dairy products within his state. Scott's criticism was dismissed by the FDA. The agency cited a highly prejudiced whitewashing of this additive, issued earlier, to justify its position.

—Ammonium hydroxide's safety was questioned by the representative of a chemical company and others as being too strong and possibly dangerous in the hands of persons untrained in chemistry. The FDA rejected the criticism and regarded the compound as safe.

—NDGA, an antioxidant used to preserve fat, was singled out by W. F. von Oettingen, M.D., who questioned the insufficiency of toxicological data in existence. The FDA stated, "We have information to show safety and this has been published." However, at later dates, both the Joint FAO/WHO Expert Committee on Food Additives and the Canadian Food and Drug Directorate cautioned that information on NDGA was inadequate. Because of insufficient toxicological data, the Canadians conducted tests and found that NDGA was unsafe. Ultimately, the Canadian findings forced the FDA to remove NDGA from the GRAS list.

—Twelve scientists objected to vitamin D's inclusion on the GRAS list because of the potential harm to infants from hypercalcemia (excessive calcium in the blood). The FDA refused to acknowledge this danger and stated that "nutrient levels of vitamin D will not produce hypercalcemia effects." Six years later, the FDA had to reverse its position and limit the amount of vitamin D that could be added to food products "to prevent possible injury to infants. Excessive amounts of vitamin D was a possible cause of infantile hypercalcemia."

Even the critical evaluations of the agency's own scientists were ignored in compiling the GRAS list. Barbara Moulton, M.D., who was a staff member at the FDA's Bureau of Medicine at the time, recalled at a later date how the agency had handled the GRAS list:

. . . I first saw [the first list of food additives that was proposed for GRAS] when it came over my desk as a Federal Register proposal. . . . I was rather taken aback at some of the substances included on this list of substances generally recognized by experts as safe. . . . I went up and down the hall and inquired whether any member of the Bureau of Medicine Staff had been asked to comment on this list before it was published by the Food and Drug Administration. And I was assured by each member of the staff of the Bureau of Medicine that they had not seen this, nor had they been asked to comment on it before it was published in the Federal Register. . . . There are memos in the FDA file over my signature pointing out to the administrative group handling this why we as physicians felt folic acid certainly should not be included as a generally recognized safe food additive when it was well-known in the administration that I thought that I had collected almost enough data to take action against it as a drug, where the burden of proof is on the Government, whereas in the food-additive situation the burden of proof is upon industry. . . . There were certain ingredients [on the list] that we in the

Bureau of Medicine felt should not have been [on] it, and we were not asked to comment on beforehand . . . there were no physicians on the staff who favored [them]. . . ."

Dr. Moulton then charged that, despite overwhelming evidence in the FDA's own files showing the potential hazards of folic acid in masking symptoms of pernicious anemia, the FDA proposed to include folic acid on the GRAS list on the basis of one obscure report about three patients who apparently suffered no adverse effects. Dr. Moulton commented:

. . . there is, on the part of many of the people in the FDA, who have the power to decide policy, a deliberate attempt to pick a single isolated statement by one physician or one scientist, who may be and frequently is not well-regarded, and which supports a liberal attitude as far as the industry point of view is concerned, and to disregard a vast amount of material by the leaders in the field medically, which takes an opposite point of view.

Moulton was joined by others in the Bureau of Medicine who were concerned about the manner in which the "safety" of the additives was being decided. The Bureau of Medicine staff had gone on record saying:

We have reviewed the list with an assumption (but not a conviction) that the proscription against poor manufacturing practices will prove adequate in a general way to prevent harmful concentrations. . . .

As a single example, we do not actually recognize calcium phytate as necessarily safe used as a sequestrant, but without more details of its customary use and of its pharmacology and without more insight into the expected interpretation of the paragraph introducing the list [i.e., good manufacturing practices and conditions of intended use], we have no actual opinion of its propriety on the list.

In addition, we have considered the list with an attitude consistent with the assumption apparently held in its preparation—namely that the substances will meet necessary standards of identity, quality, and purity even though specifications are not stated. At least, it leaves unanswered the questions of just what allowances of impurities will constitute good manufacturing practices when substances are used for the purposes specified.

After the FDA had collated all the responses received, the Food and Pharmacology divisions prepared a joint memorandum entitled "Defense of the White List." In part, the memorandum stated:

In our final evaluation of the safety of a substance we have taken cognizance of the fact that all opinions are not of equal value, and thus have weighed the most heavily the opinions of scientifically recognized and often world-renowned experts. Common sense as well as scientific principles require us to accept the opinions of some and to reject the opinions of others. The Administration has long recognized the validity of this policy with respect to scientific matters and employs it in our day-to-day operations.

Despite the official statement in this memorandum, the formulation of the GRAS list lacked respectability as a scientific project. The FDA had arbitrarily rejected comments that did not suit its viewpoint. And in announcing that 900 world-renowned scientists were formulating the list, the FDA appears to have been practicing window dressing.

The FDA's GRAS list began with 189 additives (only three of the originally suggested additives were not included). The list continued to lengthen; as new additions were proposed they were added to the list without any pretense of scientific consultation. Ultimately, the GRAS list grew to include about 700 chemical additives. The FDA's lax policy made it virtually impossible to tell which chemicals were food additives, how many there were, and who—if anyone—had tested and evaluated their safety. If keeping track of them was difficult, regulating them was impossible.

The proposed inclusion of new additives on the GRAS list often was published in the Federal Register, but this was not always the case. In some instances, Winton B. Rankin, assistant to the commissioner of the FDA, merely sent out letters to various food processors indicating that certain additional substances had been placed on the list. This casual procedure caused HEW Assistant General Counsel William Goodrich to warn FDA Assistant Commissioner Kenneth W. Kirk, "Sooner or later these . . . letters are bound to get us into trouble."

The FDA had allowed the original intention of the law to be completely distorted. Instead of demanding scientific data, the FDA had totally acquiesced to the food processors' own interpretation, expressed clearly in a trade journal:

Contrary to the opinion held by many people in the food industry, the law confers no special authority on the FDA for deciding that an ingredient is GRAS. If experts who are qualified to evaluate the safety of a particular ingredient generally recognized as safe under the conditions of its intended use, then according to the language of the law itself . . . it is not subject to the provisions of the additive law.

Food additives on the GRAS list automatically enjoy certain privileges. They are exempt from the legal definition of a food additive and, therefore, are not subject to regulations concerning food additives. In order to remove an additive from the list, the FDA must demonstrate the harmfulness of the additive. But even when scientific evidence shows that a compound on the GRAS list may be hazardous, the FDA has failed to act promptly and decisively. One FDA official stated that the agency is not bound to remove a substance from the GRAS list on the basis of isolated evidence of potential danger that isn't widely accepted by scientists. "GRAS doesn't have to mean unanimously recognized as safe," he added.

Although the FDA ignored the critical evaluations of outside scientific experts of its own choosing, as well as qualified scientists within the agency, in formulating the original GRAS list, the agency gave great weight to data submitted by food processors. After the FDA had published the original GRAS list in the Federal Register, a food additives committee of the Flavoring Extracts Manufacturing Association of the United States (FEMA) conducted its own industry-wide survey, concerning the identity, composition, and uses of more than a thousand flavoring agents. The questionnaires were collated, and the substances were reviewed by a panel of toxicologists and pharmacologists who decided on safety. These additives are termed "deemed GRAS by FEMA."

Following an intense internal struggle, the FDA issued a regulation allowing most food flavoring agents on the FEMA list to be used under conditions approximating the GRAS-list items. The FDA retained vague legal control over these additives, while granting them GRAS privileges. Of some 1,400 food flavorings and adjuncts in use, only 191 were covered by FDA "white lists" of official approval and only 343 were granted "extension" status (i.e., tentatively allowed). On the basis of its own review, FEMA decided that 662 food flavoring additives could be considered GRAS. The remainder have been used in food without any independent scientific review of their safety.

In the decade after the original GRAS list was formed, toxicity testing became more sophisticated. The lack of reported cases of human toxicity was recognized as an untrustworthy factor in determining a substance's safety.

As the use of one substance after another was questioned in the late 1960s, the GRAS list threatened to become an explosive issue. In former President Nixon's Consumer Message of 1969, the FDA was directed to reevaluate the entire GRAS list, rather than the mere 100 items that the agency planned to review.

Reviewing the entire GRAS list brought a multitude of problems. The task required far more resources, both in terms of manpower and funds, than were available. Even with unlimited funding, performing chronic toxicity tests on all GRAS items would probably swamp all of the animal testing facilities available within the United States, as well as those in some foreign countries. A number of decisions had to be made about how to maintain adequate control over a fantastically complex operation.

As a result, the FDA adopted several industrial management techniques. Alan T. Spiher, Jr., of the FDA was assigned as project manager for the GRAS review. A Program Evaluation and Review Technique (PERT), developed originally for the Polaris Missile Project in 1958, was used as an operational research tool. Industry was sent a questionnaire that was to provide the FDA with data about the amount of the additive being consumed and with any available toxicity information.

The questionnaire was prepared by the NAS–NRC, and the FDA arranged to distribute a revised questionnaire if the first one failed to provide the required information.

The FDA recognized that food processors who were using GRAS additives probably had not done further safety studies after the initial GRAS classification. Consequently, recent pertinent toxicity information would not necessarily be obtained from files of the food processors using the additives. The FDA planned a review of the toxicological literature of the last 50 years.

The FDA anticipated subjecting most, if not all, of the existing GRAS additives to screening tests for teratogenic and mutagenic effects, and for reproductive performance (i.e., mating efficiency, survival rate, and weight gains of offspring, etc.). To speed up the operation, the FDA planned to use contractors, and a computerized storage and retrieval system.

As the GRAS review proceeded, it came under critical attack. Epstein voiced some of the objections:

The consumer, the taxpayer, you, and I are now being asked to foot the bill for safety evaluation of profitable food chemicals which the industry has generally regarded or treated as being generally regarded as safe, and which will be tested at our expense. . . . This is to my mind somewhat of a strange situation, whereby you and I will be expected to foot the bill for profitable food chemicals which have been illegally—the word "illegal" has to be qualified depending on whether one is dealing with the GRAS or the so-called gray list or various subcategories—but I submit, improperly treated as being safe in the past. . . . I would venture to wager that if indeed the financial onus for safety evaluation of profitable food chemicals were placed on the food manufacturer as indeed the law demands, this list of 640 food additives on the GRAS list would miraculously shrink overnight to something like 50 to 75.

At the beginning of the GRAS review, it was estimated that the entire study might eventually cost as much as $20 million. By the end of 1974, with the end not in sight, this mark had already been reached.

Additional criticism of the GRAS review centered around the FDA's policy of requesting the NAS–NRC to evaluate additive safety data. One governmental observer remarked:

The NAS is being constantly called on by the FDA to get them off the hook. The question comes up as to whether the NAS has now become the full deciding arm of the FDA. The industry men on the panels or those who are under obligation to industry create a situation which is like an author reviewing his own book.

Epstein contended that "close identification of the NAS–NRC Food Protection Committee with industrial interests" makes it singularly inappropriate as a major source of "independent advice" to the FDA. The Food Protection Committee was originally organized at the request and with the financial support of the food and chemical industries. It consults at frequent intervals with members representing these supporters.

Epstein charged that "anyone can buy the data to support his case," and he gave as an example that the NAS–NRC's panel for monosodium glutamate review was supported "strongly by the food, chemical, and packaging industries."

After John W. Olney, M.D., reported in 1969 that brain lesions were induced by monosodium glutamate in test animals, the FDA requested the NAS–NRC to review the additive. Of the seven scientists appointed by the NAS–NRC to investigate monosodium glutamate, two had received research funds from major manufacturers and food-processor users of the additive. Two more were employed by toxicological divisions of major chemical companies. Another panel member was founder of a research and testing laboratory that, on occasion, had performed animal studies on monosodium glutamate under contract with a large manufacturer of the additive. At the same time as he was serving on the review panel, he testified in behalf of the Grocery Manufacturers of America, a lobbying organization opposed to stringent food additive regulations.

When the panel's report exonerated monosodium glutamate, Olney termed it "an industry-arranged whitewash" made by a group with almost no experience in neuropathology. Olney charged:

Those who were unable to confirm the findings [of neurological damage in infant animals] turned out to be almost exclusively from a certain element of the scientific community . . . who maintain close ties to the food and drug industries. . . . Some members of the team specialize in generating made-to-order evidence, while others are asked by the FDA through the NAS to evaluate the evidence.

The NAS–NRC review of cyclamates had also come under sharp criticism. The FDA had requested several reviews by the NAS–NRC, and based on the 1968 review, which affirmed the "safety" of cyclamates, the FDA allowed their use to continue. Dr. John J. Schrogie of the FDA's Bureau of Medicine and Dr. Herman F. Kraybill of the FDA's Bureau of Science both served on the review panel. When the report was issued, Schrogie and Kraybill, in a detailed memorandum to FDA Commissioner Ley, wrote:

This report of the Food Protection Committee represents a largely uncritical review of the available material. Conclusions of studies are included without proper regard for the quality of methodology originally used. Studies lacking adequate statistical design are given equal weight with sounder studies; many clinical and epidemiological studies yielding questionable conclusions are given uncritical acceptance. Because such conclusions are included, possibly erroneous results gain added stature and interpretive errors are perpetuated.

It is not our intention to direct attention solely to reports of potentially toxic effects. The quality of studies is often mediocre on both sides of the issue. Although questions of safety have been raised, they have not as yet been resolved satisfactorily in either direction.

This report, in general, suggests a level of knowledge on many aspects of this topic [cyclamates] which simply does not exist. It should have pointed more critically to the current deficiencies in information as a basis for further action. . . .

A "special interest" charge was made against the NAS–NRC by Philip M. Boffey (see also pages 187–88). Boffey charged that the NAS–NRC, when asked to judge food additive safety, has "continuously acted in the interests of the food industry" and has "downplayed the likelihood of such long-term hazards as cancer, genetic defects, and birth defects." He cited as an example the case of the food dye FD&C Red No. 2. (see pages 172–75)

"No one has charged that committee [Food Protection Committee] members are guilty of blatant conflicts of interest in the sense that they profit directly from the recommendations they make," Boffey said. "Rather, the complaint is that the committee members are just a bit too close to industry—too sympathetic to its problems—to permit objective judgment in a situation where the economic stakes are high and the scientific advice is subject to varying interpretations."

Another reason for the Food Protection Committee's "leniency," Boffey explained, "is that it has long been dominated by scientists who tend to be more concerned about immediate, acute effects than about long-term, chronic effects." He continued:

The Committee's panels have seldom included anyone primarily expert in mutagenesis or teratogenesis, and the members expert in carcinogenesis have been a small minority. Yet in many cases the most alarming evidence of hazards associated with a particular chemical has involved precisely these long-term effects.

Referring to the 1969 NAS report on "toxicological insignificance" (see page 157), Boffey said that the committee asked industry scientists to render a "sensitive judgment" on the safety of the tens of thousands of natural and synthetic food chemicals found in the food supply. Five of the nine-member task force, Boffey said, "were directly employed by food or chemical companies, and a sixth headed a commercial laboratory which serves the food and chemical industries." He charged:

These are the very industries which have been responsible for introducing chemicals into the food supply and whose profits would be affected by a get-tough attitude toward chemicals or by a requirement that all chemicals be extensively tested. In addition to its obvious bias, the committee lacked in-depth expertise concerning such long-term hazards as cancer.

The FDA's use of NAS–NRC for additive safety review also has been criticized by congressmen. Senator Charles H. Percy charged that the NAS–NRC had been "insensitive" to conflicts of interest among the scientists it chose to advise the government on subjects such as food additive safety. Percy suggested that the academy should follow the example of the American Bar Association, whose code of ethics forbids judges from hearing cases involving parties to whom they have financial or personal ties.

During the congressional hearings on DES, congressmen questioned the FDA's revision of a regulation requiring the FDA's Commissioner:

. . . to be guided by the principles and procedures for establishing the safety of food additives stated in current publications of the National Academy of Sciences–National Research Council. The [congressional] committee recommends that FDA *not rely* upon principles and procedures advanced by any single outside group in matters of this kind. . . .

The congressional committee also noted that the FDA's delegation of power to the NAS–NRC appeared to endow such institutions "with unusual regulatory effect."

As a result of this series of stinging charges, the NAS–NRC took steps in 1972 to avoid conflicting interests. Candidates for panels are now required to file statements declaring any potential conflicts. These "bias statements" are then used as a guide in achieving a "balanced viewpoint" among panelists.

The FDA reacted to these criticisms by turning to the Federation of American Societies for Experimental Biology (FASEB) to review the GRAS list. Although the FDA decided to bypass the NAS–NRC, it was kept as an appeals body for judgments rendered by the FASEB.

Officials of the FASEB regarded the GRAS review as a "new and unusual endeavor" for a panel of nine scientists. At present, the panel is reviewing the available literature on each additive, as compiled in a series of monographs being prepared for the FDA under separate contracts. Research sponsored by the FDA will fill some gaps.

Detailed statements of each panelist's "bias statements" were required by the FASEB. However, unlike the NAS–NRC, the FASEB decided to bar any member from evaluating a particular food additive if companies manufacturing or using the additive have financially supported the member's research.

Any possible value of the present GRAS review is limited by the same features that marked an earlier Drug Efficacy Study. The review consists largely of sifting through old data, long in the files, much of which is from industry or from their privately contracted testing laboratories. The review consists of relatively few new studies conducted with more sophisticated testing methods and techniques. Nor is there any indication that clinical reports on allergic reactions are being considered.

Close scrutiny of the GRAS review, as it has proceeded, has demonstrated that the project is more of a public relations' stunt than a scientific exercise. FDA Commissioner Schmidt announced at a news conference:

> Our goal in this review is to reassure the FDA and the American people that hundreds of ingredients—both chemical and natural—long added to the food supply are in fact safe for that purpose.

At the same news conference, the former director of the FDA's Bureau of Foods, Dr. Virgil O. Wodicka, added that he did not expect any of the additives under review to be proved unsafe. But, he added, it was nevertheless important to prove their safety.

Thus, it appears that the FDA already had decided, prior to the review, that all additives on the GRAS list would be cleared for safety. The agency had prudently retained an escape hatch, by reserving the right to have the NAS–NRC as final arbiter, in the unlikely event that FASEB might raise embarrassing doubts about the safety of any additive. The GRAS review, currently in progress, bears features strangely similar to those displayed in the formulation of the original list in the late 1950s.

Food interests have long opposed the establishment of efficacy for food additives; and the FDA has never required efficacy to be demonstrated. During the Delaney Hearings in 1958, the following exchange took place between George Faunce, Jr., vice president and general counsel of Continental Baking Company (testifying in behalf of the American Bakers Association), and Congressman John D. Dingell:

Faunce: We are opposed to having the FDA determine whether or not a proposed new food additive has any functional value. If the Secretary [of HEW], upon examination of a proposed new food additive, finds that it is without hazard to the health of man or other animal, the question of what its function is should be of no concern to him. That is an economic determination which is the prerogative of the potential user. Nor should the functional value of a proposed new food additive be a relevant factor to be used by the Secretary in arriving at his determination. In other words, the question of functional value should not be injected at all in a bill concerned solely with the safety of an additive. . . .

Dingell: Could you illustrate, perhaps, a purpose for which some useless chemical or useless substance [might] be added to the food?

Faunce: A substance is not useless if, assuming its safety [has been demonstrated], it is used in a product, and the product is improved, and it improves its sale. You cannot tell, I do not see how you can say it was a useless product.

Dingell: Then you are telling me that a manufacturer should have a blank check to add any substance he wants, as long as it is not harmful; is that right?

Faunce: That is right.

Dingell: Is that right?

Faunce: That is my position.

Faunce's position was supported by Charles Wesley Dunn, general counsel for the Grocery Manufacturers of America, Inc., who was also a prime framer of the present federal food laws:

Where a food additive is actually safe under the conditions of its use, the question of its functional value, that is, its industrial functional value, is clearly one for a food manufacturer to decide in his discretionary exercise of the food-manufacturing art; and it is not one for the Government to decide under a pure-food law, directed to assure the safety of food and not its functional use.

Lawrence A. Coleman, in behalf of the Manufacturing Chemists' Association, Inc., concurred:

We join with what we are informed is the overwhelming consensus of food manufacturers that any legislation in this field should concern itself only with the safety of food additives in their intended use and should not deal with any concept as the functional value of the additive. We believe that no food additive will be purchased by a food processor unless the purchaser believes it has some value, functional or otherwise. It is for the purchaser and not the government to say whether any product has value. Value is to be determined in the marketplace, and not by administrative decision.

Although the FDA has consistently acquiesced to industry's viewpoint, this concept has been challenged on numerous occasions. The Food and Nutrition Section of the American Public Health Association endorsed the position that additives should not be used unless they are proven to benefit the consumer, as well as being safe.

Epstein suggested that regulatory agencies need to view each petition for a new additive by asking:

Does the chemical in question serve a socially and economically useful purpose for the general population? If not, why introduce it and accept potential hazards without general matching benefits? Such considerations clearly apply to the use of monosodium glutamate in baby foods and cyclamates for the public at large. The self-evident need for efficacy, now generally accepted for drugs, should be extended to all synthetic chemicals. I would think the majority of these . . . 600-odd chemicals on the GRAS list would disappear from use [if an efficacy regulation would be in effect]; in fact, there is no demonstrable efficacy for many of these.

An example of how the list of food additives continues to be extended needlessly is shown in a recent incident. A petition requested that industry be allowed to use sodium acid pyrophosphate (SAPP) in the curing of frankfurters, wieners, bologna, garlic bologna, knockwurst, and other cooked sausage products. Since the USDA controls meat processing safety, the decision needed to be made by that agency. Adding SAPP to the meat stuffing of such cooked sausage products makes the blend more acid. This speeds up the curing (color fixing), and cuts cooking time by about 20 minutes. The resulting economic savings are clearly beneficial for the sausage processors, but these savings are not necessarily passed along to consumers as lower prices.

The USDA requested interested persons, groups, and officials to submit comments about SAPP. Nearly 90 percent of the 447 comments received came from individual consumers, consumer organizations, and state officials who opposed the use of SAPP in frankfurters. Most of the supporting comments came from sausage processors.

SAPP was not a critically important additive for sausage processors. Other additives—glucono delta lactone, citric acid, sodium ascorbate, and erythorbic acid—that have official government sanction are used for the same purpose. Some opponents viewed the SAPP proposal as an opportunity to halt the continuous, needless, and potentially hazardous proliferation of food additives. Why, asked the opponents of SAPP, was it necessary to introduce yet another chemical additive into our food supply? One homemaker filed the comment, "The use of additives has to stop somewhere, and it would be wonderful if this could be the turning point."

Donald W. Moos, Director of Washington State's agriculture department, was among the state officials who raised objections: "For many years we have had acceptable sausage products without sodium acid pyrophosphate. This chemical does nothing to benefit the consumer of the product. It only serves as an expedient . . . to further shorten the manufacturing process."

Staff members of two USDA divisions also opposed the sanctioning of SAPP for use in cooked sausages. Members of the USDA's Consumer and Marketing Service (CMS) expressed the view that the strong opposition by consumers be respected. In an interoffice memorandum, the CMS staff suggested that the broad antiadulteration provisions of the Wholesome Meat Act of 1967 gave the USDA legal authority to reject the SAPP proposal. Staff members of USDA's Products Standards Division, a group responsible for meat additive review, also opposed SAPP's use. They said that products made with SAPP would be "less nutritious, less wholesome, and not any cheaper."

Despite the opposition from the public, as well as from within its own agency, the USDA announced that manufacturers would be permitted to use SAPP in frankfurters and other cooked sausage products. When the USDA's decision was criticized, an agency spokesman was reported as saying that the protesters "told us they didn't like SAPP and didn't want it, but they didn't provide any data that was truly useful, and industry did." Consumers and officials alike need to ponder over the implications of this statement. Should consumers be forced to accept food additives they don't want and don't need? Should additives be officially sanctioned merely because they serve food processors as a means of providing shortcuts that increase profits? In theory, at least, the FDA and the USDA have repudiated this philosophy. Should decisions be weighed solely on the basis of technical data, without consideration of the consumers' wishes that their food remain free of questionable ingredients? If this is the case, requesting comments from all interested parties serves no real purpose, except to create an *impression* that the governmental agency is concerned about the consumers.

Although the question of SAPP's safety was not an issue when the USDA requested comments, this question *was* raised shortly after the additive was officially sanctioned. The Products Standards Division of the USDA cautioned that the use of SAPP raised "a serious wholesomeness question." A memorandum from this division, circulated throughout the USDA, cautioned that "many frankfurters and almost all bologna is eaten without further cooking. . . . If this reduction in smoking and cooking takes place in a routine manner in plants using unlimited amounts of rework, the results could be disastrous." (*Rework* is a term for processed meat products that cannot be marketed due to some defect, such as ruptured casings, and are salvaged and reblended in new batches of ingredients.) The memorandum warned that the bacterial level in the product can be raised by the addition of such reworked materials during the processing. When the reduced processing time made possible by SAPP is coupled with the effect of summertime weather, an ideal environment is created "for the growth and development of those spoilage and food-poisoning organisms which have survived the reduced heating cycle".

Another question regarding SAPP's safety was raised by Haven C. Sweet, Assistant Professor of Biological Sciences at Florida Technological University. Before the USDA approved the use of SAPP in frankfurters, the FDA had approved its use as a buffering agent in baking powder, muffins, cake mixes, doughnuts, waffles, and self-rising flour. SAPP also has been in use to minimize the amount of cooked-out juices in hams, bacon, pork loins, and cooked ham. When Sweet asked the FDA to supply him with SAPP's safety data, the agency sent him the 1964 report by the Joint FAO/WHO Expert Committee on Food Additives. This report quoted an earlier study done by Dr. G. J. van Esch and colleagues in Germany in 1957, as well as another document, prepared in 1970, which presented no new evidence.

While scrutinizing the data, Sweet noticed certain discrepancies.

He obtained the original van Esch study and compared it to the expert committee report of the study. Van Esch and his colleagues had reported that rats fed a 5 percent phosphate mixture showed less rapid development, reduced fertility, and reduced lifespan than the controls. The expert committee report had *deleted* this conclusion, and claimed the *opposite*. Sweet charged either "incompetence" or "motives of deliberate deception." Not only had SAPP's safety not been proven, "but there are indications that considerable damage may result." Sweet pointed out:

. . . although an 11 percent decline in lifespan at 0.6 percent feeding level (the SAPP level in frankfurters) is not statistically significant, it still may be a real phenomenon. . . . When one considers the possibility of an 11 percent reduction in lifespan of all persons who consume hot dogs, the number of years lost would be staggering.

Sweet asked for "an immediate moratorium" on SAPP's use, and a "thorough and honest research program to evaluate its safety."

The policy of allowing the number of food additives used to increase is rationalized by the Joint FAO/WHO Expert Committee on Food Additives, which stated in a report:

An increase in the number of food additives on a permitted list does not imply an over-all increase in [the amount of] additives used; the different additives are largely used as alternatives. . . . From the toxicological point of view there is less likelihood of long exposure, or of high or cumulative dose levels being attained, if a wide range of substances is available for use.

This peculiar view, endorsed by food additive proponents, must be rejected. The proliferation of food additives has reached a point where it is impossible to judge their safety or to monitor their use adequately.

According to cancer researcher William E. Smith:

It seems clear that food additive legislation to safeguard consumers could evolve more soundly if food industries agreed upon their fundamental needs for genuinely useful additives, and then sought approval for a minimum of necessary, thoroughly studied substances mutually and generally agreed upon as safe and beneficial.

Smith's view was affirmed by Wilhelm C. Hueper, M.D., when he was Chief of the Environmental Cancer Section of the NCI:

It becomes necessary . . . for the ensuring of an adequate health protection of the general public, to limit the number of permitted food additives . . . to the smallest number which still meets the essential economic requirements of the industries producing, processing, and merchandising foodstuffs and the protective demands of the general public consuming them.

If the federal regulatory agencies would limit food additives to those that were thoroughly tested for safety *and* efficacy, the American public would prosper from a higher level of quality food. Processed foods—cake mixes, frozen pies, TV dinners, dehydrated potatoes, dry soup mixes, frozen fish sticks, and instant imitation fruit drinks, to name a few—usually use many more additives than conventional foods. A drastic cutback of such food products in the marketplace would benefit both the health and the pocketbook of consumers, since such items are generally low in essential nutrients and high in cost. Even in the absence of so-called convenience foods, American shoppers would have a greater variety of foods from which to select than has ever before been available. For years home economics teachers and other professionals concerned with nutrition have attempted to educate the public about the "basic four" or "basic seven" food groups. There is general agreement that these efforts, which have tended to oversimplify a complex subject, have been feeble and ineffective. They have been offset by mass media advertising of convenience foods, snack foods, and even "fun foods." People have been convinced that these foods were developed because of public demand, but in reality, the demand was created by means of vigorous advertising campaigns, after these foods had been formulated. The media convinced the public that such items were truly desirable and even necessary.

Consumers must be reeducated in order to make wise food selections: to place a bag of potatoes in the shopping cart rather than instant mashed potatoes or potato chips; to use fresh rather than maraschino cherries; to drink orange juice rather than imitation orange drink; to eat low-fat ground-round beef rather than luncheon meat; and to use natural cheese rather than imitation processed cheese food spread. *Wise food choices can reduce automatically the total intake of food additives.*

Food dyes have had a particularly poor safety record and should be shunned especially. Food dyes serve *only* a cosmetic purpose. Food interests attempt to justify using food dyes by saying that consumers might reject their products otherwise. At one time, the FDA required each dye-treated orange to be stamped "color added." This control was eliminated when industry claimed it was too costly and time consuming, even though some citrus growers still find it a worthwhile practice to stamp each piece of fruit with its brand name or variety.

Instead of dye-treated oranges, citrus interests should try to reeducate the public. The industry should launch an advertising campaign to explain that, at certain times of the year, oranges may appear green but nevertheless be ripe. Enlightened consumers will come to accept such normal colored fruit, especially if there are no dye-colored oranges in the marketplace. Both in the Caribbean area and in Central American countries, the sale of oranges with a green color is customary, and there is no public demand for uniform "orange" color in the fruit. If artificially-colored foods are not found in the marketplace the consumer will not give weight to the attractiveness of appearance as a basis of choice.

Similarly, frankfurter processors could reeducate consumers about their products, which appear gray unless treated with the color fixatives sodium nitrite and sodium nitrate. Traditionally, consumers have accepted the grayness of pork sausages; they also can learn to accept a grayness in frankfurters.

Enlightened consumers have begun to choose foods that may not appear attractive, if they are convinced that such foods are of superior quality. British housewives were reported to be paying *higher* prices for blemished fruits than for perfect looking ones, because they believe that the blemished fruits have received fewer pesticide treatments. Similarly, those who shop at health food stores willingly pay higher prices for produce that is not as large and doesn't look as attractive as their supermarket counterparts.

Another way to eliminate the use of food dyes with citrus fruit is to apply various bioregulatory agents to fruit after it has reached maturity, either before or after harvest. This induces the formation and accumulation of carotenoid pigments, which can color lemons, oranges, and grapefruits from pale yellow to orangish red. This process also would increase the formation and accumulation of provitamin A carotenoids, increasing the fruit's nutrients. The process is being studied at a fruit and vegetable chemistry laboratory at the USDA, with partial funding from the Florida and California citrus industries. If it is successful, the citrus interests will need to promote the novel-colored fruit for consumer acceptance.

Consumers also must be taught to avoid foods containing synthetic food flavorings and their adjuncts. This group of additives presently poses, according to one critic, "one of the areas of greatest toxicological uncertainty."

Many food processors have become aware of a growing consumer interest in foods with natural flavors. Ice cream companies, especially, have been responsive. In a press release about its ice cream made with natural colors and flavors, one well-established firm reported:

These natural flavors are different from what many people are used to. Most people identify vanilla with the flavor that comes from the little brown bottle in the kitchen, and that's what most vanilla ice cream tastes like. But that usually is a flavoring substance called vanillin. It's artificial. The flavor in true vanilla ice cream comes from actual vanilla beans— clearly visible as specks in [our] ice cream. The flavors are subtle and refreshing, and for a change, you can see everything that you are eating in your ice cream. . . . the color is not going to be what a lot of people have come to expect. Our natural strawberry ice cream, for example, is a very pale shade, unlike the vivid pink color some companies produce. That's because our color comes exclusively from nearly three dozen ripe strawberries blended into every half gallon.

The press release also pointed out that the butter pecan ice cream included more than 50 pecans in each half gallon.

Another commercial ice cream made with all natural ingredients advertised:

Because I want you to know all the natural ingredients in my [Brand name] Ice Cream, they are printed clearly on the carton. . . . Mine . . . is a more expensive ice cream because the fresh ingredients, the real natural ingredients, are more costly to come by than synthetic flavors and additives. . . . Only real raspberries with the eaten-in-the-fields fresh flavors are used in my [raspberry] Ice Cream. And not just a raspberry here or there. I try to make sure every quart of ice cream is at least one-sixth juicy raspberries.

Food interests have been telling the public that synthetic food flavorings must be used because supplies of natural flavorings for such popular flavors as raspberries or strawberries would be insufficient to meet consumer demands. This argument is faulty and needs to be challenged. If demands increase, more farmers will grow such crops as raspberries and strawberries. Market demands will be met. The real reasons for synthetic flavoring are economy, stability and uniformity, and other features of concern to food interests. However, it should be apparent to food processors that a constantly growing number of consumers *willingly pay higher prices* for quality food.

The public should understand that the durability and long shelf life processors give to foods benefit storekeepers more than consumers. But food processors and sellers have other options to retard or prevent food spoilage. Frequent baking and delivery could stop bakery goods from going stale. Refrigeration or freezing of bread retards molding, so that mold-retarding agents are unnecessary.

A harmless saline solution process for drying fruit has been known since 1907. This process could be used in place of the toxic sulfur dioxide. In some instances, sun-drying, freeze-drying, or other drying methods—greatly improved through technological progress—can be used without hazard and with minimal nutritional losses.

In some instances, both alpha tocopherol (vitamin E) and ascorbic acid (vitamin C), which are nontoxic antioxidants, can be used instead of the questionable butylated compounds.

Freezing is one of the least damaging food processing methods. Many food items could be additive-free if they were frozen. One company sells nitrite-free frankfurters by virtue of the fact that the frankfurters are frozen. Another firm freezes cakes shortly after they are baked so they can be formulated additive-free.

Presently, supermarkets devote relatively little space to refrigerators and freezers. Future supermarkets should make greater use of refrigerators and freezers to retard spoilage. This would automatically reduce the total number of food additives needed.

Grinding coffee has been commonplace in many supermarkets, with self-service in an aisle or to order at the checkout counter. Similarly, flours and cereals could be freshly ground, and thus the use of fumigants, bleaches, aging agents, and freshness preservers could be eliminated. Whole grains, stored cool, dry and protected from insect infestation, have a long shelf life. Electrified grinding mills are available, but no one has taken the initiative to use them. Food processors and sellers need to think along different lines than in the past. Their great technological skills should be applied to meet consumer needs, and the drive for novelty and innovation that serves no real purpose needs to be rechanneled.

At times, food processors have been pressured to use unnecessary food additives by food additive sellers. BHT and BHA, for example, have been added to vacuum-packed tins of nuts, a totally unnecessary practice. In one instance, a dry cereal processor added these antioxidants to his product until consumer complaints convinced the seller they should be withdrawn. In another case, a wheat germ processor used one of these antioxidants. Again, consumer reactions convinced him that he should stop using the additive with his product.

Some food companies have shown interest in voluntary nutritional labeling or in supplying nutritional composition of their products upon request. Food companies must also recognize the need to disclose the use of food additives, as well as food components. Such information should not be regarded as "trade secrets" but as information vital to the consumer.

Vague labeling phrases, such as "antioxidant," "freshness preserver," or "oxygen interceptor," tolerated by the FDA and the USDA, are insufficient, since certain people may be highly sensitive to a specific substance. The label "artificial color" does not help a tartrazine-sensitive individual. The phrases "thickening agents," "spices," or "vegetable oils" do not safeguard those individuals who may be highly sensitive. All additives, whether in nonstandardized or standardized foods, should be listed on labels. Since federal agencies have shown apathy about this situation, enlightened food processors must initiate this practice.

Food processors should also place a notice on food labels if products have been reformulated. People who are allergic to certain substances usually read labels carefully. But, after using a product for a while, they may forget, and a reformulated product may be potentially harmful to them.

The Metropolitan Washington, D.C., chapter of the Allergy Foundation of America cited several cases of children who suffered adversely after consuming food products in which ingredients had been changed. A year-old child's painful urinary tract infection was traced to a drink to which vitamin C recently had been added. A 13-year-old girl's eczema condition suddenly worsened. The cause was traced to cranberry juice, to which dextrose had recently been added. In both cases, the children had tolerated the products for long periods before reformulations, and their parents had no longer bothered to check labels.

Some food processing practices are classified as "additives" by the FDA. When the review of the GRAS list was proposed, the

FDA specified that foods modified by new or unconventional processing methods may require food additive regulations. Currently, such products are considered GRAS.

Unusual methods of heat treatment, dehydration, or fumigation may alter the food's components, introduce new substances to it, or lower its nutritional value. Under the new procedures for GRAS review, food companies would have to follow food additive safety regulations to obtain FDA approval of these products. The regulations also applied to foods that have been significantly altered by genetic breeding or selection.

The need to test genetic breeding safety was impressed upon officials in 1967. The USDA, in conjunction with the Pennsylvania Agricultural Experiment Station, had developed a new potato variety, called Lenape, expressly for potato chip processing. The new strain was assumed safe, and potato seeds were distributed.

Shortly afterward, a Canadian research team reported that Lenape contained twice as many glycoalkaloids, naturally occurring poisons in potatoes, as were normally found. It was believed that the toxins could survive the frying in potato chip processing. Under certain conditions, the poison level would be high enough to produce gastrointestinal upsets in humans.

This incident should alert food processors, as well as scientists and regulatory agencies concerned with food additive safety, to a broader view of their responsibilities. Food processors must regard qualities such as attractive appearance, uniformity, and long shelf life as minor factors. Nutritional food values must become the prime concern. In order to better serve consumer needs, food processors must rechannel their energies. Food processors already possess enormous technological skills and facilities, in addition to operational efficiency. No drastic alterations would be required to redirect present research to emphasize the nutritional qualities of food rather than the further extension of shelf life, color and flavor uniformity, and other features that require numerous additives. Conceivably, the food processors could meet the challenge of providing basic research in nutrition, biochemistry, and toxicology. Food interests could educate and train their researchers to have a scientific awareness of these important concerns, rather than have them view food manipulation and engineering merely as subjects of physical and chemical technology.

Perhaps food processors will meet this challenge by allotting more funds for basic food research. As recently as 1966, they spent only $12 million for research, compared with $1.4 billion for advertising and about $123 million for research on promotional devices.

An official governmental report noted:

The biological information is probably less available in the case of food additives than for other regulated chemicals (drugs and pesticides, for example). . . . One reason . . . for a lack of information is the relatively unsophisticated biological science which has been applied to that research and testing done in behalf of food additives. . . . *Up to now there has been little incentive on the part of food additive manufacturers to make large investments in behalf of an understanding of biological effects."* [emphasis added]

Perhaps these stirrings have already begun. George F. Stewart, editor of *Food Technology*, cautioned his colleagues:

Most practicing food technologists have very little nutrition background. They little appreciate the impact of their efforts on the nutritive value of food and the nutritive well-being of consumers. If we do not pay proper attention to the nutritional problems associated with food technology, we run the risk of eventually producing an abundance of palatable, convenient staple foods that are not capable of meeting man's nutrient needs. We run the risk of undermining the nutritional well-being of our nation.

Author's Notes

Chapter 1: Consumer Be Damned!

page 1, lines 1–13
Senator Abraham S. Ribicoff, U.S. Senate, Hearings before the Subcommittee on Executive Reorganization and Government Research, Committee on Government Operations: *Chemicals and the Future of Man*, 92d Congress, 1st session, April 6–7, 1971, pp. 1–2.

page 1, lines 15–16
Howard J. Sanders, "Food Additives," *Chemical and Engineering News*, October 10, 1966, p. 102.

page 1, lines 18–20
Robert M. Hadsell, "Food Processing: Search for Growth," *Chemical and Engineering News*, August 23, 1971, p. 19.

page 1, lines 22–25
Senator Gaylord Nelson, U.S. Senate, "Food Protection Act of 1972," *Congressional Record*, February 14, 1972, No. 18.

page 1, line 27–page 2, line 6
"Program and Financial Plan, 1970–1974," Food and Drug Administration, p. 3.

page 2, lines 8–9
Herbert L. Ley, address to the 12th Annual Food and Drug Law Institute, FDA Educational Conference, December 3, 1968, p. 4.

page 2, lines 11–12
"Food Additives" (editorial), *The Lancet*, August 16, 1969.

page 2, lines 14–23
Senator Gaylord Nelson, "Food Protection Act of 1972."

page 2, lines 25–32
U.S. House of Representatives, Hearings before the Select Committee to Investigate the Use of Chemicals in Food Products, 81st Congress, 2d Session, 1950: "Chemicals in Food Products," Part 1, 1951; "Chemicals in Foods and Cosmetics," Part 2, 1951; "Chemicals in Foods and Cosmetics," 1952; "Food Additives," 1958. By the time the last hearing was called, in 1958, the word "chemical" had been dropped from the term "chemical food additives" since industry representatives had voiced strenuous objections. By 1973, Alexander M. Schmidt, Commissioner of the FDA, was referring to food additives as "food ingredients" and "good food ingredients."

page 2, line 36–page 3, line 3
"Expansion in Food Additives Use Since 1958," 19th Report by the Committee on Government Operations, Regulation of Food Additives—Nitrites and Nitrates, 92d Congress 2d session, August 15, 1972, pp. 3–4.

page 3, lines 4–15
Chemical and Engineering News, October 10, 1966, p. 104.

page 3, lines 16–17
Arthur D. Little, Inc., graph printed in Chemical and Engineering News, October 10, 1966, p. 106.

page 3, lines 17–20
Chemical and Engineering News, October 10, 1966, p. 103.

page 3, lines 21–24
U.S. House of Representatives, Hearings before the Committee on Interstate and Foreign Commerce: "Color Additives," 86th Congress, 2d session, 1960. U.S. Senate, Hearings before a Special Subcommittee of the Committee on Labor and Welfare, to amend Section 402(d) of the Federal Food, Drug, and Cosmetic Act. 89th Congress, 1st session, 1965 (additives in candy); Hearings before the Subcommittee on Reorganization and International Organizations of the Committee on Government Operations: "Interagency Coordination in Environmental Hazards (Pesticides)," 88th Congress, 1st session, Parts 1–7, 1963; extending to Part 8, 1964.

page 3, lines 25–28
"Expansion in Food Additives Used Since 1958," op. cit., p. 4.

page 3, line 29
U.S. House of Representatives, Hearings before a Subcommittee of the Committee on Government Operations: "Cyclamate Sweeteners," 91st Congress, 2d session, June 10, 1970. 92d Congress, 1st session, September and October, 1971; Hearings before a Subcommittee of the Committee on Government Operations: "Regulations of Diethylstilbestrol (DES), Its Use as a Drug for Humans and in Animal Feeds," 92d Congress, 1st session, Part 1, November 11, 1971; Part 11, December 13, 1971;

"Regulation of Diethylstilbestrol," July 20, 1972; and Part 3, August 15, 1972; "Regulation of Food Additives and Medicated Animal Feeds," March 1971.

page 3, line 29–page 4, line 13
1st Report by the Committee on Government Operations: "Recall Procedures of the Food and Drug Administration," 92d Congress, 1st session, October 21, 1971; 12th Report: "Regulation of Diethylstilbestrol and Other Drugs Used in Food Producing Animals," 93d Congress, 1st session; 19th Report: "Regulation of Food Additives— Nitrites and Nitrates," 92d Congress, 2d session, August 15, 1972.

page 4, lines 13–18
Dr. Alan T. Spiher, Jr., "The GRAS List Review," *FDA Papers*, December 1970–January 1971.

page 4, lines 19–31
The figure of five pounds of food additives per capita was released by Richard L. Hughes of Arthur D. Little, Inc., and printed in *Chemical and Engineering News*, August 23, 1971, p. 19; the figure of per capital sugar consumption is from USDA records from 1960 through 1972, reproduced in *Nutrition Today*, July–August 1973, p. 26; the remainder of the figures of per capita food additive consumption are from Richard L. Hall, "Food Additives," *Nutrition Today*, July–August 1973, pp. 21, 26. Regarding the danger of overconsumption of the food additive sugar, John Yudkin, M.D., stated, "If a small fraction of what is already known about the effects of sugar were to be revealed about any other material used as a food additive, that material would promptly be banned." Lewis K. Dahl and coworkers have found that overconsumption of table salt induces, among other problems, hypertension. Low-residue foods, resulting from diets high in refined starch (and sugar), have been implicated in a wide variety of health problems by Dr. Denis P. Burkitt and Dr. T. L. Cleave.

page 4, lines 31–34
"Expansion in Food Additives Used Since 1958," *op. cit.*, p. 4.

page 5, lines 1–25
Senator Gaylord Nelson, "Food Protection Act of 1972," *op. cit.*

page 5, lines 31–33
Methods of railroad financing in the United States were in public disfavor in the 1870s. Discontent was greatly increased by a report on railroad freight rate discrimination. At about the time of the publication of this report, Vanderbilt arrived in Chicago in his private car which was sidetracked in railroad yards. As he dined with friends, Clarence Dresser, a free-lance reporter, entered the car unannounced and asked about the proposed discontinuance of a fast mail train to Chicago. Vanderbilt had explained that the train did not pay. "Are you working for the public or for your stockholders?" asked Dresser. "The public be damned! I'm working for my stockholders," was Vanderbilt's reply. These words, uttered in anger, became widely quoted. "The public be damned" came to be regarded as typifying an attitude of official contempt of the public's interests.

Chapter 2:   The Consumer Is Misinformed

page 6, lines 1–8
Peter Barton Hutt, "Safety Regulation in the Real World," Address to the 1st Academy Forum on the Design of Policy on Drugs and Food Additives, National Academy of Sciences, Washington, D.C., May 15, 1973.

page 6, lines 10–19
Dr. J. David Baldock, "How Risky Are Most Food Additives?" Address to the Food Editors Conference, Virginia Polytechnic Institute and State University, Blacksburg, Virginia, April 2, 1973.

page 6, line 22
Jean Mayer, Ph.D., *Life*, November 28, 1969, p. 44.

page 6, lines 24–27
Wilhelm C. Hueper, M.D., "The Potential Role of Nonnutritive Food Additives and Contaminants as Environmental Carcinogens." Symposium on Potential Cancer Hazards from Chemical Additives to Foodstuffs, International Union Against Cancer, Rome, August 10, 1956.

page 7, lines 1–5
G. Roche Lynch, *Opening Address* to Conference: *Problems Arising from the Use of Chemicals in Food,* September 1951, printed in *Chemistry and Industry,* 1951, pp. 923–33.

page 7, lines 7–24
U.S. Senate, Congressional Hearings before the Subcommittee on Executive Reorganization and Government Research of the Committee on Government Operations: "Chemicals and the Future of Man," 92d Congress, 1st session, April 1971, p. 39.

page 7, lines 25–26
Congressman L. H. Fountain, U.S. House of Representatives, Congressional Hearings before the Subcommittee of the Committee on Government Operations: "FDA Regulations of the New Drug Serc," 92d Congress, 2d session, September 1972, p. 89.

page 7, lines 28–30
G. Edward Damon, "Primer on Food Additives," *FDA Consumer,* May 1973, reprint.

page 8, lines 26–28
Senator Gaylord Nelson, U.S. Senate, "Food Protection Act of 1972," *Congressional Record,* February 14, 1972. No. 18.

page 8, line 33–page 9, line 4
Winton B. Rankin, quoted in *Philadelphia Evening Bulletin,* October 21, 1969.

page 9, lines 7–10
The Washington Post, February 22, 1971, quoted by Nelson, "Food Protection Act of 1972," *op. cit.* The statement was made by a representative of Fritz, Dodge and Olcott, a food additives manufacturer.

page 9, lines 14–18
Jane E. Brody, "Drink Preservative Found to Produce a Carcinogen," *The New York Times*, December 21, 1971, p. 26.

page 9, lines 19–22
"FDA Acts to Restrict Use of Brominated Vegetable Oils in Foods, Soft Drinks," *The Wall Street Journal*, January 6, 1970.

page 9, lines 23–26
"Food Color Suspected, FDA Orders Testing," *The Record* (Bergen, New Jersey), September 12, 1971, p. A–16.

page 9, lines 27–29
Chemical and Engineering News, April 8, 1974, p. 8.

page 9, line 30–page 10, line 16
12th Report to the Committee on Government Operations: "Regulations of DES and Other Drugs Used in Food Producing Animals," 1973, pp. 24–26.

page 10, line 20–page 11, line 19
19th Report to Committee on Government Operations: "Regulations of Food Additives—Nitrites and Nitrates," 1972, pp. 11–16.

Chapter 3: The Very Small Tip of the Iceberg

page 13, line 1
"Food Additives" (editorial), *The Lancet*, August 16, 1969, p. 361.

page 13, lines 3–4
Philip H. Abelson (editorial), *Science*, November 7, 1969.

page 13, lines 6–8
John J. Hanlon, "Man's Health and His Environment," colloquium, University of Illinois, December 1968.

page 13, lines 11–15
Franklin Bicknell, *Chemicals in Food & In Farm Produce: Their Harmful Effects* (London: Faber & Faber, 1960). This quotation by Dr. Bicknell was from a subsequent American printing in which Dr. Bicknell wrote an introduction for American readers.

page 13, lines 17–24
Samuel S. Epstein, statement "Adverse Human Effects Due to Chemical Pollutants" at the Ribicoff Hearings: "Chemicals and the Future of Man," April 1971, p. 45. At the time, Dr. Epstein was chief of the Laboratories of Carcinogenesis and Toxicology, Applied Microbiology and Histology, the Children's Cancer Research Foundation, Inc., at Boston; presently, he is Swetland Professor of Environmental Health and Human Ecology, Case Western Reserve University at Cleveland.

page 13, line 26–page 14, line 2
W. V. Applegate, letter to the editor, *Nutrition Today*, September–October 1973, p. 26.

page 14, lines 4–7
Eleanor Williams, Address to the New Jersey Dietetics Association, Metropolitan District of New Jersey; quoted in article, "Dietician Cautions on Food Additives," *Sunday Star-Ledger* (Newark, New Jersey), December 10, 1972.

page 14, lines 10–14
Stephen D. Lockey, address to the Annual Congress of the American College of Allergists, Atlanta, Georgia, June 1973; reported in "Allergic Reaction Tied to Allergens in Food Additives," *Medical Tribune*, June 6, 1973.

page 14, lines 25–38
Robert Ho Man Kwok, M.D., "Chinese Restaurant Syndrome," letter to editor, *The New England Journal of Medicine*, Vol. 278, No. 14, April 4, 1968, p. 796; "Post-Sino-Cibal Syndrome," editorial & correspondence, *Ibid.* Vol. 278, No. 20, May 16, 1968, pp. 1122–24; *Ibid.* Vol. 279, No. 2, July 11, 1968, pp. 1, 5–6.

page 15, lines 1–15
"Food Additives: Health Question Awaiting an Answer," *Medical World News*, September 7, 1973, p. 73; and correspondence with Dr. Marguerite G. Stemmermann.

page 15, lines 16–32
William R. Henderson and Neil H. Raskin, "Hot-Dog Headache: Individual Susceptibility to Nitrite," *The Lancet*, December 2, 1972, pp. 1162–63.

page 15, line 33–page 16, line 15
"Type of Rheumatism Is Tied to Sodium Nitrate in Food," *Medical Tribune*, January 8, 1970.

page 16, lines 16–27
Related by Stephen D. Lockey, Sr., M.D. of Lancaster, Pennsylvania.

page 16, line 28–page 17, line 2
Related by Rita L. Don, M.D., of El Paso, Texas, in letter of May 1, 1968.

page 17, lines 3–18
Ben F. Feingold, M.D., "Adverse Reactions to Food Additives, with Special Reference to Hyperkinesis and Learning Difficulties," address to the A.M.A., Allergy Section, New York City, June 19, 1973.

page 17, lines 19–34
Thomas H. Sternberg, M.D., and Stanley M. Bierman, M.D., "Unique Syndromes Involving the Skin Induced by Drugs, Food Additives and Environmental Contaminants," *Archives of Dermatology*, Vol. 882, 1963, pp. 779–88; "The Dutch Margarine Sickness," *Food & Cosmetics Toxicology*, Vol. 1, No. 1, September 1963, pp. 92–93; "More About the Dutch Margarine Sickness," *Ibid.* Vol. 1, No. 2, December 1963, p. 265.

page 18, lines 1–23
The story of monochloroacetic acid is mainly drawn from testimony before the original Delaney Hearings (1950) in the first volume issued, "Chemicals in Food Products," pp. 25–26, 48–49; 51, 73, 150, 467, 516–17.

page 18, line 24–page 19, line 4
Information about the Halloween candy is related by Loren B. Sjostrom and Charles J. Kensler of Arthur D. Little, Inc.; *Chemical and Biological Hazards in Food*; edited by J. C. Ayres, A. A. Kraft, H. E. Snyder, & W. W. Walker (Ames, Iowa: Iowa State University Press, 1962), pp. 54–55. Information about the Christmas popcorn is related by Franklin D. Clark in his address to the FDA–Food Law Institute Conference, Washington, D.C., November 28, 1960.

page 19, lines 5–11
Information about lithium chloride is drawn mainly from testimony before the original Delaney Hearings (1950), *op. cit.*, pp. 23–24; 48; 467; 514–16; 517; 638; and from *The Merck Index*, 8th ed., p. 622.

page 19, lines 12–22
"Cobalt, Beer and Heartache," *Food & Cosmetics Toxicology*, Vol. 10, No. 1, February 1972, pp. 99–100; "Some Additives Have Been Banned Because of Questionable Safety or Unethical Use," *Chemical and Engineering News*, October 10, 1966, p. 108.

page 20, lines 10–13
Information about agene is drawn mainly from testimony before the original Delaney Hearings (1950), *op. cit.*

page 20, lines 14–18
"Cobalt, Beer and Heartache," *op. cit.*

page 20, lines 19–22
Chemical and Engineering News, October 10, 1966, *op. cit.*, p. 108.

page 20, lines 23–27
"Drug Company to Ask FDA to Reconsider on Cyclamate," *Medical Tribune*, September 26, 1973; and Richard D. James, "Remember Cyclamates? Maybe They Weren't So Harmful After All." *The Wall Street Journal*, July 2, 1973, pp. 1, 15.

page 20, line 28–page 21, line 6
Information about DES is drawn mainly from Congressional Hearings: "Regulation of Diethylstilbestrol," U.S. House of Representatives, the Subcommittee of the Committee on Government Operations, 92d Congress, 1st session, November 11,

1971, Part 1, and December 13, 1971, Part 2 (Chairman, Congressman L. H. Fountain); U.S. Senate, Committee on Health of the Committee on Labor and Public Welfare, 92d Congress, 2d session, July 20, 1972 (Chairman, Senator Edward M. Kennedy).

page 21, lines 7–11
G. Löfroth and T. Gejvall, "Diethyl Pyrocarbonate: Formation of Urethan in Treated Beverages," *Science*, Vol. 174, December 17, 1971, pp. 1248–50.

page 21, lines 12–15
Information about dulcin is drawn mainly from testimony before the original Delaney Hearings (1950), *op. cit.*

page 21, line 16–page 23, line 17
Information about the banned food dyes is drawn mainly from "Appendix B, Chronological History of Synthetic Colors in the United States," *Food Colors* (Washington, D.C.: National Academy of Sciences, 1971), pp. 43–44.

page 23, lines 18–21
Information about lithium chloride and monochloracetic acid is from the Delaney Hearings: "Chemicals in Food Products," 1950, *op. cit.*

page 23, lines 22–26
Canadian Food and Drug Directorate Trade Information Letter, September 20, 1967: "USDA Bars Use of NDGA in Most Meat Food Products." USDA release, September 18, 1968; *Federal Register*, November 22, 1967; *Idem*, April 11, 1968.

page 23, lines 27–31
Information about oil of calamus: *Canadian Food and Drug Directorate Trade Information Letter*, August 26, 1968; also *Food and Cosmetics Toxicology*, Vol. 6, No. 6, December 1968, p. 771.

page 23, line 32–page 24, line 2
Information about polyoxyethylene-8-stearate is from the Delaney Hearings: "Chemicals in Food Products," 1950, *op. cit.*

page 24, lines 3–6
"Food Additives," *Chemical and Engineering News*, October 10, 1966, p. 108.

page 24, lines 7–10
Information about thiourea is from the Delaney Hearings: "Chemicals in Food Products," 1950, *op. cit.*

page 24, lines 11–23
"Food Additives: Health Questions Awaiting an Answer," *Medical World News*, *op. cit.*, pp. 73–80.

Chapter 4: The Mirage of Safety

page 25, lines 1-9
L. Golberg, "Safety of Environmental Chemicals—The Need and the Challenge," *Food & Cosmetics Toxicology*, Vol. 10, No. 4, August 1972, pp. 523-24.

page 25, lines 17-22
Joan Arehart-Treichel, "Agonizing Over Foods and Drugs: How Safe?" *Science News*, Vol. 103, June 2, 1972, p. 362.

page 25, lines 24-26
P. R. Peacock, "Coloring Matter in Foods," from conference, Problems Arising from the Use of Chemicals in Food; printed in *Chemistry and Industry* (Great Britain, 1951), pp. 932-33.

page 25, line 28-page 26, line 8
Peter Barton Hutt, "Safety Regulation in the Real World," address to the 1st Academy Forum on the Design of Policy on Drugs and Food Additives, National Academy of Sciences, Washington, D.C., May 15, 1973.

page 26, line 10
"The Eventful History of BHT," *The Lancet*, November 20, 1965, p. 1058.

page 26, lines 12-14
Lewis Herber, *Our Synthetic Environment* (New York: Alfred A. Knopf, 1962), p. 96.

page 27, lines 5-6
Senator Abraham Ribicoff, opening statement of "Chemicals and the Future of Man," *op. cit.*, p. 3.

page 27, line 7
In 1967, when James L. Goddard was Commissioner of the FDA, he admitted before the Food Protection Committee that "we do not have the kind of clinical research underlying food chemistry that we have underlying drug chemistry."

page 27, lines 9-13
"Application of Supreme Court Decisions to Foods Questioned," *Food Chemical News*, October 1, 1973; Cortez F. Enloe, Jr., M.D., "For Whom the Bell Tolls" (editorial), *Nutrition Today*, Vol. 8, No. 4, July-August 1973, p. 14.

page 27, lines 14-15
The highest figure currently quoted for intentional food additives is 3,900, by Congressman Benjamin S. Rosenthal, in his speech, "The Foodmakers," *Congressional Record*, Vol. 118, No. 94, June 12, 1972. The highest figure currently quoted for the grand total of intentional food additives and incidental contaminants is over 20,000, according to an editorial "Food Additives," in *The Lancet*, August 16, 1969, p. 361.

page 27, lines 16-20
"Food Hazards, What About the Additives?" *Food Facts from Rutgers*, March-April 1972, p. 7.

page 31, lines 4–8
Lucinda Franks, "F.D.A. Approves a Challenged Dye," *The New York Times*, December 19, 1974, pp. 1, 51.

page 31, line 33–page 32, line 6
"Advisory Committee on Protocols for Safety Evaluations: Panel on Reproduction Report on Reproduction Studies in the Safety Evaluation of Food Additives and Pesticide Residues," *Toxicology and Applied Pharmacology*, Vol. 16, 1970, pp. 264–96. See Section 111, "Need for Reproduction Tests in Safety Evaluation of Food Additives and Pesticides." Although the quotation discussed the detection of changes in reproductive organs, the committee pointed out that the comment applied to other biological systems as well.

page 34, lines 7–9
Dr. A. J. Kowalk and R. L. Gillespie of the FDA's Division of Toxicology recommended that the FDA consider withdrawing approval for use of DES in medicated feed until an analytical method sensitive to *one part per trillion* could be developed, since the extreme potency of the drug as a carcinogen and its very high hormonal activity was comparable to the activity of the few parts per trillion of physiologic estrogens normally found in fattening cattle. See the 12th Report by the Committee on Government Operations, "Regulations of Diethylstilbestrol and Other Drugs Used in Food Producing Animals," December 10, 1973, p. 30. "The Potent Prostaglandins," *Chemical Progress*, December 1973, pp. 4–5.

page 34, lines 15–17
Undetected aflatoxin activity was reported in *Evaluation of Environmental Carcinogens: Report to the Surgeon General.* Prepared by the Ad Hoc Committee on the Evaluation of Low Levels of Environmental Chemical Carcinogens, Department of Health, Education and Welfare, 1971. It was quoted by Surgeon General Jesse L. Steinfeld, in his address, "Environment and Cancer: Detecting and Eradicating Hazards in Our Environment" at the 24th Annual Symposium on Fundamental Cancer Research, University of Texas, Houston, March 3, 1971. Dr. Steinfeld warned that failure to detect the presence of a compound may mean that the compound is present in concentrations far below the detectable limit of the analytical method used, but that such "subdetection levels" are difficult to distinguish from "zero."

page 34, lines 18–20
Extensive fetus-deforming effects were discovered in chick embryos when the dioxin, or a distillate predominantly consisting of it, was present at concentrations of little more than a trillionth of a gram per gram of egg. In chick tests dioxin appeared to be a million times more potent than the fetus-deforming agent thalidomide. See Thomas Whiteside, *Defoliation: What Are Our Herbicides Doing to Us?* (New York: Ballantine, 1970), p. 46.

page 35, lines 6–8
Harold C. Hodge, "Research Needs in the Toxicology of Food Additives," *Food and Cosmetics Toxicology*, Vol. 1, No. 1, September 1963, pp. 27–28.

page 35, lines 12–19
J. M. Young and K. V. Sanderson, "Photosensitive Dermatitis and Renal Tubular Acidosis After Ingestion of Calcium Cyclamate," *The Lancet*, Vol. II, No. 7633, December 13, 1969, No. 7633.

page 35, line 20–page 36, line 2
"Mustard Contains a Powerful Poison," *Consumer Bulletin*, July 1968, pp. 33–34; also *Medical Times*, November 1966.

page 36, lines 3–16
"Denver Physician Warns Against Licorice," *Health Bulletin*, September 1970, p. 4.

page 36, lines 17–21
The Washington Post, August 11, 1968, reporting the findings of Drs. Jerome W. Conn, David R. Rovner, and Edwin L. Cohen from the University of Michigan.

page 36, lines 22–28
Harold J. Robinson, M.D.; Frank S. Harrison, M.D.; and Joseph T. Nicholson, M.D.; "Cardiac Abnormalities Due to Licorice Intoxication," *Pennsylvania Medicine*, Vol. 74, 1971, pp. 1971.

page 36, lines 26–35
Health Education and Welfare News (press release), January 28, 1972, p. 2. Even the one gram daily recommended as the upper limit for the average adult was far from reassuring. One gram equals seven 12-ounce bottles or five 16-ounce bottles of the standard diet drink, or 60 small saccharin tablets. As more foods and beverages were being sweetened with saccharin, the one gram maximum could be exceeded. In July 1970, it was estimated that the highest average daily adult intake of saccharin was unlikely to exceed 0.21 of a gram, and the "safe" level at that time was estimated between 0.225 and 0.335 gram. But by June 1971, the FDA reported that few persons consumed more than 0.2 grams of saccharin daily, and consumption by heavy users was estimated at about 0.5 gram. Thus, within less than a year, intake by heavy users had more than doubled. The earlier set of figures was reported in *The New York Times* on July 23, 1970, based on the Food Protection Committee's report; the latter set, from *The Wall Street Journal*, on June 23, 1971, based on figures released by then FDA Commissioner Charles Edwards.

page 36, line 36–page 37, line 7
John G. Fuller, *200,000,000 Guinea Pigs* (New York: G. P. Putnam's Sons, 1972), p. 164.

page 37, lines 8–12
"Red Food Coloring, How Safe Is it?" *Consumer Reports*, February 1973, p. 132.

page 37, line 27–page 38, line 2
Hearings: "Regulations of Diethylstilbestrol," Part 2, December 13, 1971, *op. cit.* "The Scientific Reasonableness of a Million to One Safety Factor for Environmental Carcinogens," p. 229. Another proposal is the use of a safety factor 5,000-fold by use of "a minimum measured cancer producing level" rather than using the no-effect level. See C. S. Weil, "Statistics, Safety Factors and Scientific Judgment in the Evaluation of Safety for Man," *Toxicology and Applied Pharmacology*, Vol. 21, 1972, pp. 454–63.

page 38, lines 3–6
Ibid., p. 229.

page 38, lines 8–12
12th Report: "Regulations of Diethylstilbestrol," 1973, *op. cit.*, p. 32.

page 38, lines 12–17
Hearings: "Regulations of Diethylstilbestrol,"Part 2, *op. cit.*; memorandum from Dr. M. Adrian Gross on carcinogenicity of diethylstilbestrol, December 5, 1971, pp. 115–18.

page 38, lines 17–29
12th Report: "Regulations of Diethylstilbestrol," *op. cit.*, pp. 32–33.

page 38, lines 30–32
Hearings: "Regulations of Diethylstilbestrol," Part 2, *op. cit.*, pp. 119–81.

page 38, line 32–page 39, line 9
Ibid., pp. 137–43.

page 39, lines 10–18
"FDA Proposes Methods Criteria for Carcinogenic Animal Drugs," *Food Chemical News*, Vol. 15, No. 18, July 23, 1973, pp. 22–31.

page 39, lines 24–32
Dr. Nathan Mantel, NCI, memorandum to Dr. Peters, NCI, regarding the FDA's modification of Mantel–Bryan Model, new rule 135.36, *Federal Register*, Vol. 38, No. 138, pp. 19226–30.

page 40, lines 7–11
Dr. Bert J. Vos, FDA files: memorandum from Deputy Director of the Division of Pharmacology and Toxicology, to Dr. Herman Kraybill, Assistant Director for Biological Research, FDA, October 6, 1969.

page 40, lines 17–21
M. C. Oberle, "Lead Poisoning: A Preventable Childhood Disease of the Slums," *Science*, Vol. 165, 1969, pp. 991–99.

page 40, lines 22–29
Samuel S. Epstein, M.D., "Potential Human Hazards Due to Some Currently Used Food Additives and Pesticides," address to the Museum of Natural History, Cleveland, Ohio, March 17, 1972, pp. 27–28.

page 40, line 34–page 41, line 5
"USDA Issues Economic Report on Banning DES," USDA press release 2052–71. Cattlemen disputed these estimates as being too low.

page 41, lines 26–28
A. B. G. Burton, "A Method for the Objective Assessment of Eye Irritation," *Food and Cosmetics Toxicology*, Vol. 10, No. 2, April 1972, pp. 209–17. A testing technique to assess eye irritancy as evidence of the safety or lack of it for commercial products

is the Draize rabbit-eye test. There can be considerable variation between assessments obtained from different laboratories.

page 42, lines 1–4
Food Protection Committee: "The Safety of Polyoxyethylene (8) Stearate for Use in Foods" (Washington, D.C.: NAS-NRC, Publication 646, December 1958), pp. 8–9.

page 42, lines 5–12
H. L. Self, "DES Residues," letter to editor, *Science*, Vol. 178, October 13, 1972, p. 117.

page 42, lines 13–15
Wilhelm C. Hueper, "Cancer Hazards in Foods and Consumer Products," address to the 11th annual convention, National Health Federation, Long Beach, California, December 29, 1965.

page 42, lines 16–23
Samuel S. Epstein, M.D., "Potential Human Hazards Due to Some Currently Used Food Additives and Pesticides," address to the Cleveland Museum of Natural History, Cleveland, Ohio, March 17, 1972, p. 21.

page 42, lines 24–25
In the field of food additive safety testing, dodging of responsibility by food manufacturers, processors, and distributors "has been and remains truly scandalous," according to Dr. Golberg. These food interests "have doggedly refused to contribute significantly" to the cost of food additive testing. "Even the cyclamate episode, which cost some food companies losses running into hundreds of millions of dollars, has not taught them the facts of life." Golberg cited the food dye crisis as an example of the food industry leaving the responsibility of safety tests to its suppliers. By contrast, the drug and cosmetics industries have, for years, supported amply financed and expertly staffed groups that "have been wrestling conscientiously" with dye problems. Golberg warned that "the food industry can no longer afford to maintain the fiction that the safety of a food additive is solely the concern of the supplier of that compound. Neither can the people of the United States allow this state of affairs to continue." See L. Golberg, "Safety of Environmental Chemicals . . . ," *op. cit.*, p. 524.

page 42, line 24–page 43, line 19
Ribicoff Hearings: "Chemicals and the Future of Man," *op. cit.*, Epstein's statement, pp. 19–20. Dr. Arnold J. Lehman, then Director of the Division of Pharmacology, FDA, termed useless the safety test data submitted with an application in 1950 for drug use of cyclamates. Dr. Lehman commented that the application was "an illustration of how an experiment should not be conducted." Data was vague. The number of test animals was too small, control groups in the experiments were discontinued too early, and too few autopsies were performed. See New Drug Application (NDA) 7258, memorandum of Dr. Lehman, February 2, 1950.

Assessing safety test data for saccharin, another artificial sweetener, has been especially complicated, since some past studies were poorly designed. The tests were conducted with impure test substances or unhealthy animals, and nearly all of the early results are of unknown relevance to humans. One scientist, attempting to evaluate saccharin safety based on past tests, described the effort as "an education in obtuseness—poor data derived from poor experiments." He added, "This is a job for a philosopher, not a scientist."

One of the many unresolved problems with saccharin arose when more recent tests induced tumors in some test animals. Were the tumors cancerous or benign? Examination of this question began in October 1969, when the FDA requested a review by the NAS–NRC, which was expected to be completed in approximately two months. In September 1972, an FDA spokesman announced that a few more months would be needed. In January 1972, the FDA restricted saccharin's use while the safety review was being completed. In May 1973, the FDA announced that evaluation was ongoing. In June 1973, the FDA extended an interim rule while the review continued. Then it was announced that the review would be completed by the end of June 1973. By September 1973, the panel of scientists was still evaluating the evidence and awaiting new test results. The NAS–NRC announced that its report would probably be finished in the autumn of 1973. At the present writing (1974) the review is still ongoing, with no information released to date regarding the malignant or benign qualities of the tumors.

page 43, lines 20–27
Leon Golberg, "Safety of Environmental Chemicals—The Need and the Challenge," *Food and Cosmetics Toxicology*, Vol. 10, No. 4, August 1972, p. 525.

page 43, lines 28–29
Samuel E. Epstein, "Potential Human Hazards . . ." *op. cit.*, p. 20.

page 43, lines 32–35
Congressman James J. Delaney, "Chemical Additives in Our Food Supply Can Cause Cancer," *Extension of Remarks*, February 21, 1957, citing letter from William E. Smith, M.D., to Delaney, January 28, 1957. Smith wrote, "Public confidence . . . cannot be enhanced by the facts that the cancer-inciting action of one of the most dangerous carcinogens was discovered by the staff of a leading chemical manufacturer, but the senior scientist who made the discovery promptly lost his job. For the nearly 20 years that have since elapsed, manufacture of this substance has continued, and it has been used to make food dyes. Meanwhile, consumers have been required to wait several decades for decisions by juries of test rats and dogs as to the safety of these dyes. While the argument has gone on, upward of half a million pounds of dyes made from this substance have been certified for use in food. . . ." Dr. Smith elaborated on these charges during the Delaney Hearings: "Food Additives," July 18, 1957, pp. 169–92.

page 43, line 36–page 44, line 5
Leon Golberg, "Safety of Environmental Chemicals . . ." *op. cit.*, p. 525.

page 44, lines 8–9
Harold C. Hodge, "Research Needs in the Toxicology of Food Additives," *Food and Cosmetics Toxicology*, Vol. 1, No. 1, September 1963, p. 30.

page 44, lines 9–13
Golberg, "Safety of Environmental Chemicals . . ." *op. cit.*, p. 525.

page 44, lines 14–19
The lack of data accessible to scientists was dramatically illustrated in the case of the herbicide 2, 4, 5–T. The federal government contracted with Bionetics Research Laboratory to test more than 200 insecticides and related products for possible carcinogenic, teratogenic, or mutagenic properties. Qualified scientists, requesting copies of the report on 2, 4, 5–T encountered extraordinary obstacles. Only after strong pressures were exerted did scientists obtain the data. When reviewing this data, scientists discovered that teratogenic qualities of the herbicide with test animals was far greater than had been officially admitted. See Thomas Whiteside, *Defoliation* (New York: Ballantine Books, 1970).

Secret industry review of food additive safety is another aspect of the problem. For example, studies on animals fed saccharin were debated at a closed-door session, *excluding the public*, held in March 1973. The meeting was sponsored by the Nutrition Foundation, Inc., an organization supported by food processors and other segments of the food industry. The session, restricted to researchers and government observers, was held to evaluate the findings of tumors induced in saccharin-fed rats. See *Chemical and Engineering News*, March 5, 1973, p. 6.

Some food additive safety data (as well as pesticide safety data) submitted to the FDA with petitions for use are inadequate for evaluation, noted Dr. Alan T. Spiher, Jr., present Acting Assistant to the Director, Office of Compliance, Bureau of Foods and Pesticides, FDA. Dr. Spiher made this statement in addressing the Eastern Experiment Station Collaborators' Conference on Food Safety, in Philadelphia, on October 29, 1968. When interviewed about the statement, Dr. Spiher explained, "I was trying to stress the need for a thorough understanding that the initial research has to be very complete and basic in nature." See "FDA Receiving Inadequate Additive Information," *Health Bulletin*, Vol. 6, No. 45, November 9, 1968, p. 1.

page 44, lines 21–25
Hearings before a Subcommittee of the Joint Congressional Committee on Atomic Energy: Testimony of Dr. Kenneth W. Kirk, Associate Commissioner of the FDA, 91st Congress, 2d session, July 30, 1968, pp. 118–19. In recent years, the FDA has relied on reviews by organizations outside the agency, such as the Food Protection Committee. The ongoing GRAS review (discussed on pages 198–212) has been under review by the Federation of American Societies for Experimental Biology (FASEB). Such reviews, like those of the FDA, may utilize summaries only. The public has no means of knowing what comprises a "review" or how thoroughly it is conducted. The FDA's increased use of outside groups came under criticism in the 12th Report by the Committee on Government Operations, *op. cit.* The Committee recommended that the FDA *not* rely upon principles and procedures advanced by any outside group in matters of establishing food additive safety (p. 12). By such reliance, the FDA "appeared to endow publications" of such outside groups "with unusual regulatory effects" (pp. 32–34).

page 44, line 26–page 45, line 5
"FDA Officials Changed Data, Inquiry Finds," *The Los Angeles Times*, May 1, 1970; "FDA Probe Needed" (editorial), *The New York Times*, May 4, 1970.

page 45, lines 6–13
"Magnuson Charges FDA May Be Suppressing Research Information," *Health*

Bulletin, January 23, 1971, p. 1. In August 1974, 14 FDA physicians, research workers and consultants testified under oath that FDA frequently suppressed unfavorable reports on new drugs, and harassed those who drafted such reports. After submitting an unfavorable report, some of the individuals would be taken off the case, and the drug study would be assigned to another physician who subsequently approved the drug. Those who testified cited numerous instances in which adverse reports on drugs had been overturned by higher-ranking FDA officials. Some of the FDA staff physicians said that after they had criticized certain drugs or FDA procedure they had been transferred to less important work, and out of their field of expertise. The group also charged that the FDA is dominated by the drug industry. Alexander M. Schmidt, Commissioner of FDA, denied the allegations. HEW Secretary Caspar W. Weinberger promised a full review of the charges.

page 45, lines 14–24
Harold M. Schmeck, Jr., "Report Criticizes FDA Over Its Scientific Effort," *The New York Times*, May 28, 1971.

page 45, lines 25–32
Report to the Secretary of Health, Education and Welfare on the Food and Drug Administration by the Citizens Advisory Committee (Washington, D.C.: HEW, October 1962). The committee was comprised of food and drug industry representatives, laymen, and scientists outside of the FDA. In recent years, the FDA has been investigated by more committees, congressional hearings, consumer advocates, media, and individual critics than any department of the federal government responsible for public protection.

page 45, line 33–page 46, line 3
During drug hearings of the Fountain Committee, May 9, 1969, this case helped to increase congressional pressure for public access to secret information in federal civilian agency files. *The New York Times* of May 5, 1972, termed the FDA's policy "one of the most secretive of Federal civilian agencies."

page 46, lines 4–12
"FDA Is Criticized on Food Additive," *The Washington Post*, April 25, 1972, p. H–11. The researcher who brought legal suit was Dale B. Hattis, a graduate student of genetics at Stanford University. Hattis contended that the FDA had granted petitions to four food processors, including three which had been using nitrite illegally as an additive in their products. None of the petitions contained any original scientific research by the companies as to whether the proposed uses of nitrite were safe. In two of the four, the petitioners had merely "expressed their belief" that nitrite is safe.

page 46, lines 13–26
Richard Halloran, "Information Act Scored as Futile," *The New York Times*, March 15, 1972, p. 19. The lawyer who brought suit was Peter H. Schuck, consultant to the Center for Study of Responsive Law. Although his suit involved access to information concerning a meat inspection program, not a food additive, his action helped increase public pressure for access to secret information in federal civilian agency files.

page 46, lines 27–35
Harold M. Schmeck, Jr., "FDA Acts to End Policy of Secrecy and Open Its Files," *The New York Times*, May 5, 1972, pp. 1, 6. The FDA's proposal appeared to emphasize data availability on drugs, other products, and factory and food inspection. Less mention was made of food additives. *The New York Times* account mentions food additives only near the end of the article.

page 46, line 36–page 47, line 3
Ibid., p. 6.

page 47, lines 6–12
Chemical and Engineering News, August 14, 1972, p. 6.

page 47, lines 17–37
Ribicoff Hearings: "Chemicals and the Future of Man," *op. cit.*, Epstein's statement, p. 57, and testimony, p. 18.

page 48, lines 17–29
"Primates as Guinea Pigs," *Food and Cosmetics Toxicology*, Vol. 10, No. 5, October 1972, pp. 710–11.

page 48, lines 32–35
"FDA Advisory Committee on Protocols for Safety Evaluations; Panel on Reproduction Report on Reproduction Studies in the Safety Evaluation of Food Additives and Pesticide Residues," *Toxicology and Applied Pharmacology*, Vol. 16, 1970, "Human Testing," p. 285.

page 49, lines 14–30
Wilhelm C. Hueper, "Potential Role of Nonnutritive Food Additives . . ." *op. cit.*, p. 242.

page 49, line 31
In 1955, prison volunteers were tested with DDT. Although this test is frequently quoted purportedly to demonstrate the "safety" of DDT for humans, the inadequacies of the tests are largely ignored. Morton S. Biskind, M.D., a specialist in pesticidal poisoning, called the tests "an intricate, carefully contrived and ingeniously composed document, perhaps a classic of its kind."

page 49, line 33–page 50, line 10
Jessica Mitford, "Experiments Behind Bars," *Atlantic Monthly*, January 1973, pp. 64–73; U.S. Senate, Hearings before the Subcommittee on Health of the Committee on Labor and Public Welfare: "Human Guinea Pigs," March and April 1973 (Senator Edward Kennedy, Chairman).

page 50, lines 10–12
Newsweek, August 25, 1969, p. 71.

page 50, lines 17–19
In one study in Tuskegee, over 400 black men with syphilis were allowed to remain untreated for up to 40 years so that experimenters could study the natural course of the disease. In another study, at Willowbrook School in New York, mentally

retarded children were purposely infected with hepatitis to study the disease. Drug testing in Kilby Prison, Alabama, resulted in the death of four inmates and hospitalization of ten percent of the entire prison population, resulting ultimately in a federal investigation. Elsewhere, prisoners have been injected with live cancer cells and blood from leukemia patients to determine whether these diseases were transmittable. A drug that induced tumors in laboratory dogs was injected in low income women in Tennessee as a three-month contraceptive and in female mental patients to regulate their menstruation. Government agencies, as well as pharmaceutical companies, have engaged in some questionable ethical practices with human experimentation. The National Council on Radiation Protection, using charity cases of terminal cancer, exposed individuals to high dosages of whole-body radiation, not for therapy, but to gather radiation data. None of the patients had been informed that the massive doses could not possibly help them and would produce extremely unpleasant side effects. All but three of the patients had only six years of schooling and had below-normal intelligence. See "Human Experimentation," *Medical World News*, June 8, 1973, pp. 37–51; *Ibid.*, October 27, 1971; Jessica Mitford, "Experiments Behind Bars," *op. cit., The Wall Street Journal*, February 22, 1973, p. 1; and U.S. Senate, Hearings Before the Subcommittee on Health of the Committee on Labor and Public Welfare: "Quality of Health Care—Human Experimentation, 1973," Part 4, April, June and July 1973, 93d Congress, 1st session.

Chapter 5: The Toxicological Imponderables

page 51, lines 1–5
L. Golberg, "Safety of Environmental Chemicals—The Need and the Challenge," *Food and Cosmetics Toxicology*, Vol. 10, No. 4, August 1972, pp. 527–28.

page 51, lines 8–10
Dr. Paul E. Johnson, quoted in "Food Additives Safety Faces Scrutiny," *Chemical and Engineering News*, March 9, 1970.

page 51, lines 13–17
Magnus Pyke, *Man and Food* (London: World University Library, 1970), p. 183.

page 51, lines 19–20
H. C. Hodge, "Research Needs in the Toxicology of Food Additives," *Food and Cosmetics Toxicology*, Vol. 1, No. 1, September 1963, p. 31.

page 51, lines 22–26
Theron G. Randolph, M.D., *Human Ecology and Susceptibility to the Chemical Environment* (Springfield, Illinois: Charles C. Thomas, 1962), p. 4.

page 52, lines 5–9
"The Fate of BHA in Man," *Food and Cosmetics Toxicology*, Vol. 1, No. 2, December 1963, p. 276.

page 52, lines 9–10
"Food Additives" (editorial), *The Lancet*, August 16, 1969, p. 361.

page 52, lines 12–14
"Primates as Guinea Pigs," *Food and Cosmetics Toxicology*, Vol. 10, No. 5, October 1972, p. 709.

page 52, lines 14–16
J. C. Dacre, *New Zealand Institute of Chemistry*, Vol. 24, 1960, p. 161.

page 52, lines 19–23
John Yudkin, M.D., "Dietary Sugar and Disease," undated, mimeographed report, p. 2.

page 52, lines 24–25
"Food Additives," *The Lancet, op. cit.,* p. 276.

page 52, lines 19–25
Janice Crossland, "Man's Best Friends," *Environment*, Vol. 15, No. 7, September 1973, p. 9.

page 52, line 34–page 53, line 6
J. R. Allen and J. F. Engblom, "Ultrastructural and Biochemical Changes in the Liver of Monkeys Given Butylated Hydroxytoluene and Butylated Hydroxyan-isole," *Food and Cosmetics Toxicology*, Vol. 10, No. 6, December 1972, p. 776; also, *Ibid*, December 1963, p. 276; April 1971, p. 296; and December 1971, p. 906.

page 53, lines 7–14
Janice Crossland, "Man's Best Friends," *op. cit.,* p. 9.

page 53, lines 15–17
Senator Abraham Ribicoff, U.S. Senate, Hearings before the Subcommittee on Executive Reorganization and Government Research, Committee on Government Operations: "Chemicals and the Future of Man," *op. cit.,* opening statement, p. 3.

page 53, lines 17–20
P. Grasso, et al., "Studies on Carrageenan and Large-bowel Ulceration in Mammals," *Food and Cosmetics Toxicology*, Vol. 11, No. 4, August 1973, p. 555.

page 53, lines 21–25
J. R. Allen and J. F. Engblom, "Ultrastructural and Biochemical Changes. . ." *op. cit.,* pp. 776–77.

page 53, line 25–page 54, line 18
"Primates as Guinea Pigs," *Food and Cosmetics Toxicology*, Vol. 10, No. 5, October 1972, pp. 708–10.

page 54, lines 19–30
Harold Kalter, *Teratology: Principles and Techniques* (Chicago: University of Chicago Press, 1964), edited by James G. Wilson and Joseph Warkany, p. 58, and from *Teratology of the Central Nervous System* (Chicago: University of Chicago Press, 1968), p. 11.

page 54, lines 33–36
Julius M. Coon, M.D., "Food Toxicology: Safety of Food Additives," *Modern Medicine*, November 30, 1970, p. 106.

page 55, lines 6–10
G. Burroughs Mider, M.D., "The Role of Certain Chemical and Physical Agents in the Causation of Cancers," paper for the National Cancer Institute, January 26, 1960, p. 5.

page 55, lines 18–20
G. Burroughs Mider, *Ibid.*, p. 5.

page 55, lines 22–25
Delaney Hearings: "Chemicals in Food Products," *op. cit.*, testimony of Dr. George L. McNew, Managing Director, Boyce Thompson Institute for Plant Research, Inc., Yonkers, New York, p. 570.

page 55, lines 25–27
McGovern Hearings: "Nutrition and Diseases," 1973, Part 2, "Sugar in Diet, Diabetes and Heart Diseases," testimony of Dr. Carolyn Berdanier, Research Nutritionist, Carbohydrate Nutrition Laboratory, USDA, p. 155.

page 55, lines 27–30
"FDA Advisory Committee on Protocols for Safety Evaluations: Panel on Reproduction Report on Reproduction Studies in the Safety Evaluation of Food Additives and Pesticide Residues," *Toxicology and Applied Pharmacology*, Vol. 16, 1970; p. 275; reference for trypan blue in the rat: D. L. Gunberg, "Variations in the Teratogenic Effects of Trypan Blue Administered to Pregnant Rats of Different Strain and Substrain Origin," *Anatomical Record*, Vol. 130, 1958, p. 310; for cortisone in the mouse: C. F. Fraser and T. D. Fainstat, "Production of Congenital Defects in the Offspring of Pregnant Mice Treated with Cortisone," *Pediatrics*, Vol. 8, 1951, p. 527; and for vitamin A deficiency in the rat: D. H. Anderson, "Effect of Diet During Pregnancy Upon the Incidence of Congenital Hereditary Diaphragmatic Hernia in the Rat," *American Journal of Pathology*, Vol. 25, 1949, p. 163.

page 55, lines 30–32
"FDA Advisory Committee Report on Protocols . . ." *op. cit.*, p. 275.

page 55, lines 32–34
K. W. Petersen, M. S. Legator, and F. H. J. Figge, "Dominant-lethal Effects of Cyclohexylamine in C57 B1/Fe Mice," *Mutation Research*, Vol. 14, 1972, p. 126.

page 56, lines 15–17
"FDA Advisory Committee on Protocols for Safety Evaluation: Panel on Carcinogenesis Report on Cancer Testing in the Safety Evaluation of Food Additives and Pesticides," *Toxicology and Applied Pharmacology*, Vol. 20, 1971, p. 435.

page 56, lines 17–20
I. Berenblum, ed., "Carcinogenicity Testing: A Report of the Panel on Carcinogenicity of the Cancer Research Commission of the UICC." Geneva: International Union Against Cancer, *UICC Technical Report Series*, Vol. 2, No. 16, 1969.

page 56, lines 21–29
American Association for the Advancement of Science, "Nova," TV program, Channel 2, WGBH Boston, January 11, 1975.

page 57, lines 3–5
John W. Olney, M.D., "Brain Lesions, Obesity and Other Disturbances in Mice Treated with Monosodium Glutamate," *Science*, Vol. 164, May 9, 1969, pp. 719–21; John W. Olney and Lawrence G. Sharpe, "Brain Lesions in an Infant Rhesus Monkey Treated with Monosodium Glutamate," *Ibid.*, Vol. 166, October 17, 1969, pp. 386–88; John W. Olney, "Glutamate-induced Neuronatal Necrosis in the Infant Mouse Hypothalamus," *Journal of Neuropathology and Experimental Neurology*, Vol. 30, No. 1, January 1971, pp. 75–90; John W. Olney, Lawrence G. Sharpe, and Ralph D. Feingin, "Glutamate-induced Brain Damage in Infant Primates," mimeographed copy, April 27, 1972, from authors, Department of Psychiatry, Washington University School of Medicine, St. Louis, Missouri.

page 57, lines 6–7
Leo Friedman, Ph.D., "Safety of Food Additives," address to the American Association for the Advancement of Science, December 28, 1969; reprinted in *FDA Papers*, March 1970, p. 4.

page 57, lines 7–8
Delaney Hearings: "Chemicals in Food Products," *op. cit.*, testimony of Dr. McNew, p. 570.

page 57, lines 9–14
J. R. Allen and J. F. Engblom, "Ultrastructure and Biochemical Changes . . ." *op. cit.*, p. 777.

page 57, lines 15–18
"Soya beans and vitamin B_{12}," *Food and Cosmetics Toxicology*, Vol. 10, No. 1, February 1972, p. 119.

page 57, lines 19–34
G. Burroughs Mider, "The Role of Certain Chemical and Physical Agents . . ." *op. cit.*, p. 24.

page 58, lines 5–15
Janice Crossland, and Virginia Brodine, "Drinking Water," *Environment*, Vol. 15, No. 3, April 1973, p. 14.

page 58, lines 16–26
"The Motion of Growth," *The Journal of the American Medical Association*, Vol. 103, No. 26, December 29, 1934, p. 2030.

page 58, lines 27–30
Winton B. Rankin, former Deputy Commissioner, FDA, raised this point during an interview. Reported by Harold M. Schmeck, Jr., "FDA to Restudy Four Substances," *The New York Times*, October 23, 1969, p. 35.

page 58, line 32–page 59, line 2
Susan M. Milner, "Effects of the Food Additive Butylated Hydroxytoluene on

Monolayer Cultures of Primate Cells," *Nature*, Vol. 216, November 11, 1967, pp. 557–60.

page 59, lines 3–6
Wilhelm C. Hueper, M.D., "Potential Role of Nonnutritive Food Additives and Contaminants as Environmental Carcinogens," *Acta Unio International Contra Cancrum*, Vol. 13, 1957, p. 241.

page 59, lines 6–8
G. Feuer and L. Golberg, *Biochemistry Journal*, Vol. 103, 1967, p. 13P, cited by Susan M. Milner, *op. cit.*, p. 560.

page 59, lines 8–10
C. Catz and S. J. Yaffe, *Journal of Pharmacology and Experimental Therapeutics*, Vol. 155, 1967, p. 152, cited by Susan M. Milner, *op. cit.*, p. 560.

page 59, lines 16–20
"Sex Differences in Organ Weights," *Food and Cosmetics Toxicology*, Vol. 1, No. 1, September 1963, p. 149.

page 59, lines 20–24
C. S. Weil, "Application of Methods of Statistical Analysis to Efficient Repeated-dose Toxicological Tests," *Toxicology and Applied Pharmacology*, Vol. 4, 1962, p. 561.

page 59, line 32–page 60, line 6
Ribicoff Hearings: "Chemicals and the Future of Man," 1971, *op. cit.*, testimony of Samuel S. Epstein, M.D., p. 11; also E. Boyland, D.Sc., "Food Additives and Contaminants and Cancer," *The Practitioner* [England], Vol. 190, No. 1140, June 1963, p. 728.

page 60, lines 7–10
Ribicoff Hearings, *op. cit.*, pp. 11, 46.

page 60, lines 15–17
Richard D. James, "Remember Cyclamates? Maybe They Weren't So Harmful After All," *The Wall Street Journal*, July 2, 1973, pp. 1, 15.

page 60, lines 18–20
Rudnick, A. W., "DES Residues," letters to editor, *Science*, Vol. 178, October 13, 1972, p. 117.

page 60, lines 21–23
House of Representatives, Hearings before a Subcommittee of the Committee on Government Operations: "Regulation of Diethylstilbestrol DES," Part 1 (Fountain Hearings), statement of Dr. Caro Luhrs, Medical Adviser to the Secretary of USDA, 92d Congress, 1st session, November 11, 1971, p. 95. Similar statements have been voiced on other occasions, as when carbon black was banned for jellybean use, or when aminotriazole was banned as an herbicide for post-harvest application in cranberry bogs, etc.

page 60, line 26–page 61, line 2
Ribicoff Hearings: "Chemicals and the Future of Man," *op. cit.*, statement of Umberto Saffiotti, M.D., p. 176.

page 61, lines 3–18
"FDA Advisory Committee on Protocols for Safety Evaluations: Panel on Reproduction Report on Reproduction Studies in the Safety Evaluation of Food Additives and Pesticide Resides," *op. cit.*, pp. 281–82.

page 61, line 19–page 62, line 13
Ibid., p. 281.

page 62, lines 14–19
Ibid., p. 280. Scientists from the National Agricultural Chemicals Association and the Manufacturing Chemists' Association, Inc., have accumulated results of reproduction studies carried out on a total of 67 compounds in the laboratories of some of the member companies.

page 62, lines 20–25
Ibid., p. 280, based on the work of Dr. William B. Deichmann, Chairman, Department of Pharmacology, University of Miami School of Medicine, Coral Gables, Florida.

page 62, lines 26–31
Ibid., p. 280, based on FDA studies.

page 62, line 32–page 63, line 2
Ibid., p. 281.

page 63, lines 12–16
R. Abraham, W. Dougherty, L. Golberg, and F. Coulston, "The Response of the Hypothalamus to High Doses of Monosodium Glutamate in Mice and Monkeys. Cytochemistry and Ultrastructural Study of Lysosomal Changes," *Experimental Molecular Pathology*, Vol. 15, 1971, p. 43.

page 63, lines 25–35
Problems in the Evaluation of Carcinogenic Hazards from Use of Food Additives, Food Protection Committee, Food and Nutrition Board, National Academy of Sciences–National Research Council, Washington, D.C., December 1959, *Publication 749*, p. 27.

page 64, lines 1–5
Beatrice Trum Hunter, *Consumer Beware! Your Food and What's Been Done to It* (New York: Simon and Schuster, 1971), pp. 42–46. Also see more recent charges: "Academy Food Committees: New Criticism of Industry Ties," *Science*, Vol. 177, September 29, 1972, pp. 1172–75; " 'Bias' Charges Against Food Protection Committee Surface Again," *Food Chemical News*, Vol. 15, No. 6, April 30, 1973, pp. 24–25; and "NAS Linked to 'Special Interests,' Nader Probers Charge," *Medical Tribune*, May 23, 1973, pp. 1, 9.

page 64, lines 6–10
Many eminently qualified professionals have supported Hueper's thesis that if a substance produces carcinogenic response in any species of test animals by any route, including repeated subcutaneous injections, the data must be evaluated. These include, among others, E. Boyland, "The Determination of Carcinogenic Activity," *International Union Against Cancer.* Vol. 13, 1957, p. 271; "Evaluation of the Carcinogenic Hazards of Food Additives," 5th Report of the Joint FAO/WHO Expert Committee on Food Additives (Geneva: WHO *Technical Report 220,* 1961), pp. 16–17; Dr. H. F. Kraybill, "Carcinogenesis Associated with Foods, Food Additives, Degradation Products, and Related Dietary Factors," Symposium on Chemical Carcinogenesis, *Clinical Pharmacology and Therapeutics,* Vol. 4, No. 1, January–February, 1963, p. 78; Franklin Bicknell, M.D., *Chemicals in Food and in Farm Produce: Their Harmful Effects* (London: Faber and Faber, 1960), p. 47; and House of Representatives, Hearings before the Committee on Interstate and Foreign Commerce: *Color Additives,* testimony of Harold L. Stewart, 86th Congress, 2d session, 1960, p. 413.

page 64, lines 11–25
Wilhelm C. Hueper, M.D., and W. D. Conway, *Chemical Carcinogenesis and Cancers* (Chicago: Charles Thomas, 1964), pp. 73–74.

page 64, lines 26–32
Wilhelm C. Hueper, "Symposium: Environmental and Occupational Cancer Hazards, Part 1," *Clinical Pharmacology and Therapeutic,* Vol. 3, No. 6, 1963, pp. 776–813.

page 64, line 33–page 65, line 7
Ibid., p. 783.

page 65, lines 11–29
House of Representatives, Hearings before Subcommittee No. 2 of the Committee of the Judiciary: "Cyclamates," 92d Congress, 1st session, September and October 1971, paper by George T. Bryan, and Erdogan Erturk, "Production of Mouse Urinary Bladder Carcinomas by Sodium Cyclamate," pp. 236–39.

page 65, line 30–page 66, line 12
Ibid., pp. 241–44.

page 66, lines 13–15
Those who have supported Bryan's thesis that the pellet implant technique is highly sensitive, reproducible by other testers, and is a useful predictive method, include: G. M. Bonser, E. Boyland, E. R. Busby, D. B. Clayson, P. L. Grover, and J. W. Jull, *British Journal of Cancer,* Vol. 17, 1963, p. 127; Boyland, Busby, C. E. Dukes, Grover, and D. Manson, *Ibid.,* vol. 18, 1964, p. 575; Clayson, *Canada Cancer Conference,* Vol. 6, 1966, p. 186; A. M. Pamukeu, C. Olson, and J. M. Price, *Cancer Research,* Vol. 26, 1966, p. 1745; and Clayson et al., *British Journal of Cancer,* Vol. 22, 1968, p. 825.

page 66, lines 16–31
Ribicoff Hearings: "Chemicals and the Future of Man," *op. cit.,* statement of Samuel S. Epstein, M.D., p. 50.

page 66, line 33–page 67, line 6
J. Verrett and J. McLaughlin, Jr., "Use of the Chick Embryo Technique in Evaluation of Toxicity of Drugs," Annual Meeting of Federation of American Societies for Experimental Biology, *Federation Proceedings*, Vol. 22, Abstract 168, 1963, p. 188.

page 67, lines 7–18
Jacqueline Verrett, Ph.D., and Jean Carper, *Eating May Be Hazardous to Your Health: The Case Against Food Additives* (New York: Simon and Schuster, 1974), p. 56. Verrett has had primary responsibility for chick embryo testing at FDA since 1963. Verrett considers chick embryo studies, like other animal studies, far from foolproof, but useful in conjunction with tests on mammals. Verrett says that chick embryo studies should never be ignored, but, she says, they frequently are.

page 67, lines 19–27
House of Representatives, Hearings before a Subcommittee of the Committee on Government Operations: "Cyclamate Sweeteners," 91d Congress, 2d session, June 10, 1970, letter submitted for the record by R. W. Kasperson, Vice President, Corporate Regulatory Affairs, Abbott Laboratories, pp. 100–101; and "Chemicals and the Future of Man," *op. cit.*, pp. 225–34.

page 67, lines 27–34
Robert L. Brent, M.D., "Drug Testing in Animals for Teratogenic Effects. Thalidomide in the Pregnant Rat," address to the Society for Pediatric Research, Atlantic City, New Jersey, 1963.

page 67, line 34–page 68, line 2
Some individuals oppose animal tests on the basis of ethics, in addition to the lack of validity. Social biologist Ashley Montagu, in the keynote address of the 1973 annual conference of the Humane Society of the United States, criticized current animal tests that inflict pain in animals when results could be obtained as efficiently through other means. Montagu suggested five alternative methods: *(1)* tissue culture, in which dispersed cells are grown in a state of continuous multiplication; *(2)* organ cultures, using aborted fetuses, persons killed accidentally or through natural death; *(3)* gas chromatography and mass spectrometry, for testing and identifying the effects of chemicals; *(4)* modeling and simulating, using a simplified analogue of the system under study; and *(5)* electrochemical methods for the study of nervous phenomena. "The fact that somewhere between 20 and 200 million animals are sacrificed annually in laboratories is largely the result of inertia of scientists," charged Montagu, "who have been trained in traditional experimental methods with which they feel comfortable."

page 68, lines 6–7
"Toxicology's Need for New Analytical Methods," *Food and Cosmetics Toxicology*, Vol. 11, No. 1, February 1973, p. 141.

page 68, line 10–page 69, line 2
12th Report . . . : "Regulations of Diethylstilbestrol . . ." *op. cit.*, p. 24.

page 69, lines 3–7
A. J. Malanoski, "Methods Development Laboratory Technical Service Division"

(USDA article), *Journal of the Association of Official Analytical Chemists*, Vol. 53, March 1970, cited in 12th Report . . . : "Regulations of Diethylstilbestrol . . ." *op. cit.*, p. 51.

page 69, lines 8–24
Hearings . . . : "Regulations of Diethylstilbestrol . . ." Part 2, *op. cit.*, memorandum of M. Adrian Gross to Drs. Leo Friedman and Daniel Banes, FDA, December 5, 1971, p. 118.

page 69, lines 25–33
12th Report . . . : "Regulations of Diethylstilbestrol . . ." *op.cit.*, p. 51.

page 70, lines 1–11
Ibid., p. 51.

page 70, lines 12–19
Ibid., p. 52.

page 70, lines 20–25
Ibid., p. 52.

page 70, lines 26–30
Ibid., p. 61.

page 70, line 30–page 71, line 6
Clayton Yeutter, Assistant Secretary of Agriculture, address to the American Meat Institute, September 24, 1973.

page 71, lines 12–16
Dr. P. Issenberg, Massachusetts Institute of Technology, address to the American Chemical Society, Boston, Massachusetts, April 1972.

page 71, lines 17–26
"Toxicology's Need for New Analytical Methods," *op. cit.*, pp. 142–44.

Chapter 6:   The Intricate Interrelationships

page 72, lines 1–2
G. Roche Lynch, *opening address*, "Problems Arising from the Use of Chemicals in Food," Conference, Great Britain, 1951; reprinted, *Chemistry and Industry*, 1951, p. 932.

page 72, lines 4–8
Theron G. Randolph, M.D., *Human Ecology and Susceptibility to the Chemical Environment* (Springfield, Illinois: Charles C. Thomas, 1962), p. 3.

page 72, lines 10–15
Sir Edward Mellanby, M.D., "The Chemical Manipulation of Foods," address at

Sanderson Well Lecture, Middlesex Hospital, England, May 4, 1951; printed in *British Medical Journal*, October 13, 1951, p. 864.

page 72, lines 17–21
William D. Ruckelshaus, address to the American Society of Toxicology, Washington, D.C., March 9, 1971.

page 72, lines 23–27
Theron G. Randolph, M.D., *op. cit.*, p. 4.

page 73, lines 11–21
"NAS Conference on Carcinogenesis Testing in the Development of New Drugs," *Food Chemical News*, Vol. 15, No. 10, May 28, 1973, p. 49.

page 73, lines 28–31
"Too Many Foods in Pursuit of Too Few Preservatives," *Food and Cosmetics Toxicology*, Vol. 11, No. 2, June 1973, p. 504.

page 73, lines 32–34
R. F. Milton, paper for the Attingham Park Conference, Soil Association, 1958, p. 10.

page 74, lines 1–2
U.S. House of Representatives, Hearings before a Subcommittee of the Committee on Government Operations: "Cyclamate Sweeteners," 91st Congress, 2d session, June 10, 1970, memorandum from Charles C. Edwards, commissioner of the FDA, to Jesse L. Steinfeld, Surgeon General, March 31, 1970, p. 54.

page 74, lines 3–5
"National Institute of Environmental Health Sciences Researchers Report on Saccharin Tissue Buildup," *Food Chemical News*, Vol. 15, No. 28, October 1, 1973, p. 11.

page 74, lines 6–14
Wilhelm C. Hueper, M.D., "Potential Role of Nonnutritive Food Additives . . ." *op. cit.*, p. 240.

page 74, lines 15–18
James J. Delaney, House of Representatives, *Extension of Remarks*, February 21, 1957, *letter* from William E. Smith, M.D. of January 28, 1957.

page 74, lines 19–22
G. Sriranga Reddy, T. B. G. Tilak, and D. Krishnamurthi, "Susceptibility of Vitamin A.-deficient Rats to Aflatoxin," *Food and Cosmetics Toxicology*, Vol. 11, No. 3, June 1973, p. 467.

page 74, lines 23–26
Leo Friedman, *Federation Proceedings*, Vol. 25, 1966, p. 137. This experiment was cited by Michael Jacobson, *Eater's Digest* (New York: Doubleday, 1972), p. 36. The late Dr. Friedman, a biologist, was acting director of the Division of Toxicology, Bureau of Foods, Pesticides and Product Safety, FDA.

page 74, lines 27–32
"The Eventful History of B.H.T." (leading article), *The Lancet*, No. 1056, November 20, 1965, p. 1057.

page 74, lines 33–34
"Toxicity of Antioxidants," *Food and Cosmetics Toxicology*, Vol. 1, No. 1, September 1963, p. 113.

page 74, line 35–page 75, line 3
E. B. Gammal, K. K. Carroll, and E. R. Plunkett, "Effects of Dietary Fat on Mammary Carcinogenesis by 7,12-Dimethylbenz-*(a)*-anthracene in Rats," *Cancer Research*, Vol. 27, 1967, p. 1737.

page 75, lines 7–14
"The Fate of BHA in Man," *Food and Cosmetics Toxicology*, Vol. 1, No. 2, December 1963, pp. 276–77.

page 75, lines 20–23
Eldon M. Boyd, M.D., *Protein Deficiency and Pesticide Toxicity* (Springfield, Illinois: Charles C. Thomas, 1972), p. viii.

page 75, line 30–page 76, line 6
Benjamin H. Ershoff, Ph.D., "Antitoxic Effects of Plant Fiber," *American Journal of Clinical Nutrition*, Vol. 27, December 1974, pp. 1395–98.

page 76, lines 7–21
Wilhelm C. Hueper, "Potential Role of Nonnutritive Food Additives . . . ," *op. cit.*, p. 242.

page 76, lines 23–31
Ribicoff Hearings: "Chemicals and the Future of Man," *op. cit.*, testimony of Robert L. Brent, M.D., p. 78.

page 76, line 32–page 77, line 6
Delaney Hearings: "Food Additives," 1957–1958, *op. cit.*, statement of Dr. William B. Deichmann, Chairman, Department of Pharmacology, University of Miami School of Medicine, Coral Gables, Florida, pp. 335–36.

page 77, lines 7–12
Francis J. C. Roe, D.M., ed., *Metabolic Aspects of Food Safety* (London: University of London, Blackwell Scientific Publications, 1970); R. F. Crampton, "Absorption from the Gastrointestinal Tract, As Applied to Food Additives," pp. 75–76.

page 77, lines 13–25
"Cobalt, Beer and Heartache," *Food and Cosmetics Toxicology*, Vol. 10, No. 1, February 1972, pp. 99–100.

page 77, lines 26–31
Lois Ann Shearer, John R. Goldsmith, Clarence Young, Owen A. Kearns, and Benjamin R. Tamplin, "Methemoglobin Levels in Infants in an Area with High Nitrate Water Supply," *American Journal of Public Health*, Vol. 14, No. 9, September 1972, p. 1174.

page 77, line 32–page 78, line 6
E. Ellis, letter to the editor, *Food and Cosmetics Toxicology*, Vol. 10, No. 1, February 1972, p. 125.

page 78, lines 9–12
"Another Check on Ethylene Oxide Sterilization," *Food and Cosmetics Toxicology*, Vol. 11, No. 5, October 1973, pp. 916–17.

page 78, lines 12–13
E. A. Hawk and O. Mickelsen, *Science*, Vol. 121, 1955, pp. 442–44.

page 78, lines 14–29
The possibility that methyl bromide fumigated foods induced myeloptic neuropathy was reported by Dr. Yoshikazu Yomura, Department of Neurology of Kanto Rosai Hospital, Kawasaki, Japan, at the 9th International Congress of Nutrition, Mexico City, 1973.

page 78, lines 30–38
D. R. King, "Effects of Fumigation for Insect Control on Seed Germination," Texas Agriculture Experimental Station, College Station, Texas, 1960.

page 79, lines 1–5
Ernest Liener, ed., *Toxic Constituents of Plant Foodstuffs* (New York: Academic Press, 1969), p. 377. Early studies showed that rats grew most rapidly when fed untreated flour; slower when flour was treated lightly with chlorine dioxide; and slowest, with heavily treated flour. This was reported by S. G. Impey and T. Moore, "Nutritive Value of Bread Made from Flour Treated with Chlorine Dioxide," *British Medical Journal*, ii, No. 5251, August 26, 1961, pp. 533–56. These studies were confirmed later by J. B. Hutchinson, T. Moran and J. Pace, "Flour Treated with Chlorine Dioxide: Multigeneration Tests with Rats," *Journal of Science and Food Agriculture*, Vol. 15, 1964, p. 725. At a later date, no adverse effects on growth rate were demonstrated by A. C. Frazer and J. G. Lines, "Studies on Change in Flour Tocopherols Following Aging and Treatment of the Flour with Chlorine Dioxide," *Ibid.*, Vol. 18, 1967, p. 203. But in all three sets of studies, the reduction of vitamin E naturally present in the flour was found to be drastically reduced by the bleach. Furthermore, *the heavy treatment of flour with chlorine dioxide causes oxidation of lipids (oils) and rancidity in such flour develops more rapidly than in untreated flour, presumably due to the loss of the natural antioxidant,* according to Liener, *op. cit.*, p. 377.

page 79, lines 5–7
David C. Herting and Emma-Jane E. Durry, "Alpha-Tocopherol Content of Cereal Grains and Processed Cereals" *Agricultural and Food Chemistry*, Vol. 17, No. 4, July–August 1969, pp. 785–90.

page 79, lines 8–19
Ernest Liener, "Toxic Constituents . . ." *op. cit.*, "Solvents," pp. 272–73.

page 79, lines 20–23
"Sulfites and Sulfur Dioxide Toxicology," *Food and Cosmetics Toxicology*, Vol. 1,

No. 1, September 1963, pp. 115–16; interaction between sulfur dioxide and other sulfur compounds with folic acid were reported by Vonderschmitt, *et al.*, *Archives of Biochemistry and Biophysics*, Vol. 122, 1967, p. 488, cited in "Too Many Foods in Pursuit of Too Few Preservatives," *Food and Cosmetics Toxicology*, Vol. 11, No. 3, June 1973, p. 504.

page 79, lines 23–26
Medical World News, Vol. 13, No. 36, September 29, 1972, "Outlook" [brief items], p. 10.

page 79, lines 32–36
"The Complexities of EDTA," *Food and Cosmetics Toxicology*, Vol. 10, No. 5, October 1972, pp. 697–700; also *Toxicology and Applied Pharmacology*, Vol. 5, 1963, p. 142.

page 79, line 37–page 80, line 5
C. E. Poling, *et al.*, 'Effects of Feeding Polyoxyethylene Preparations to Rats and Hamsters," *Food Research*, Vol. 21, 1956, p. 337.

page 80, lines 6–11
R. J. Emerick and O. E. Olson, "Effect of Nitrate and Nitrite on Vitamin A Storage in the Rat," *Journal of Nutrition*, Vol. 78, 1962, p. 73; "Effects of Nitrate and Nitrite on Vitamin A Storage," *Food and Cosmetics Toxicology*, Vol. 1, No. 2, December 1963, pp. 277–78; G. E. Mitchel, C. O. Little, and T. R. Greathouse, "Influence of Nitrate and Nitrite on Carotene Disappearance from the Rat Intestine," *Life Sciences*, Vol. 4, 1964, p. 385; "Hazards of Nitrate, Nitrite, and Nitrosamines to Man and Livestock," *Accumulation of Nitrate* (Washington, D.C.: National Academy of Sciences, 1972), pp. 46–75.

page 80, lines 12–32
Delaney Hearings: "Chemicals in Food Products," 1950, *op. cit.*, statement of Dr. Paul B. Dunbar, Commissioner of FDA, pp. 24–25.

page 80, line 36–page 81, line 3
"Carmine and the Mouse Embryo Again," *Food and Cosmetics Toxicology*, Vol. 10, No. 3, June 1972, pp. 427–28, cites work of G. Schüter in Germany.

page 81, lines 3–6
"Sodium Saccharin Possible Mutagenicity Noted," *Food Chemical News*, Vol. 15, No. 10, May 28, 1973, p. 39.

page 81, lines 8–10
Ibid., p. 40. The impurity, orthotoluene sulfonamide, has been found at levels as high as 5,650 ppm in sodium saccharin. See also Jane E. Brody, "Sugar Substitute Gets New Scrutiny," *The New York Times*, November 5, 1973.

page 81, lines 10–15
Ben F. Feingold, M.D., *Introduction to Clinical Allergy* (Springfield, Illinois: Charles C. Thomas, 1973), pp. 155–56.

page 81, lines 19–34
Wilhelm C. Hueper, M.D., "Carcinogens in the Human Environment," *Archives of Pathology*, Vol. 71, April 1961, p. 359. "Flour Bleaches and Improvers," leading article, *British Medical Journal*, No. 5252, September 2, 1961, pp. 631–32; "Flour Improvers" (editorial), *Ibid.*, No. 5268, December 23, 1961, p. 1695.

page 82, lines 1–3
Ernest Liener, "Toxic Constituents . . ." *op. cit.*, pp. 372–73.

page 82, lines 4–13
Ibid., pp. 176–78.

page 82, lines 14–20
"More Violative Chlordane Residues Found by APHIS," *Food Chemical News*, Vol. 15, No. 33, November 5, 1973, p. 10. Although this article deals mainly with the problem of chlordane residues, unidentified microbials in veal calves was also discussed.

page 82, line 21–page 83, line 3
B. M. Ulland, J. J. Weisburger, Elizabeth K. Weisburger, J. M. Rice, and R. Cypher, "Thyroid Cancers in Rats from Ethylene Thiourea Intake," *Journal of the National Cancer Institute*, Vol. 49, 1972, p. 583; also *The Sciences*, November 1972; "Spectrum," *Environment*, Vol. 14, No. 8, October 1972, p. 22. USDA researchers have found that the toxicity of another fungicide (thiabendazole), permitted in the wax applied to citrus fruits, apples, and pears, *increased* in the pulp during storage.

page 83, lines 5–6
N. Gannon and J. H. Bigger, "The Conversion of Aldrin and Heptachlor to the Epoxides in Soils," *Journal of Economic Entomology*, Vol. 51, No. 1, 1958, pp. 1–2; and E. P. Lichtenstein and K. R. Schultz, "Breakdown of Lindane and Aldrin in Soils," *Ibid.*, Vol. 52, No. 1, 1959, pp. 118–19.

page 83, lines 7–9
B. Davidow and J. L. Radomski, "Metabolite of Heptachlor, Its Analysis, Storage, and Toxicity," *Federation Proceedings*, Vol. 2, No. 1, 1952, p. 336.

page 83, lines 11–12
The increased toxicity of heptachlor's conversion in sunlight was reported by Dr. Charles Hammer, Georgetown University, before the American Chemical Society, 1973.

page 83, lines 12–14
The increased toxicity of parathion's conversion in sunlight was reported by J. R. Grunwell and R. Erickson, before the American Chemical Society, 1973.

page 83, lines 15–21
Thomas H. Maugh, II, "DDT: An Unrecognized Source of Polychlorinated Biphenyls," *Science*, Vol. 180, May 11, 1973, pp. 578–79; also G. F. Fries, "PCB Residues: Their Significance to Animal Agriculture," *Agricultural Science Review*, 3rd Quarter, 1972, pp. 19–24.

page 83, lines 21–25
The increased toxicity of PCB's conversion products was reported by Christoffer Rappe, K. Andersson, A. Norsrom, B. Rasmuson, and H. Swahlin, University of Umea, Sweden, before the American Chemical Society's annual meeting, Chicago, August 27, 1973. Equally surprising chance combinations form from other chemicals in the environment. Bis (chloromethyl) ether, an industrial carcinogen under present investigation, was found to form spontaneously from formaldehyde and acid chlorine ions in humid air. See *Chemical and Engineering News*, February 11, 1974.

page 83, line 26–page 84, line 6
D. Dickinson and T. W. Raven, "Stability of Erythrosine in Artificially Colored Canned Cherries," *Journal of Science of Food and Agriculture*, Vol. 13, 1962, p. 650; also Delaney Hearings: "Chemicals in Food Products," 1950, *op. cit.*, p. 73.

page 84, lines 9–11
"Toxicology's Need for New Analytical Methods," *Food and Cosmetics Toxicology*, Vol. 11, No. 1, February 1973, p. 144.

page 84, lines 13–19
Chemistry, May 1972, p. 4, cited in *Miller News Review*, September 21, 1972, p. 2.

page 84, line 20–page 85, line 2
Kevin P. Shea, "The New-Car Smell," *Environment*, Vol. 13, No. 8, October 1971, pp. 2–9; "Plasticizers: Getting into Blood," *Chemical and Engineering News*, February 15, 1971, pp. 12–13; "Plasticizers: New Entry on List of Suspected Contaminants," *Science News*, Vol. 100, November 13, 1971, p. 324; and "Phthalate Effect on Health Still Not Clear," *Chemical and Engineering News*, September 18, 1972, pp. 14–15.

page 85, lines 3–33
"Evidence Mounts Linking Vinyl Chloride and Cancer," *Chemical and Engineering News*," February 18, 1974, p. 6; also Robert J. Kelsey, "FDA May Revoke PVC's Prior Sanction Status," *Food and Drug Packaging*, Vol. 30, No. 7, April 11, 1974, pp. 1, 25. Persons in contact with polyvinyl chloride food packaging material may, under certain conditions, also be at risk. A condition termed "meat-wrapper's asthma" has been recently reported: "We have recently treated three patients who are employed as meat wrappers and who had severe respiratory problems. In all three, the onset of respiratory difficulty followed exposure to fumes produced by cutting with a hot wire a plastic film made of the common polymer, polyvinyl chloride. We are reporting these cases because *we suspect the phenomenon is not uncommon*, yet it has not been reported previously in the medical literature." [emphasis added] See *The Journal of the American Medical Association*, November 5, 1973.

page 85, line 34–page 86, line 12
Richard D. Lyons, "Plastic Liquor Bottles Face Ban Over Suspicious Toxic Effect," *The New York Times*, May 9, 1973.

page 86, lines 13–24
William B. Mead, "Boxes from Recycled Paper Contaminate Food, U.S. Says," *The*

Record (Bergen, New Jersey), September 28, 1971, p. 1; also "EPA, FDA Crackdown on Toxic Pollutants," *Chemical and Engineering News*, July 16, 1973, p. 10.

page 86, line 30–page 88, line 8
G. Löfroth, and T. Gejvall, "Diethyl Pyrocarbonate: Formation of Urethan in Treated Beverages," *Science*, Vol. 174, December 17, 1971, pp. 1248–50; Harold M. Schmeck, Jr., "FDA Urges Ban on Preservative," *The New York Times*, February 11, 1972, p. 61.

page 88, line 9–page 90, line 5
"Accumulation of Nitrate," *op. cit.*, "Carcinogenic, Mutagenic, and Teratogenic Effects of Nitrosamines," pp. 66–68; "Nitrites, Nitrates, and Nitrosamines in Food—A Dilemna," (Chicago, Illinois: Institute of Food Technologists, November 1972); I. A. Wolff and A. E. Wasserman, "Nitrates, Nitrites and Nitrosamines," *Science*, Vol. 177, July 7, 1972, pp. 15–19; C. L. Walters, Michael C. Archer, and Steven R. Tannenbaum, "Nitrosation in the Environment: Can It Occur?" *Science*, Vol. 179, January 5, 1973, pp. 96–97; W. J. Aunan, "Update of the Nitrosamine Issue," paper for the Reciprocal Meat Conference, Iowa State University, Ames, Iowa, June 1972; Steven R. Tannenbaum, "Nitrite and Nitrosame Content of Foods: Unsolved Problems and Current Research," paper for the Reciprocal Meat Conference, *Ibid.*, June 1972.

page 90, lines 7–10
William Lijinsky and Samuel S. Epstein, "Nitrosamines as Environmental Carcinogens," *Nature*, Vol. 225, No. 5227, 1970, pp. 21–23; also Fountain Hearings: "Regulation of Food Additives and Medicated Animal Feeds," March 1971, *op. cit.*, testimony of Dr. William Lijinsky, Eppley Institute, University of Nebraska Medical Center, Omaha, Nebraska, pp. 11–147; and Dr. Lijinsky's submitted statement for the record, pp. 147–67.

page 90, lines 10–21
"USDA Reports Results of Dimethylnitrosamine Survey," USDA press release, December 14, 1971; "Carcinogens in Meat," *Chemical and Engineering News*, February 21, 1972, p. 16.

page 90, lines 22–33
19th Report by the Committee on Government Operations: "Regulations of Food Additives—Nitrites and Nitrates" (Washington, D.C.: U.S. Government Printing Office, 1972), p. 23.

page 90, line 34–page 91, line 10
"USDA and FDA Issue Joint Ban on Buffered Premixes," USDA press release, November 14, 1973.

page 91, lines 11–16
R. K. Elespuru and W. Lijinsky, "The Formation of Carcinogenic Nitroso Compounds from Nitrite and Some Types of Agricultural Chemicals," *Food and Cosmetics Toxicology*, Vol. 11, No. 5, October 1973, pp. 807–16. Lowell Klepper, assistant professor of Agronomy at University of Nebraska, reported that 90 percent

of all chemical classes of commercial herbicides he tested caused nitrite buildup. See "Nitrite Ion Charged with Murder," *Chemical Week*, March 14, 1973.

page 91, lines 17–24
"Regulations of Food Additives—Nitrites and Nitrates," *op. cit.*, p. 25.

page 92, lines 6–8
Robert Shapiro, "Reactions of Uracil and Cytosine Derivatives with Sodium Bisulfite," letter to editor, *Journal of the American Chemical Society*, January 28, 1970, pp. 422–24.

page 92, lines 10–13
Report on the Review of Preservatives in Food Regulations 1962, Ministry of Agriculture, Fisheries, and Food (London: HMSO, 1972).

page 92, lines 16–29
Arnold J. Lehman, M.D., "Nitrates and Nitrites in Meat Products," *Association of Food and Drug Officials of the United States, Quarterly Bulletin*, Vol. 22, 1958, p. 138.

page 92, line 30
Barry Commoner, "The Balance of Nature," *The Journal of the Soil Association*, Vol. 15, No. 2, April 1968, pp. 76–77.

page 92, line 31–page 93, line 4
Kevin P. Shea, "Canned Milk," *Environment*, Vol. 15, No. 2, March 1973, pp. 6–11.

page 93, lines 5–10
Howard, G. Rapaport, M.D., and Shirley Motter Linde, *The Complete Allergy Guide* (New York: Simon and Schuster, 1970), p. 68.

page 93, lines 25–29
Irving J. Selikoff, M.D., "Second Sunday," NBC television program, March 9, 1969, p. 15 (printed script).

page 94, lines 10–14
Wilhelm C. Hueper, "Potential Role of Nonnutritive Food Additives . . ." *op. cit.*, p. 238.

page 94, lines 15–23
W. C. Cutting, "Toxicity of Silicones," *Stanford Medical Bulletin*, Vol. 10, No. 23, 1952.

page 94, lines 24–27
The Merck Index; Chemical Abstracts, Vol. 46, 1952, No. 7707.

page 94, lines 28–32
"Coming Up: New Artificial Sweetener," *Medical World News*, June 7, 1974, pp. 52 G-I.; Harold M. Schmeck, Jr., "F.D.A. To Approve A New Sweetener," *The New York Times*, July 26, 1974.

page 94, line 33–page 96, line 4
John W. Olney, M.D., *Memorandum to Commissioner, Food and Drug Administra-*

tion, Washington, D.C., August 16, 1974, pp. 5–6; "Aspartame Sugar Substitute May Cause Brain Damage in Children," *Congressional Record*, Senate, September 24, 1974, S 17340–43.

page 96, lines 9–11
D. M. Shankel, "Nutritional Synergism of Ultraviolet Light and Caffeine in *Escherichia coli*," *Journal of Bacteriology*, Vol. 84, 1962, p. 410.

page 96, lines 12–14
Jane E. Brody, "Conferees Study Asbestos Hazard," *The New York Times*, January 25, 1973.

page 96, lines 15–19
"Pesticide Synergists and Human Health," *Science News*, September 9, 1972; and Julian McCaull, "Mix with Care," *Environment*, Vol. 13, No. 1, January/February 1971, p. 39.

page 96, lines 21–22
Congressional Hearings, Subcommittee of Commerce on Appropriations: "Report on Environmental Health Problems," 86d Congress, 2d session, March 1960, p. 78.

page 96, lines 23–24
"Silent Alabama Autumn: A Tale of Two Pesticides," *Science News*, September 29, 1973.

page 96, lines 26–27
Janice Crossland and Virginia Brodine, "Drinking Water," *Environment*, Vol. 15, No. 3, April 1973, p. 15.

page 96, lines 29–30
Chemistry, May 1973, p. 20, cited in *Miller News Review*, May 24, 1973.

page 96, lines 30–31
"Synergism," *Food and Cosmetics Toxicology*, Vol. 3, No. 4, October 1965, p. 640.

page 96, line 34–page 97, line 2
Samuel S. Epstein, M.D., "Potential Human Hazards Due to Some Currently Used Food Additives and Pesticides," address to the Cleveland Museum of Natural History, Cleveland, Ohio, March 17, 1972.

page 97, lines 4–5
Arthur R. Tamplin and John W. Gofman, *"Population Control" Through Nuclear Pollution* (Chicago: Nelson–Hall Co., 1970), p. 43.

page 97, lines 5–7
Paul Brodeur, *Asbestos and Enzymes* (New York: Ballantine, 1972), p. 37.

page 97, lines 8–10
Report by the Task Force on Environmental Health and Related Problems, HEW (Washington, D.C.: U.S. Government Printing Office, 1967).

page 97, lines 22–25
"Risk of Drug Interaction May Exist in 1 out of 13 Prescriptions," *The Journal of the American Medical Association*, Vol. 220, No. 10, June 5, 1972, p. 1287.

page 97, line 29–page 98, line 12
36th Report by the Committee on Government Operations: "Regulation of Cyclamate Sweeteners," 91st Congress, 2d session (Washington, D.C.: U.S. Government Printing Office, 1970), pp. 6–7.

page 98, lines 13–27
J. M. Talbot and B. W. Meade, "Effect of Silicones on the Absorption of Anticoagulant Drugs," letter to the editor, *The Lancet*, June 19, 1971, p. 1292.

pages 98, lines 30–32
House of Representatives, Committee on Government Operations, news release, August 16, 1972, p. 2.

page 98, line 35–page 99, line 2
The Merck Index indicates many pharmaceutical incompatibilities, including food additives. Ascorbic acid, for example, which is used as a food additive, should not be formulated with sodium nitrite, theobromine, sodium salicylate, or methenamine (an antiseptic). See *Chemical Abstracts*, Vol. 46, No. 7707; sodium nitrite is incompatible with food additives, such as sulfites and tannic acid, as well as some pharmaceuticals.

page 99, lines 7–13
"Food–Drug Interactions," *Chemical and Engineering News*, September 13, 1971, p. 47.

Chapter 7:   The Interference with Vital Processes

page 100, lines 1–4
George Gaylord Simpson, "The Crisis in Biology," *The American Scholar*, Summer, 1967, p. 367.

page 100, lines 6–7
Medical Research: A Midcentury Survey, Vol. 2, Unsolved Clinical Problems in Biological Perspective (Boston: Little Brown, 1955), p. 4.

page 100, lines 9–17
Leo Friedman, Ph.D., Acting Director of the Division of Toxicology, Bureau of Foods, Pesticides and Product Safety, address to the American Association for the Advancement of Science, December 28, 1969.

page 100, lines 19–20
Dr. René Dubos, *Mirage of Health* (New York: Harper, 1959), p. 171.

page 100, line 22–page 101, line 3
Otto Folin, Ph.D., Hamilton Kahn Professor of Biological Chemistry, *Harvard Health Talks: Preservatives and Other Chemicals in Foods: Their Use and Abuse* (Cambridge, Massachusetts: Harvard University Press, 1914), pp. 39–40.

page 101, lines 5–10
Julius J. Coon, M.D., "Food Toxicology: Safety of Food Additives," *Modern Medicine*, November 30, 1970, p. 105.

page 101, lines 12–15
W. B. Gibson and F. M. Strong, Department of Biochemistry, College of Agriculture and Life Sciences, University of Wisconsin, "Metabolism and Elimination of Sulfite by Rats, Mice and Monkeys," paper, September 20, 1972, printed in *Food and Cosmetics Toxicology*, Vol. 11, No. 2, April 1973, p. 185.

page 101, lines 17–20
R. M. W. Cunningham, Ph.D., Department of Health, Canberra, "Chemical Additives to Food as Factors Possibly Contributing to Disease," *The Medical Journal of Australia*, May 29, 1954, pp. 819–22.

page 101, lines 21–24
W. N. Aldridge, ed., *Mechanisms of Toxicity*, Biological Council Co-ordinating Committee for Symposia on Drug Action (London: Macmillan, 1971). This volume contains the proceedings of a symposium on the mechanisms of toxicity, London, April 1970.

page 101, lines 28–32
John W. Olney, M.D., "Brain Lesions, Obesity, and Other Disturbances in Mice Treated with Monosodium Glutamate," *Science*, Vol. 164, May 9, 1969, pp. 719–21.

page 101, line 33–page 102, line 2
"Long-Term Effects of Food Additives," *Medical World News*, September 24, 1971, p. 13. M.I.T. studies are being funded from National Institute for Environmental Health Sciences, National Cancer Institute, and the American Meat Institute Foundation. Investigators will conduct in-depth studies, among other things, of the effects of nitrosamines. The program is being coordinated by Gerald N. Wogan, a toxicologist.

page 102, line 8–page 103, line 8
Ernest Freese and Chingju W. Shen, Laboratory of Molecular Biology, National Institute of Neurological Diseases and Stroke, and Enid Galliers, "Function of Lipophilic Acids as Antimicrobial Food Additives," *Nature*, Vol. 241, February 2, 1973, pp. 321–25; also E. Ginsberg, D. Salomon, T. Sreevalsan, and E. Freese, "Growth Inhibition and Morphological Changes Caused by Lipophilic Acids in Mammalian Cells," *Proceedings of the National Academy of Sciences*, Vol. 70, No. 8, August 1973, pp. 2457–61.

page 103, lines 14–24
Susan M. Milner, Department of Pathology, University of Cambridge (England), "Effects of the Food Additive Butylated Hydroxytoluene on Monolayer Cultures of Primate Cells," *Nature*, Vol. 216, November 11, 1967, pp. 557–60.

page 103, lines 25–29
A. J. Day, A. R. Johnson, M. W. O'Halloran, and C. J. Schwartz, "The Effect of the Antioxidant Butylated Hydroxytoluene on Serum Lipid and Glycoprotein Levels in the Rat," *Australian Journal of Experimental Biology and Medical Science*, Vol. 37, 1959, p. 295; J. P. Frawley, F. E. Kohn, J. H. Kay, and J. C. Calandra, "Progress Report on Multigeneration Reproduction Studies in Rats Fed Butylated Hydroxytoluene," *Food and Cosmetics Toxicology*, Vol. 3, 1965, p. 377; and A. R. Johnson and F. R. Hewgill, "The Effect of the Antioxidants, Butylated Hydroxyanisole, Butylated Hydroxytoluene and Propyl Gallate on Growth, Liver and Serum Lipids and Serum Sodium Levels of the Rat," *Australian Journal of Experimental Biology and Medical Science*, Vol. 39, 1961, p. 353.

page 103, line 30–page 104, line 1
Mechanisms of Toxicity, op. cit., paper by E. Farber and associates.

page 104, lines 4–11
Otto Warburg, Director, Max Planck–Institute for Cell Physiology, Berlin, *The Prime Cause and Prevention of Cancer* (Bethesda, Maryland: National Cancer Institute, 1967), pp. 5–6.

page 104, lines 13–18
Accumulation of Nitrate (Washington, D.C.: National Academy of Sciences, 1972), p. 57.

page 104, lines 19–35
"Research Links Tumor Virus with Normal Cells," *New Directions*, Vol. 3, No. 4, Summer 1973, p. 1.

page 105, lines 1–5
"Facts on Pollution's Genetic Hazards," *Medical World News*, September 29, 1972, p. 10. This is a report on the work of biochemists Robert Shapiro and Barbara Braverman at New York University.

page 105, lines 5–7
"A Carcinogenic Sterilizer?" *Ibid.*, June 14, 1974, p. 13. This is a report on the work of Dr. Herbert S. Rosenkrantz, College of Physicians and Surgeons, Columbia University.

page 105, lines 16–27
Ralph W. Gerard, M.D., *Food for Life* (Chicago University of Chicago Press, 1952), Chapter 5, "Enzymes."

page 105, line 28–page 106, line 3
Ibid., pp. 170–71.

page 106, lines 13–24
Ibid., pp. 161–62.

page 106, lines 32–35
Toxicants Occurring Naturally in Foods, first edition (Washington, D.C.: National Academy of Sciences, 1966), pp. 105, 107.

page 106, line 36–page 107, line 2
R. F. Milton, "Cell Nutrition," paper for the Attingham Park Conference, Soil Association of England, 1958.

page 107, lines 3–6
Chemical and Engineering News, June 25, 1973, p. 12. Dr. David G. Lygre, Central Washington State University, reported at American Chemical Society Northwest Regional Meeting, that the enzyme glucose 6-phosphatase catalyzes the terminal reaction in the synthesis of glucose. It can also convert glucose to glucose 6-phosphate. Under acidic conditions, both saccharin and cyclamate compete with glucose 6-phosphate.

page 107, lines 7–8
Food and Cosmetics Toxicology, Vol. 11, No. 5, October 1973, p. 887. The information was contained in a discussion of a recently published book on sorbic acid: E. Lück, *Sorbinsaure*, Chemie, Biochemie, Mikrobiologie, Technologie. Vol. 2, Biochemie, Mikrobiologie (Hamburg: Behr, 1972).

page 107, line 9
Mechanisms of Toxicology, *op. cit.*

page 107, lines 10–11
"Flour Bleaches and Improvers," leading article, *British Medical Journal*, No. 5252, September 2, 1961, pp. 631–32; also A. H. Conney and J. J. Burns, "Metabolic Interactions Among Environmental Chemicals and Drugs," *Science*, Vol. 178, November 10, 1972, pp. 576–86.

page 107, lines 20–21
Christine M. Botham, D. M. Conning, Jo Hayes, M. H. Litchfield, and T. F. Mc-Elligott, "Effects of Butylated Hydroxytoluene on the Enzyme Activity and Ultrastructure of Rat Hepatocytes," *Food and Cosmetics Toxicology*, Vol. 8, 1970, p. 1.

page 107, lines 21–23
"Metabolic Interactions. . . ." *op. cit.,* p. 577. It is recognized that the same toxic property of a pesticide that effectively kills insects also carries a potential toxicity for the cells of other living organisms. Pesticides do not act selectively against the cells of the target insect, but also act on cells of plants and animals, including humans.

page 107, lines 27–30
The Secret of Life: Enzymes (Chicago: National Enzyme Company), 1958.

page 107, line 34–page 108, line 1
Ibid. Saliva analyses for enzyme levels were conducted at Michael Reese Hospital.

page 108, lines 1–3
Ibid. Urine analyses for enzyme levels were conducted by Dr. Eckardt in Germany.

page 108, lines 4–10
R. F. Milton, "Cell Nutrition," *op. cit.*

page 109, lines 11–18
John R. Holum, *Elements of General and Biological Chemistry* (New York: John Wiley, 1962).

page 109, lines 19–28
"Second Line of Cancer Defense?" *Medical World News*, April 2, 1971, p. 23.

page 109, line 19–page 110, line 14
"Metabolic Interactions . . ." *op. cit.*, p. 576.

page 110, lines 13–34
R. A. Holman, M.D., "Civilization and Cancer," paper for the International Conference on Nutrition and Vital Substances, September 1961.

page 111, lines 15–24
H. Ghadimi, S. Kumar, and F. Abaci, "Studies on Monosodium Glutamate Ingestion. I. Biochemical Explanation of Chinese Restaurant Syndrome," *Biochemical Medicine*, Vol. 5, 1971, p. 447.

page 111, lines 25–31
L. M. Dalderup (Amsterdam), letter to editor, *The Lancet*, i, 1971, p. 1358, cited in *Food and Cosmetics Toxicology*, Vol. 10, No. 4, August 1972, p. 586.

page 111, line 35–page 112, line 3
Science News, April 29, 1972, p. 282.

page 112, lines 4–28
"NIEHS Researchers Report on Saccharin Tissue Buildup," *Food Chemical News*, Vol. 15, No. 28, October 1, 1973, pp. 10–11. Studies were conducted at Analytical and Synthetic Chemistry Section, National Institute of Environmental Health Sciences, by Hazel B. Mathews, Minerva Fields, and Lawrence Fishbein; reported in *Agricultural and Food Chemistry*, September–October 1973.

page 112, lines 29–32
"Food Additives" (editorial), *The Lancet*, August 16, 1969, pp. 361–62.

page 112, line 33–page 113, line 2
Food and Cosmetics Toxicology, Vol. 8, No. 4, August 1970, pp. 409–412.

page 113, lines 3–11
"Food Additives" (editorial), *The Lancet, op. cit.*, cites figures on human adipose BHT accumulations from the work of A. J. Collins and M. Sharratt, *Food and Cosmetics Toxicology*, Vol. 6, 1968, p. 79. These authors also noted that dicophane (a DDT metabolite) *nearly doubled* in the adipose tissue of the average American, from 5.3 ppm in 1950 to 10.3 ppm in 1962.

page 113, lines 21–23
R. L. Vought, F. A. Brown, and J. Wolff, "Erythrosine: An Adventitious Source of Iodide," *Journal of Clinical Endocrinology and Metabolism*, Vol. 34, 1972, p. 747.

page 113, lines 23–27
Food Colors (Washington, D.C.: National Academy of Sciences, 1971), p. 12.

page 113, lines 28–34
Jane E. Brody, "Study Hints That Yogurt May Reduce Cholesterol," *The New York Times*, June 23, 1974. Investigation of the effects of surfactants was conducted by Dr. George V. Mann, associate professor of biochemistry and medicine at Vanderbilt University.

page 114, lines 1–9
Linda P. Posati and Michael J. Pallansch, "Bradykinin Inhibition by Butylated Hydroxyanisole," *Science*, Vol. 168, April 3, 1970, pp. 121–22.

page 114, lines 9–10
Ibid., p. 122.

page 114, lines 11–25
These findings were reported by two different groups at the 28th Northwest Regional Meeting of the American Chemical Society, Pullman, Washington, June 15, 1973. Dr. Adam L. Lis, Nucleic Acid Laboratory, Medical School, University of Oregon, Portland, reported on the neuromuscular disorders caused by creatinine-5-oxime injected into rats; Drs. D. I. and R. K. McLaughlin reported on the symptoms noted in the treated animals.

page 114, lines 30–31
Alastair Frazer, "The Need for More Biochemical Information in the Field of Food Safety Evaluation," paper at the 2d Nuffield Conference, contained in Francis J. C. Roe, ed., *Metabolic Aspects of Food Safety* (Oxford: Blackwell Scientific Publications, 1970), pp. 2–3.

page 114, line 32–page 115, line 2
Wilhelm C. Hueper, "Potential Role of Nonnutritive Food Additives . . ." *op. cit.*, p. 243.

page 115, lines 3–10
Alastair Frazer, "The Need for More Biochemical Information . . ." *op. cit.*, pp. 6–7.

page 115, lines 13–17
"Metabolism in the Gut," *Science News*, July 11, 1970; and S. Kojuma and H. Ichibagase, *Chemical Pharmacology Bulletin*, Vol. 14, 1966, p. 971.

page 115, line 18–page 116, line 2
The Ad Hoc Committee on Nonnutritive Sweeteners, Summary and Conclusions from an Interim Report to the United States Food and Drug Administration (Washington, D.C.: Food Protection Committee, National Academy of Sciences–National Research Council, November 1968), pp. 5–6.

page 116, lines 3–9
Wilhelm C. Hueper, "Potential Role of Nonnutritive Food Additives . . ." *op. cit.*, p. 240.

page 116, line 14–page 117, line 8
"The Gut Flora of Man and Laboratory Animals," *Food and Cosmetics Toxicology*, Vol. 11, No. 4, August 1973, pp. 679–83; and "Metabolism in the Gut," *Science News, op. cit.*

page 117, lines 9–22
Wilhelm C. Hueper, "Potential Role of Nonnutritive Food Additives . . ." *op. cit.,*
p. 245.

page 117, lines 23–27
Ernest Liener, *Toxic Constituents of Plant Foodstuffs, op. cit.,* p. 361.

page 117, line 27
Elmer W. Fisherman, M.D. and Gerald Cohen, M.D., "Chemical Intolerance to
BHA and BHT and Vascular Response as an Indicator and Monitor of Drug
Intolerance," *Annals of Allergy,* Vol. 31, No. 3, March 1973, p. 133.

page 117, lines 27–28
Ben F. Feingold, M.D., "Recognition of Food Additives as a Cause of Symptoms of
Allergy," *Annals of Allergy,* Vol. 26, June 1968, p. 310.

page 117, lines 28–29
Jerry E. Bishop, "Alza Seeks Way to Make Food Additives, Sugar That Won't Be
Absorbed Into Body," *The Wall Street Journal,* June 18, 1973, p. 32.

page 117, lines 29–31
P. Millburn, R. L. Smith, and R. T. Williams, "Biliary Excretion of Foreign
Compounds. Biphenyl, Stilbestrol, and Phenolphthalein in the Rat: Molecular
Weight, Polarity and Metabolism as Factors in Biliary Excretion," *Biochemistry
Journal,* Vol. 105, 1967, p. 1275.

page 117, lines 32–34
"Food Additives" (editorial), *The Lancet,* August 16, 1969, *op. cit.,* p. 362.

page 117, line 35–page 118, line 10
Jerry E. Bishop, "Alza Seeks Way to Make Food Additives, Sugar That Won't Be
Absorbed . . ." *op. cit.*

page 118, lines 21–30
Bert J. Vos, M.D., Food and Drug Administration, memorandum to A. J. Lehman,
M.D., on artificial sweeteners, November 1968 Report of NRC Ad Hoc Committee,
December 8, 1968, cited in Fountain Hearings: "Cyclamate Sweeteners," *op. cit.,*
liver pathology, p. 20.

page 118, line 35–page 119, line 2
Christine M. Botham, D. M. Conning, Jo Hayes, M. H. Litchfield, and T. F.
McElligott, "Effects of Butylated Hydroxytoluene on the Enzyme Activity and
Ultrastructure of Rat Hepatocytes," *Food and Cosmetics Toxicology,* Vol. 8, 1970,
p. 1.

page 119, lines 2–3
P. J. Creaven, W. H. Davies, and R. T. Williams, "The Effect of Butylated
Hydroxytoluene, Butylated Hydroxyanisole and Octyl Gallate upon Liver Weight
and Biphenyl 4-hydroxylase Activity in Rats," *Journal of Pharmacology and
Pharmaceuticals,* Vol. 18, 1966, p. 485; D. Gilbert and L. Golberg, "BHT Oxidase. A
Liver-microsomal Enzyme Induced by the Treatment of Rats with Butylated

Hydroxytoluene," *Food and Cosmetics Toxicology*, Vol. 5, 1967, p. 481; D. Gilbert, A. D. Martin, S. D. Gangolli, R. Abraham, and L. Golberg, "The Effect of Substituted Phenols on Liver Weights and Liver Enzymes in the Rat: Structure-activity Relationships," *Food and Cosmetics Toxicology*, Vol. 7, 1969, p. 603; G. Feuer, I. F. Gaunt, L. Golberg, and F. A. Fairweather, "Liver Response Tests. VI. Application to a Comparative Study of Food Antioxidants and Hepatotoxic Agents," *Food and Cosmetics Toxicology*, Vol. 3, 1965, p. 457; and J. G. Nievel, "Effect of Coumarin, BHT and Phenobarbitone on Protein Synthesis in the Rat Liver," *Food and Cosmetics Toxicology*, Vol. 7, 1969, p. 621.

page 119, line 5
I. F. Gaunt, G. Feuer, F. A. Fairweather and D. Gilbert, "Liver Response Tests. VI. Application to a Comparative Study of Food Antioxidants and Hepatotoxic Agents," *Food and Cosmetics Toxicology*, Vol. 3, No. 3, September 1965, pp. 457–469.

page 119, line 6
A. R. Johnson and F. R. Hewgill, "The Effect of the Antioxidants, Butylated Hydroxyanisole, Butylated Hydroxytoluene and Propyl Gallate on Growth, Liver and Serum Lipids and Serum Sodium Levels of the Rat," *Australian Journal of Experimental Biology and Medical Science*, Vol. 39, 1961, p. 353.

page 119, lines 7–11
Wilhelm C. Hueper, "Potential Role of Nonnutritive Food Additives . . ." *op. cit.*, p. 240.

page 119, lines 12–21
Ben F. Feingold, M.D., "Adverse Reactions to Food Additives," paper for the annual meeting of the American Medical Association, Section on Allergy, New York City, June 19, 1973, p. 6.

page 119, lines 22–28
Isobel Jennings, M.D., *Vitamins in Endocrine Metabolism* (Springfield, Illinois: Charles C. Thomas, 1970).

page 119, line 29–page 120, line 16
John C. D. Plant, Ian Percy, Tom Bates, J. Gastard, and Y. Hita De Nercy, "Incidence of Gallbladder Disease in Canada, England and France," *The Lancet*, August 4, 1973, pp. 249–50.

page 120, lines 17–19
Ribicoff Hearings: "Chemicals and the Future of Man," *op. cit.* Dr. Epstein testified that there are certain areas "for which there has been as yet little or no toxicological concern," including psychobehavioral effects and the possibility that environmental chemicals can induce psychobehavioral effects.

page 120, line 24–page 121, line 30
Sir Edward Mellanby, M.D., "Diet and Canine Hysteria Experimentally Produced by Treated Flour. Preliminary Report," *British Medical Journal*, Vol. 2, December 14, 1946, pp. 885–93. Colter Rule, M.D., claimed that many patients in mental

hospitals in the southern United States in the 1930s were there because of vitamin B deficiencies related to the ingestion of bleached white flour. After the cause was identified, a change of diet alone produced remission of symptoms in many individuals.

page 121, line 31–page 122, line 3
"Flour Improvers" (editorial), British Medical Journal, No. 5268, December 23, 1961, p. 1695.

page 122, lines 5–25
John Stokes, C. L. Scudder, and A. G. Karczmar, Department of Pharmacology, Stritch School of Medicine, Loyola University, "Effects of Chronic Treatment with Established Food Preservatives on Brain Chemistry and Behavior of Mice," Federation Proceedings, Vol. 31, No. 2, 1972, p. 596.

page 122, lines 26–31
Boyce Rensberger, "Two Food Additives Linked to Mice Defects," The New York Times, April 15, 1972.

page 122, line 32–page 123, line 12
"Sodium Nitrite Hazard," Chemical and Engineering News, October 25, 1971, p. 26. Dr. Hillel I. Shuval and associates, Hebrew University–Hadassah Medical School, Jerusalem, reported findings with rat experiments at a meeting of the American Public Health Association, Minneapolis, October 1971.

page 123, lines 13–19
Ben F. Feingold, M.D., "Adverse Reactions to Food Additives," paper for the American Medical Association Annual Convention, Section on Allergy, New York City, June 19, 1973, p. 6.

page 123, lines 20–27
"Food Additives Are Linked to Child Behavior Problems," Medical Tribune, July 25, 1973, pp. 1, 30.

page 123, line 28–page 124, line 32
Ben F. Feingold, M.D., "Recognition of Food Additives as a Cause of Symptoms of Allergy," Annals of Allergy, Vol. 26, June 1968, pp. 309–13; and "Adverse Reactions . . ." op. cit., pp. 6–7; and John R. Vane, "Prostaglandins and the Aspirin-like Drugs," Hospital Practice, March 1972, p. 61, cited by Feingold in abbreviated version of "Adverse Reactions . . ." p. 3.

page 124, line 33–page 125, line 2
Consumer Bulletin, January 1970, p. 5. Dr. Lawrence D. Dickey of Fort Collins, Colorado, reported on the two cases at a conference held in autumn, 1969.

page 125, lines 5–12
Jane E. Brody, "Discovery of Rare Cancer Spurs Concern About Environment," The New York Times, March 23, 1974, p. 13.

Chapter 8: Individual Susceptibility

page 126, lines 1–2
Jesse L. Steinfeld, Surgeon General of the United States, "Environment and Cancer: Detecting and Eradicating Hazards in Our Environment," keynote address to the 24th Annual Symposium on Fundamental Cancer Research, University of Texas, Houston, March 3, 1971, p. 7.

page 126, lines 4–8
Professor Roger J. Williams, "The Biology of Behavior," *Saturday Review*, January 30, 1971, pp. 17–19, 61.

page 126, lines 10–20
Theron Randolph, M.D., *Human Ecology and Susceptibility to the Chemical Environment* (Springfield, Illinois: Charles C. Thomas, 1962), p. 4.

page 126, lines 22–27
Ben F. Feingold, M.D., "Adverse Reactions to Food Additives," paper to the Annual Convention of the American Medical Association, Section on Allergy, New York City, June 19, 1973, p. 5.

page 127, lines 1–7
William C. Grater, M.D., address to the Annual Convention of the American Medical Association, Section on Allergy, New York City, 1969, reported in article "Allergist Warns on Risks of Food Additives," *Medical Tribune*, August 18, 1969, p. 10.

page 127, lines 10–13
Eugene Cowen, M.D., "Hidden Allergens, Vehicles and Excipients," *Annals of Allergy*, Vol. 25, March 1967, pp. 161–64.

page 127, lines 16–23
Thomas H. Steinberg, M.D., and Stanley M. Bierman, M.D., "Unique Syndromes Involving the Skin Induced by Drugs, Food Additives and Environmental Contaminants," *Archives of Dermatology*, Vol. 88, December 1963, pp. 779–88.

page 127, lines 26–33
Howard G. Rapaport, M.D., and Shirley Motter Linde, *The Complete Allergy Guide* (New York: Simon and Schuster, 1970), p. 212.

page 127, line 37–page 128, line 5
Ibid., p. 13.

page 128, lines 5–9
Ibid., p. 200.

page 128, lines 10–24
Elmer W. Fisherman, M.D., and Gerald Cohen, M.D., "Chemical Intolerance to BHA and BHT and Vascular Response as an Indicator and Monitor of Drug Intolerance," *Annals of Allergy*, Vol. 31, No. 3, March, pp. 126–133. Drs. Fisherman

and Cohen have been using the Sequential Vascular Response Test with sensitive individuals at the Allergy Clinic, U.S. Veterans Administration West Side Hospital, Chicago. The technique of testing is to pierce the ear lobe and insert the test material.

page 128, lines 25–34
Otto Saphir, *et al.*, Michael Reese Hospital, Chicago, United Press International, April 10, 1961, cited by Lewis, *Our Synthetic Environment, op. cit.*, p. 119.

page 129, lines 5–14
Theron Randolph, M.D., *Human Ecology* . . . , *op. cit.*, p. 5.

page 129, lines 16–17
Donald C. Nilsson, M.D., "Sources of Allergenic Gums," *Annals of Allergy*, Vol. 18, May 1960, pp. 518–24.

page 129, lines 22–27
Ibid., p. 519; also Albert H. Rowe, M.D., and Albert H. Rowe, Jr., M.D., *Food Allergy, Its Manifestations and Control* (Springfield, Illinois: Charles C. Thomas, 1972), p. 534.

page 129, lines 27–34
George Thosteson, M.D., Ask Your Doctor (syndicated column), "Very Little Danger in Most Food Additives," *The Philadelphia Inquirer*, October 27, 1972.

page 130, lines 1–27
Donald C. Nilsson, M.D., "Sources of Allergenic Gums," *op. cit.*, p. 519.

page 131, lines 14–18
Howard G. Rapaport and Shirley Motter Linde, *The Complete Allergy Guide, op. cit.*, p. 200.

page 131, lines 19–25
Ben F. Feingold, M.D., *Introduction to Clinical Allergy* (Springfield, Illinois: Charles C. Thomas, 1973), p. 152.

page 131, lines 26–31
Howard G. Rapaport and Shirley Motter Linde, *The Complete Allergy Guide, op. cit.*, p. 200.

page 131, line 32–page 132, line 9
Ibid. p. 312.

page 132, lines 10–25
Information sheet, Abel Allergy Testing Laboratories.

page 132, line 26–page 133, line 3
Edmund F. Finnerty, M.D., "Urticaria and Sodium Benzoate," *Cutis*, Vol. 8, No. 5, Nov. 1971, pp. 484–85; also see Edmund F. Finnerty, "Urticaria, Preservatives and Problems." *Ibid.*, Vol. 13, No. 5, May 1974, p. 818. Adverse reactions to benzoic acid compounds were also reported by Gerd Michaëlsson, Lars Pettersson and Lennart Juhlin, M.D., "Purpura Caused by Food and Drug Additives," *Medical*

Challenge, May 1974, p. 23. Individuals who suffer adverse reactions to aspirin and salicylates may also experience reactions to benzoic acid and its derivatives, through cross sensitivity. Aspirin, as salicylic acid, has the identical organic structure as benzoic acid, except for $OCOCH_3$ added onto the number two position. A majority of all margarines contain sodium benzoate. See N. M. Kudelko, M.D., "Oleomargarine: A Potent and Significant Complex Allergen," *Cutis*, Vol. 14, July 1974, pp. 132–36. Other margarines contain EDTA, citric acid, potassium sorbate, natural isopropyl citrate or stearyl citrate. Some of these additives have also produced adverse reactions in individuals. EDTA, and especially calcium disodium EDTA, may be a significant allergen, resulting in widespread eczematous eruptions. See J. Z. Raymond and P. R. Gross, "EDTA: Preservative Dermatitis," *Archives of Dermatology*, Vol. 100, 1969, p. 436.

page 133, lines 4–6
Howard G. Rapaport and Shirley Motter Linde, *The Complete Allergy Guide, op. cit.*, p. 207.

page 133, lines 6–31
Theron Randolph, *Human Ecology . . . op. cit.*, p. 71.

page 133, line 32–page 134, line 2
Daniel Henninger, "Secret Killers," *The National Observer*, July 29, 1972.

page 134, lines 3–9
Ben F. Feingold, M.D., "Recognition of Food Additives as a Cause of Symptoms of Allergy," *Annals of Allergy*, Vol. 26, June 1968, p. 311.

page 134, lines 10–20
Hyman H. Gordon, M.D., "Untoward Reactions to Saccharin," *Cutis*, Vol. 10, July 1972, pp. 78–81; also Subcommittee on Nonnutritive Sweeteners, Committee on Food Protection, Food and Nutrition Board, National Research Council, "Safety of Saccharin and Sodium Saccharin in the Human Diet." Washington, D.C.: National Academy of Sciences, 1974, pp. 33–34.

page 134, lines 21–24
Howard G. Rapaport and Shirley Motter Linde, *The Complete Allergy Guide, op. cit.*, p. 314.

page 134, line 25–page 135, line 12
Elmer W. Fisherman and Gerald Cohen, "Chemical Intolerance to BHA and BHT . . . ," *op. cit.*, pp. 126–133.

page 135, lines 13–18
Joan Arehart-Treichel, "Agonizing Over Food and Drugs: How Safe?" *Science News*, Vol. 103, June 2, 1973, p. 362; cases of Dr. Stephen D. Lockey, Sr., allergist, Lancaster, Pennsylvania.

page 135, line 19–page 136, line 9
John J. Shea, M.D., allergist, Dayton, Ohio, correspondence to author, 1966; also correspondence from patient to author, 1966; a similar case was reported by Rita L. Don, M.D., El Paso, Texas, correspondence, May 1, 1968.

page 136, lines 15–30
"Tenox, 2, Eastman Antioxidant for Animal Fats," *Bulletin 1*, 1952; "Tenox, Eastman Food-Grade Antioxidants," *Bulletin 6*, 1953; "Tenox R, Key to Feed Markets for Animal Fats," 1954; "Tenox, Antioxidants for Edible Animal Fats," *Bulletin G-105* (Kingsport, Tennessee: Tennessee Eastman Co., 1958).

page 136, line 34–page 137, line 5
Consumers' Research Bulletin, March 1955, p. 4.

page 137, lines 6–19
Robert Ho Man Kwok, M.D., "Chinese Restaurant Syndrome," *The New England Journal of Medicine*, Vol. 278, No. 14, April 4, 1968, p. 796; "Post-Sino-Cibal Syndrome" (editorial and correspondence), *Ibid.*, Vol. 278, No. 20, May 16, 1968, pp. 1122–24; *Ibid.*, Vol. 279, No. 2, July 11, 1968, pp. 105–6.

page 137, lines 20–27
Studies were conducted by Dr. Herbert H. Schaumburg, assistant professor of neurology, and Dr. Robert Byck, assistant professor of pharmacology, at Albert Einstein College of Medicine. Their findings were reported by Earl C. Gottschalk, Jr., "Relief May Be in Sight for Those Who Suffer from Chinese Cooking," *The Wall Street Journal*, July 11, 1968, p. 25; *Idem.*; "Flavoring Agent Tied to Strange Ailment from Chinese Food," *Ibid.*, February 14, 1969.

page 137, lines 28–34
Studies were conducted at New York University School of Medicine and reported by Gottschalk, "Relief May Be in Sight . . ." and "Flavoring Agent . . ." *Ibid.*

page 138, line 3–page 139, line 12
"Food Additives: Health Questions Awaiting an Answer," *Medical World News*, September 7, 1973, p. 73; and Marguerite G. Stemmermann, M.D., internist, Owen Clinic Institute for Nervous and Mental Disorders, Huntington, West Virginia, correspondence to author, November 7, 1973, and February 25, 1974; also correspondence from patient's mother to author, March 9, 1974, and March 23, 1974.

page 139, lines 13–16
Ben F. Feingold, *Introduction to Clinical Allergy, op. cit.*, p. 156.

page 139, lines 16–21
Ben F. Feingold, statement at roundtable discussion, College of Allergists, cited by Howard G. Rapaport, *The Complete Allergy Guide, op. cit.*, p. 210.

page 139, lines 21–23
Ben F. Feingold, *Introduction to Clinical Allergy, op. cit.*, p. 157.

page 139, line 28–page 140, line 12
Ben F. Feingold, "Adverse Reactions to Food Additives," paper for the annual meeting of the American Medical Association, Section on Allergy, New York City, June 19, 1973, p. 6 (of typescript).

page 140, lines 13–17
Ibid., p. 15.

page 140, lines 18–27
Ibid., p. 17.

page 140, line 28–page 141, line 7
Ibid., p. 19. Franklin Bicknell, M.D., made the point that dyes with the nitro or azo groups are suspect. In many cases they can, or could be converted within the body into an aromatic amine with the position *para* to the amino-group blocked by a large substituent (an atom or group substituted for another or entering a molecule in place of some other part that is removed), so that subsequently the cancer-inducing *ortho*-hydroxyamine group is formed. As an example, Bicknell cited the body's formation of the cancer-inducing *ortho*-hydroxyamine from 2-naphthylamine or, presumably, of *ortho*-hydroxyamine from the azo dye Sudan 1 (demonstrated as cancer inciting with test animals and a dye that had been widely used in Great Britain during the 1940s to color margarine). For Bicknell's discussion and diagrams of food dye chemical structures, see Bicknell, *Chemicals in Food and in Farm Produce: Their Harmful Effects* (London: Faber and Faber, 1960), pp. 148–52.

page 141, lines 25–33
Stephen D. Lockey, Sr., M.D., "Reactions to Hidden Agents in Foods, Beverages and Drugs," *Annals of Allergy,* Vol. 29, September 1971, p. 461.

page 141, line 33–page 142, line 3
Albert H. Rowe and Albert Rowe, Jr., *Food Allergy, op. cit.,* p. 188.

page 142, lines 10–22
Max Samter, M.D., and Ray F. Beers, Jr., M.D., "Intolerance to Aspirin: Chemical Studies and Consideration of Its Pathogenesis," *Annals of Internal Medicine,* Vol. 68, May 1968, p. 975. Drs. Samter and Beers are associated with the University of Illinois College of Medicine.

page 142, lines 23–29
L. Juhlin, G. Michaëlsson, and O. Zetterström, "Urticaria and Asthma Induced by Food and Drug Additives in Patients with Aspirin Hypersensitivity," *Journal of Allergy,* Vol. 50, 1972, p. 92; and G. Michaëlsson, et al., "Purpura Caused by Food and Drug Additives," *Archives of Dermatology,* Vol. 109, January 1974, pp. 49–52. These studies were conducted at the University Hospital, Uppsala University, Uppsala, Sweden.

page 142, lines 29–31
"Tartrazine Sensitivity," *Food and Cosmetics Toxicology,* Vol. 11, No. 4, August 1973, p. 685.

page 142, lines 32–35
"Foods, Vitamins Loaded with Peril for People with Allergies," *The Philadelphia Bulletin,* January 17, 1972.

page 142, lines 35–36
Ben F. Feingold, *Introduction to Clinical Allergy, op. cit.,* p. 193.

page 143, lines 1–4
Elmer W. Fisherman and Gerald Cohen, "Chemical Intolerance to BHA and BHT . . ." *op. cit.*, p. 128.

page 143, line 5–page 144, line 3
Francis Chafee, M.D., and Guy A. Settipane, M.D., "Asthma Caused by FD&C Approved Dyes," *The Journal of Allergy*, Vol. 40, No. 2, Aug. 1967, pp. 65–72. Dr. Chafee is a consulting physician to the staff of Rhode Island Hospital and Dr. Settipane is assistant physician and director of the allergy clinic, Rhode Island Hospital.

page 144, lines 4–19
Theron Randolph, *Human Ecology*. . . . *op. cit.*, pp. 71–73.

page 144, lines 23–30
Case reported by Stephen D. Lockey, Sr., M.D., correspondence to author, May 12, 1972; also Stephen D. Lockey, "The Clinical Sensitizing Properties of Food Additives and Other Commercial Products," paper for the 28th Annual Congress of the American College of Allergists, Dallas, Texas, March 9, 1972, pp. 4–5 (devoted to case histories of individual sensitivity to food dyes); also Stephen D. Lockey, "Allergic Reactions Due to FD&C Yellow No. 5, Tartrazine, an Aniline Dye Used as a Coloring and Identifying Agent in Various Steroids," *Annals of Allergy*, Vol. 17, September-October 1959, pp. 719–21.

page 144, line 32–page 145, line 9
Francis Chafee and Guy A. Settipane, "Asthma Caused by FD&C Approved Dyes," *op. cit.*, p. 70.

page 145, lines 17–30
Ben F. Feingold, "Adverse Reactions to Food Additives" (abbreviated paper), June 1973, p. 8.

Chapter 9: The Agents of Irreversible Effects: Carcinogens

page 146, lines 1–7
William E. Smith, M.D., letter to Congressman James J. Delaney, January 28, 1957, read by Delaney in U.S. House of Representatives, *Extension of Remarks*, February 21, 1957.

page 146, lines 9–14
Umberto Saffiotti, quoted by Jean Carper, "Danger of Cancer in Food." *Saturday Review*, September 5, 1970, p. 49.

page 146, lines 17–21
German Research Council meeting on the prophylaxis of cancer, Bad Godesberg, May 1954. This meeting included 39 scientists from 11 West European countries, notably distinguished public health officials and representatives of major pharmaceutical and chemical industries.

page 146, lines 23–25
Symposium on cancer prevention, 6th International Cancer Congress, sponsored by the International Union Against Cancer, Sao Paulo, Brazil, July 1954. The resolutions were published in its journal, *Acta Unio Internationalis contra Cancrum*, Vol. 11, No. 1, 1955, pp. 72–76.

page 147, lines 5–7
Marvin S. Legator, quoted in "The Heat is On Chemical Additives," *Business Week*, October 23, 1971, p. 83.

page 147, lines 10–18
Ribicoff Hearings: "Chemicals and the Future of Man," opening statement, *op. cit.*, pp. 2–3.

page 147, lines 20–23
Samuel Epstein, testimony before the U.S. Senate Committee on Commerce, 1973, quoted in *Let's Live*, August 1973, p. 2.

page 147, line 27
Irving J. Selikoff and E. Cuylor Hammond, joint background paper for the opening session of the annual seminar for science writers, American Cancer Society, St. Augustine, Florida, March 22, 1974, quoted by Jane E. Brody, "Discovery of Rare Cancer Spurs Concern About Environment," *The New York Times*, March 23, 1974.

page 147, lines 32–34
John R. Goldsmith, quoted in "Man's Use of His Habitat May Be Causing Cancer," *Star-Ledger* [Newark, New Jersey], January 12, 1975, p. 53.

page 147, line 37–page 148, line 18
Wilhelm C. Hueper, statement at the Delaney Hearings, *op. cit.*, August 7, 1957, p. 372.

page 148, line 19–page 149, line 10
William Cramer, D.Sc., Ph.D., "The Origin of Cancer in Man," *The Journal of the American Medical Association*, Vol. 119, No. 4, May 23, 1942, pp. 309–16. Dr. Frank J. Rauscher, Jr., director of the National Cancer Institute, in a report on cancer, mentioned studies of individual differences among humans in their resistance to cancer. Some people may have a biochemical characteristic making them susceptible to carcinogens in the environment. Such individuals have an inborn tendency to produce large amounts of an enzyme, hydrocarbon hydroxylase, which is capable of converting certain environmental chemicals into cancer-causing forms. See *The New York Times*, November 1, 1974.

page 149, lines 11–17
Morton Mintz, "Death Rate for Cancer Hits 22-Year-High," *Sunday Star-Ledger*, (Newark, New Jersey), April 8, 1973.

page 149, lines 18–25
Dr. Gori was quoted in *Chemical and Engineering News*, January 10, 1972, p. 6. Gori was confirming what Dr. Otto Warburg had said in 1966.

page 149, line 26–page 150, line 2
William Cramer, "The Origin of Cancer in Man," *op. cit.*

page 150, lines 3–12
William E. Smith, letter to Delaney, *op cit.*

page 150, lines 13–27
Problems in the Evaluation of Carcinogen Hazards. . . . Food Protection Committee, op. cit., p. 9.

page 150, line 28–page 152, line 2
"Memo Describes Cancer Dangers," *Community Nutrition Institute Weekly Report,* March 29, 1973, p. 5.

page 152, lines 3–16
Roy Hertz, M.D., senior physician at Rockefeller University, New York, statement at "Hearings: Regulations of Diethylstilbestrol, Part 1," *op. cit.,* November 11, 1971, pp. 68, 72.

page 152, lines 17–20
M. H. C. Williams, "Occupational Tumors of the Bladder," in R. Raven, ed., *Cancer* (London: Butterworth and Co., 1958), Vol. 3, pp. 337–80.

page 152, lines 20–25.
Granville F. Knight, M.D., W. Coda Martin, M.D., Rigoberto Iglesias, M.D., and William E. Smith, M.D., "Possible Cancer Hazards Presented by Feeding Diethylstilbestrol to Cattle," paper for the Symposium on Medicated Feeds (New York: Medical Encyclopedia, 1956), p. 168.

page 152, line 26–page 153, line 19
William Cramer, "The Origin of Cancer. . . ." *op. cit.* "The Chemical Abstracts Service Registry Number System had registered some 1.8 million chemical compounds, and the list is growing by the addition of some 250,000 chemicals each year. Approximately 300 to 500 new chemical compounds are introduced annually into commercial use. Of those which are or may be used commercially, synthetic (man-made) organic chemicals are of special concern because frequently they are alien to the natural environment, and in some instances their modification, redistribution, or persistence have already had some dangerous effects," from *Toxic Substances,* prepared by the Council on Environmental Quality, April 1971, p. 3.

page 153, lines 20–32
R. M. Hicks, J. St. Wakerfield, and J. Chowanrei, "Co-Carcinogenic Action of Saccharin in the Chemical Induction of Bladder Cancer," *Nature,* Vol. 243, 1973, pp. 347–49.

page 153, line 33–page 154, line 12
Dr. Kai Setälä, Paul Holsti, and Sinikka Lundbom, "Criteres d'evaluation des dangers de cancerisation les actions co-cancerigens," *Acta Unio Internationale Contra Cancrum,* Vol. 13, 1957, pp. 280–89. These pathologists stated that a great number of these synthetic detergents used as food additives, including emulsifiers, lipophilic-hydrophilic-, surface-tension lowering-, nonpolar-polar compounds and wetting agents, possess strong tumor-promoting and/or cocarcinogenic properties.

The most potent ones are to be found among nonionic compounds that contain long-chain fatty acids in their molecules and which, at the same time, are comparatively water-soluble. Certain polyoxyethylene sorbitant fatty acid esters, especially, are in this category.

page 154, lines 13–18
Samuel Epstein, statement at the Ribicoff Hearings: "Chemicals and the Future of Man," *op. cit.,* p. 46.

page 154, lines 19–31
Wilhelm C. Hueper, "Potential Role of Nonnutritive Food Additives . . ." *op. cit.,* p. 226.

page 154, line 32–page 155, line 9
Dr. Alan T. Spiher, Jr., assistant to the director of Office of Compliance, FDA, memorandum on "modification of the anticancer proviso" to Dr. Albert C. Kolbye, Jr., deputy director of Bureau of Foods and Pesticides, FDA, December 5, 1969.

page 155, lines 13–16
George P. Larrick, Commissioner of FDA, statement at the *Delaney Hearings*; "Food Additives," *op. cit.,* April 15, 1958, p. 454. Larrick's statement is worth quoting verbatim, since it reflects his total ignorance of the nature of carcinogenesis: ". . . we see no more reason to single out cancer production for specific mention in the legislation than to single out production of high blood pressure, destruction of the blood-forming elements of the body, or production of nephritis, diabetes, or a host of other disorders."

page 155, lines 28–33
Some of the headlines chosen from articles attacking the Delaney Clause reflected their flavor: "That Pesky Food Additives Law," *Business Week,* March 12, 1960, p. 113; "For Realistic Legislation" (editorial), *Everybody's Poultry Magazine,* March 1960, p. 8; and "Political Quackery, Food and Drug Laws Need a Dose of Common Sense" (editorial), *Barron's National Business and Financial Weekly,* February 1, 1960, p. 1.

page 155, line 33–page 156, line 2
G. Burroughs Mider, "The Role of Certain Chemical and Physical Agents . . ." *op. cit.,* p. 23.

page 156, lines 3–14
Arthur S. Flemming, Secretary of Health, Education and Welfare, statement at the Hearings before the Committee on Interstate and Foreign Commerce: "Color Additives," 86th Congress, 2d session, May 6, 1960, p. 501. Despite Flemming's statement, at a later date he was receptive to the idea of modifying the Delaney Clause.

page 156, lines 25–31
"Change in Feed Additives Rules Urged," *Chemical and Engineering News,* August 20, 1962. Delaney opposed the FDA backed bills to permit the use of suspected carcinogens under special conditions proposed in the new drug amendment bills

being suggested in the early 1960s. He had the vision to see that the proposed legislation would weaken public protection, which it did.

page 156, lines 31–35
12th Report by the Committee on Government Operations: "Regulation of Diethylstilbestrol," *op. cit.*, p. 36, gives a summary of the discussions that took place during the Fountain Hearings, demonstrating how members of congress had been hoodwinked.

page 157, lines 1–6
36th Report by the Committee on Government Operations, "Regulation of Cyclamate Sweeteners," *op. cit.*, p. 11, gives a summary of the illegality of the FDA's actions in reclassifying cyclamates as "drugs."

page 157, line 15–page 158, line 18
Morton Mintz, "Cancer Report Outlines Danger in Chemicals," *Sunday Star-Ledger* (Newark, New Jersey), December 19, 1971, pp. 61, 65.

page 158, lines 23–29
Edward's "apology" is cited by Nicholas Wade, "Delaney Anti-Cancer Clause: Scientists Debate on Article of Faith," *Science*, Vol. 177, August 18, 1972, p. 588.

page 158, lines 29–30
"Butz 'Regrets' DES Ban," USDA news release, August 2, 1972.

page 158, line 30–page 159, line 2
"DES Ban Overturned by U.S. Appeals Court," *Community Nutrition Institute Weekly Report*, February 21, 1974, p. 8.

page 159, lines 2–18
The concept of "imminent hazard" as applied by FDA and USDA was sharply reversed by another federal agency in 1974. The Environmental Protection Agency (EPA), in suspension of two suspected human carcinogens, aldrin and dieldrin, declared that the continued use of these pesticides would constitute an "imminent hazard." In response to an EPA petition, the United States Court of Appeals, District of Columbia, clearly indicated that the term "imminent hazard" "was broad enough to apply to carcinogens whose effect would not be felt until many years hence." See Luther J. Carter, "Cancer and the Environment (1): A Creaky System Grinds On," *Science*, October 18, 1974, pp. 239–42.

page 159, lines 22–28
"FDA Puts Crimp In Cyclamate Comeback," *Chemical and Engineering News*, September 16, 1974, p. 5.

page 159, lines 28–31
Harold M. Schmeck, Jr., "Cyclamate Peril Denied by Maker," *The New York Times*, November 14, 1974.

page 159, lines 31–33
Barbara Gibbons, "Cyclamate Makers Fight FDA," *Boston Herald American*, December 16, 1974, p. 11.

page 159, line 33–page 160, line 1
C.H., "FDA Turns Back Bid to Reinstate Cyclamates," *Science*, November 1, 1974, p. 422.

page 160, lines 4–23
Barbara J. Culliton, "Delaney Clause: Defended Against an Uncertain Threat of Change," *Science*, Vol. 179, February 16, 1973, pp. 666, 668; also Morton Mintz, "Debate Continues on Clause That Bans Cancer Agents in Foods," *The Washington Post*, 1973, reprinted in *Media and Consumer*, March 1973, p. 2.

page 160, lines 33–36
"Evaluation of Environmental Carcinogens," *Report to the Surgeon General of the U.S. Public Health Service by the Ad Hoc Committee on Evaluation of Low Levels of Environmental Chemical Carcinogens* (Bethesda, Maryland: National Institutes of Health, April 22, 1970).

page 161, lines 1–6
"Guidelines for Estimating Toxicologically Insignificant Levels of Chemicals in Food," *Report of a Task Force* (Washington, D.C.: Food Protection Committee, NAS–NRC, 1969). In sharp contrast to FDA's limited definition of carcinogenic substances as those that actually cause cancerous tumors, the EPA established a broader precedent-setting criterion for determining the carcinogenicity of a substance. When EPA suspended all major uses of the pesticides aldrin and dieldrin in 1974, the agency stated that, for purposes of carcinogenicity testing, tumorigenic substances and carcinogenic substances are *synonymous*. See "EPA Broadens Its Definition of Carcinogen," *Chemical and Engineering News*, October 14, 1974, p. 13.

page 161, lines 7–29
The problem of evaluating tumorigenicity has been an obstacle in the case of saccharin, as well as emulsifiers. The cancer-inciting properties of certain pesticides are also related to tumor evaluation. For example, malignant tumors developed in one strain of mice after the pesticide dieldrin was administered, but tumors did not develop in other strains of mice—or in dogs, rats, or primates. The mouse strain in which the malignant tumors developed was known already as being highly susceptible to tumor-inducement. Consequently, the committee evaluating the data did not feel that the balance of evidence indicated a carcinogenic hazard, despite the malignant tumors. See R. D. O'Brien, Division of Biological Sciences, Cornell University, letter to editor, "Pesticide Regulation," *Science*, October 19, 1973. Despite this conclusion about dieldrin, G. Burroughs Mider, M.D., Associate Director in Charge of Research, National Cancer Institute, had advised: "If one is searching for a carcinogenic effect, the use of the most susceptible experimental subjects seems advisable," in "The Role of Certain Chemical and Physical Agents in the Causation of Cancers," *op. cit.*, p. 22.

Chapter 10: The Agents of Irreversible Effects: Teratogens

page 162, lines 1–3
Karlis Adamsons, statement at the U.S. Senate Hearings Before the Select Committee on Nutrition and Human Needs: "Obesity and Fad Diets," 93d Congress, 1st session, Part 1, April 12, 1973, p. 34.

page 162, lines 6–7
James D. Ebert, address at the 4th International Conference on Birth Defects, National Foundation March of Dimes, Vienna, Austria, September 1973.

page 162, lines 9–12
Ribicoff Hearings: "Chemicals and the Future of Man," opening statement, *op. cit.*, p. 3.

page 162, lines 14–21
FDA Advisory Committee on Protocols . . . : op. cit. "Teratogenicity," p. 271, cited in: R. McIntosh, K. K. Merritt, M. R. Richards, M. H. Samuels, and M. T. Bellows, "The Incidence of Congenital Malformations: A Study of 5,964 Pregnancies," *Pediatrics*, Vol. 14, 1954, pp. 505–22; and J. Warkany and H. Kalter, "Congenital Malformations," *The New England Journal of Medicine*, Vol. 265, 1961, pp. 993–1001.

page 162, lines 25–27
Report of the Secretary's Commission on Pesticides and Their Relationship to Environmental Health, Parts 1 and 2, U.S. Department of Health, Education and Welfare, December 1969 (Washington, D.C.: U.S. Printing Office, 1969), p. 657.

page 163, lines 1–4
Alan T. Spiher, memorandum to Albert C. Kolbye, December 5, 1969, *op. cit.*

page 163, lines 7–18
James G. Wilson, "Present Status of Drugs as Teratogens in Man," *Teratology*, Vol. 7, Feb. 1973, pp. 3–16. A program to detect possible birth defect outbreaks early through computer monitoring of about one million yearly births is being undertaken by the Center for Disease Control, funded by the National Institute of Child Health and Human Development. Some 1,500 hospitals are cooperating. The aim is to detect unusual patterns of birth defects that may suggest environmental causes. See *Chemical and Engineering News*, November 19, 1973, p. 16.

Wilson's figure of 3 to 5 percent human birth defects is lower than reported in 1961. J. Warkany, and H. Kalter, "Congenital Malformations," *The New England Journal of Medicine*, Vol. 265, 1961, pp. 993–1001, reported that from 4.0 to 7.5 percent of all human deliveries yield individuals with developmental defects that will interfere with survival or result in clinical disease before the end of the first year of life. The variance of such statistics results from subjective evaluations of what constitutes teratogenic effects. Dow Chemical Company, for example, redefined teratogenicity as "that degree of embryotoxicity which seriously interferes with normal development or survival of the offspring." This definition excluded minor deformities that Dow's herbicide caused in rat fetuses, including underweight, subcutaneous swelling, delayed bone formation, and growth of ribs in the lumbar region. By excluding these commonly accepted signs of teratogenicity, Dow concluded that the product was not teratogenic. See "Dow Redefines Word It Doesn't Like," *Science*, April 21, 1972, p. 262.

page 163, lines 18–21
FDA Advisory Committee on Protocols for Safety Evaluation. . . . op. cit., p. 272.

page 163, lines 22–32
Hermann Heinz, "Chemical Causes of Birth Defects," in Morris Fishbein, ed., *Birth Defects* (Philadelphia: Lippincott, 1963), pp. 181–198. Insufficiency of fetal oxygen supplies, and therefore fetal nutrition, are impaired either by restricting the placental blood flow, such as from nicotine, or by some other factor. Methemoglobinemia from sodium nitrate or sodium nitrite should be one factor considered.

page 163, line 33–page 164, line 8
The Testing of Chemicals for Carcinogenicity, Mutagenicity and Teratogenicity (Ottawa: Health Protection Branch, Health and Welfare, Canada, September 1973), p. 136.

page 164, lines 9–16
FDA Advisory Committee on Protocols for Safety Evaluation . . . : op. cit., p. 272.

page 164, lines 17–22
"Scientist Group Urges Stiffer Delaney Clause," *Medical Tribune*, March 7, 1973, p. 26; and "Need to Extend Delaney Rule to Other Synthetics Seen," *Idem.*, April 7, 1971, p. 1; and Senator Gaylord Nelson, press release, December 20, 1973.

page 164, lines 23–33
Samuel Epstein, testimony at the Ribicoff Hearings: "Chemicals and the Future of Man," *op. cit.*, p. 21.

page 165, lines 1–10
FDA Advisory Committee on Protocols for Safety Evaluation . . . op. cit., p. 279.

page 165, lines 13–14
The Testing of Chemicals . . . . op. cit., p. 138.

page 165, lines 15–17
"Sulfite and the Stomach," *Food and Cosmetics Toxicology*, Vol. 11, No. 5, October 1973, p. 911.

page 165, lines 17–19
Dr. Kurt Hirschborn of Mount Sinai Medical Center warned about the damage to male genes carrying sperm cells. See Jane E. Brody, "Most Pregnant Women Found Taking Excess Drugs," *The New York Times*, March 18, 1973.

page 165, lines 20–22
The Testing of Chemicals . . . : op. cit., p. 138. Protein-binding drugs are potentially hazardous to the fetus (as well as the newly born) because of possible interactions with other drugs that also bind to proteins. Sulfonamides, for example, may displace

other drugs or metabolites such as bilirubin from the limited binding surfaces and cause near fatal reactions. See A. H. Anton and R. E. Rodriquez, *Science*, Vol. 180, 1973, p. 974.

page 165, lines 22–24
"Antibiotics as Teratogens," *Health Bulletin*, April 2, 1966, p. 5.

page 165, lines 27–31
The Testing of Chemicals . . . : *op. cit.*, p. 137.

page 165, line 31–page 166, line 3
FDA Advisory Committee on Protocols for Safety Evaluation . . . : *op. cit.*, p. 272.

page 166, lines 3–5
J. J. Nora, A. H. Nora, R. J. Summerville, R. M. Hill, and D. G. McNamara, "Maternal Exposure to Potential Teratogens," *The Journal of the American Medical Association*, Vol. 202, 1967, pp. 1065–69.

page 166, lines 5–9
Jane E. Brody, "Most Pregnant Women Found Taking Excess Drugs," *op. cit.*; Jean L. Marx, "Drugs During Pregnancy: Do They Affect the Unborn Child?" *Science*, Vol. 180, April 13, 1973, pp. 174–175; Jerry E. Bishop, "Birth Defects Traced to Convulsion Drug Taken During Pregnancy by Epileptics," *The Wall Street Journal*, November 15, 1973; Thomas H. Maugh, II, "LSD and the Drug Culture: New Evidence of Hazard," *Science*, Vol. 179, March 23, 1973, pp. 1221–22. Lithium ion, used for manic-depressive psychiatric disorders, was found to expose individuals to high serum levels of the substance. It passed through the placenta into the fetus, causing damage or death to the liver cells of the fetus. Lithium carbonate, given to pregnant mice, increased the incidence of cleft palate in offspring. See "Lithium: Useful Drug or Hazardous Teratogen?" *Food and Cosmetics Toxicology*, Vol. 11, No. 1, February 1973, p. 139.

E. J. Quillegan advised that pregnant women should be given only about one-tenth of the drugs they usually are given, since almost all drugs cross the placenta. Diuretics may cause loss of body fluids and blood volume, which can markedly lower oxygen transfer, with resulting brain damage. Excessive glucose and vitamin C intake are transferred to fetal blood by carrier molecules, so their fetal concentration may exceed those of the mother. See E. J. Quillegan, *Obstetrical and Gynecological News*, May 1, 1973, p. 53.

page 166, lines 12–17
Jane E. Brody, "Most Pregnant Women Found Taking Excess Drugs," *op. cit.*

page 166, lines 17–19
Ibid.

page 66, lines 19–22
Jane E. Brody, "Doctors Find Pattern of Birth Defects Among Children of Alcoholic Mothers," *The New York Times*, July 3, 1973.

page 166, line 22–page 167, line 2
FDA Advisory Committee on Protocols for Safety Evaulation . . . : *op. cit.*, p. 272.

page 167, lines 5–8
James G. Wilson, "Teratogenic Interaction . . ." *op. cit.*, p. 436. Benzoic acid, a commonly used food preservative, was demonstrated to act synergistically with aspirin. It increased the percentage of malformations in test rats significantly. See Carole A. Kimmel, James G. Wilson, and Herbert J. Schumacher, "Studies on Metabolism and Identification of the Causative Agent in Aspirin Teratogenesis in Rats," *Teratology*, Vol. 4, No. 1, February 1971.

page 167, line 10–page 168, line 8
FDA Advisory Committee on Protocols for Safety Evaluation . . . : *op. cit.*, pp. 273–78.

page 168, lines 8–18
For discussions of placental transfer see: cyclamates: *Congressional Hearings*: "Cyclamate Sweeteners," June 10, 1970, *op. cit.*, memorandum of Drs. Philip H. Derse, P. O. Nees, James L. Goddard and K. J. Kirk, p. 23; saccharin: "Saccharin Seeks the Fetus," *Food and Cosmetics Toxicology*, Vol. II, No. 1, February, 1973, pp. 145–46; sodium nitrite: *Accumulation of Nitrate. . . . op. cit.*, p. 70; also *Chemical and Engineering News*, October 25, 1971, p. 26; diethylstilbestrol: *Congressional Hearings*, "Regulations of Diethylstilbestrol," Part 1, November 1971, *op. cit.*, p. 90; food dyes and artificial flavorings; Drs. Feingold and Lockey, *op. cit.*; caffeine: H. V. Malling, "Chemical Mutagens as a Possible Genetic Hazard in Human Populations," *American Industrial Hygiene Association Journal*, reprinted, Ribicoff Hearings: "Chemicals and the Future of Man," *op. cit.*, p. 261; salicylates: James G. Wilson and Josef Warkany, eds., *Teratology, Principles and Techniques* (Chicago: University of Chicago Press, 1965), p. 7; dioxins: "War Herbicide Report Stirs Controversy," *Chemical and Engineering News*, March 11, 1974, pp. 18–19; "Vietnam Foliage Hit Hard by Herbicides," *Idem.*, March 4, 1974, pp. 6–7. (Although the NAS study of 2,4,5-T used in South Vietnam minimized the damage done to human health and plant life, critics charged that the chemical contaminant, dioxin, induced human birth defects and ecological disaster. Experimentally, dioxin was teratogenic to mice, killed 50 percent of male guinea pigs after a single dose of only 0.0006 mg/kg body weight.) "Dioxin Fed to Pregnant Rats Said to Kill Their Fetuses," *Medical Tribune*, September 29, 1971, p. 20; alcohol: *The New York Times*, July 3, 1973, *op. cit.*; nicotine: "Smoking Stunts Fetal Growth," *Medical World News*, February 2, 1973, p. 19; PCBs: August Curley, V. W. Burse, and Mary E. Grim, "Polychlorinated Biphenyls: Evidence of Transplacental Passage in the Sherman Rat," *Food and Cosmetics Toxicology*, Vol. 11, No. 3, June 1973, pp. 471–76; *Chemical and Engineering News*, April 16, 1973, p. 12 (the California sea lion population was reported to have a rising incidence of premature birth and death of pups, attributed to high concentrations of PCBs.); lead: "Lead Pollution Believed to Pose Threat to Human Embryo," *Medical Tribune*, May 16, 1973; mercury: "Pregnant Women Warned About Hg in Canned Tuna," *Medical Tribune*, May 2, 1973; cadmium: O. J. Lucis, R. Lucis, and K. Aterman, "Transfer of Cadmium and Zinc from the Mother to the Newborn Rat," paper for the Federation of American Societies for Experimental Biology, 55th annual meeting, April 13, 1971 (cadmium is sequestered in the placenta by intracellular proteins that resemble the cadmium-binding proteins in the mother's liver. Trace quantities of

cadmium that do not penetrate this defense mechanism in the placenta then become bound to the fetal liver); pesticides: R. T. Rappolt, Sr., et al., "Kern County: Annual Generic Pesticide Input; Blood Dyscrasias; p,p′ = DDE and p,p′ = DDT Residues in Human Fat, Placentas with Related Stillbirths and Abnormalities," *Industrial Medicine and Surgery*, Vol. 37, 1969, p. 513; Howard G. Rapaport, *The Complete Allergy Guide, op. cit.*, pp. 35–36 (Dr. Rapaport, the allergist, suggested that the pregnant woman who eats highly allergenic foods is creating a troublesome pattern, since part of the food can pass through the linings of the stomach and intestines, into the bloodstream, and through the placenta of the developing embryo, and precondition the embryo for allergenicity). Wilhelm C. Hueper, "The Potential Role of Nonnutritive Additives . . ." *op. cit.*, p. 227. Dr. Hueper reported, "It is likely that at least some of the cancers observed at birth or in infants and children are attributable to an exposure of the maternal organism before or during pregnancy or lactation to carcinogenic agents which passed the placental barrier or were secreted in the milk." Toxins ingested by lactating women may affect breastfed infants. Food additives such as cyclamates, sodium nitrite, and antibiotics; contaminants such as nitrosamines, pesticides, dioxin, strontium 90; and drugs, nicotine, marijuana, and alcohol may contaminate breastmilk. Some substances, such as DDT and its breakdown products, even *may concentrate* in the milk. Like the fetus, the newborn infant's detoxification mechanisms are not fully developed, and the infant is not equipped to cope with toxins as efficiently as the adult.

page 168, lines 19–22
FDA Advisory Committee on Protocol for Safety Evaluation . . . : *op. cit.*, p. 278.

page 168, lines 23–25
Jane E. Brody, "Doctors Find Pattern of Birth Defects . . . Alcoholic Mothers," *op. cit.*

page 168, lines 26–28
Stanley J. Carpenter, Ph.D., address to the 57th annual meeting, Federation of American Societies for Experimental Biology, Atlantic City, New Jersey, 1973, reported in *Medical Tribune*, May 16, 1973. Dr. Carpenter reported that the highest lead concentrations were in placental and fetal membranes, as well as within the tissues of the embryo.

page 168, lines 29–31
"Pregnant Women Warned about Hg in Canned Tuna," *op. cit.*

page 168, line 32
Jay M. Arena, M.D., "Contamination of the Ideal Food," *Nutrition Today*, Winter 1970, pp. 2–8. For discussions of contaminants of breastmilk see: nitrosamines; "Smoking Stunts Fetal Growth," *op. cit.*; pesticides: *Ibid.*; cyclamates: Ben F. Feingold, *Annals of Allergy*, June 1968 (Dr. Doris Calloway, of the University of California at Berkeley, reported that mothers who ingested cyclamate-containing food could excrete them in breastmilk causing diarrhea in suckling infants.); nitrate: Janice Crossland and Virginia Brodine, "Drinking Water," *op. cit.*, p. 14 (mothers, who are themselves unaffected by nitrate, may pass it on to their infants in breastmilk).

page 168, line 32–page 169, line 4
Jacqueline Verrett, Ph. D., and Jean Carper, *Eating May Be Hazardous to Your Health, the Case Against Food Additives* (New York: Simon and Schuster, 1974), p. 143.

page 169, lines 5–23
FDA Advisory Committee on Protocol For Safety Evaluation. . . . : *op. cit.*p. 273.

page 169, lines 25–33
Ibid., p. 274.

page 169, line 25–page 170, line 11
"Mom's Diet: Key to Child's Growth, Neonatal Retardation Tied to Fetal Malnourishment," *Medical World News,* January 5, 1973, pp. 28–36; also *The Relationship of Nutrition to Brain Development and Behavior* (Washington, D.C.: Food and Nutrition Board, NAS–NRC, June 1973); U.S. Senate, Hearings Before the Select Committee on Nutrition and Human Needs: "Maternal, Fetal and Infant Nutrition," Part 1, "Consequences of Malnutrition," 93d Congress, 1st session, June 1973.

page 170, lines 13–17
The Testing of Chemicals . . . : *op. cit.,* p. 160. Teratology testing is less standardized than carcinogenic testing. Reproductive studies check for deformed fetuses and offspring, especially for bone structure and soft tissue changes. The relevance of such tests for humans is uncertain. They are more uniform, however, than mutagenic tests. See "Food Additive Safety Faces Scrutiny," *Chemical and Engineering News,* March 9, 1970.

page 170, lines 24–34
Both humans and commonly used test animals possess chorioallantoic placentae. The chorioallantois is a very vascular fetal membrane composed of more or less fused chorion and the adjacent wall of the allantois. However, the placentae of humans and test animals differ. The human placenta is hemochorial, consisting essentially of fetal villi hanging in a maternal blood pool. The chorioallantoic placenta of rodents and rabbits is a complex hemoendothelial type, consisting of closely juxtaposed and highly modified fetal and maternal cells, permeated by a labyrinth of blood sinuses. Although humans have only the chorioallantoic placenta, rodents and rabbits have the yolk-sac placenta as well. See *The Testing of Chemicals, op. cit.,* p. 145.

page 170, line 35–page 171, line 5
Ibid., p. 150.

page 171, lines 5–18
Ibid., pp. 152–53.

page 171, lines 19–26
For discussions of teratogenic properties of compounds see: fungicides: T. Petrova-Vergieva and L. Ivanova-Tchemishanka, "Assessment of the Teratogenic Activity of Dithiocarbamate Fungicides," *Food and Cosmetics Toxicology,* Vol. 11,

No. 2, April 1973, pp. 239–44; herbicides: see materials on dioxins, *op. cit.*; also "Targets for Dioxin," *Food and Cosmetics Toxicology*, Vol. 11, No. 4, August 1974, pp. 693–94; NTA: "U.S. Report Linking NTA, Birth Defects in Rats Seen Killing Role in Detergents," *The Wall Street Journal*, December 21, 1970, p. 8; salicylates and azo dyes: *FDA Advisory Committee on Protocol for Safety Evaluation* . . . : *op. cit.*, p. 274.

page 171, lines 28–30
Cited by James S. Turner, *The Chemical Feast* (New York: Grossman, 1970), p. 14.

page 171, lines 31–32
Cyclamate Hearings, June 1970, *op. cit.*, p. 16.

page 171, line 33–page 172, line 2
Ibid., letter from D. A. Hillman and F. C. Frazer to editor of *Pediatrica*, August 1969, p. 16.

page 172, lines 3–6
Arthur H. Wolff, Assistant Surgeon General, *memo for the Record*, October 15, 1969. Wolff drafted his memo three days before the dramatic and unexpected cyclamates ban, and pointed out that the "diabetic state itself appears to be etiologically associated with a higher prevalence of congenital defects as well as still births and neonatal mortality."

page 172, lines 7–9
Lawrence Fishbein, M.D., National Institute for Environmental Health Sciences, testimony at the Ribicoff Hearings: "Chemicals and the Future of Man," *op. cit.*, April 6, 1971, p. 32.

page 172, lines 15–21
A. I. Shtenberg, and E. V. Gavrilenk, "Influence of the Food Dye Amaranth Upon the Reproductive Function and Development of Progeny in Tests on Albino Rats," *Vop. Pitan*, Vol. 29, No. 2, 1970, p. 66; T.F.X. Collins and J. McLaughlin, "Teratology Studies on Food Colorings, Part 11, Embryotoxicity of R. Salt and Metabolites of Amaranth in Rats." *Food and Cosmetics Toxicology*, Vol. 11, No. 3, June 1973, pp. 355–65. Test results by the Soviet scientists as well as those at FDA were not confirmed by industry sponsored tests. Both Soviet and FDA testers began tests on day one of rat pregnancies, and induced embryotoxicity. Industry testers began tests on day six of rat pregnancies, and failed to induce embryotoxicity. The discrepancy between test results demonstrates the importance of crucial time periods when testing for teratogenic agents.

page 172, lines 22–26
Leo Friedman, statement at opening meeting of the advisory committee, quoted in "Red 2 Panel Stresses Timing of Embryotoxicity Testing," *Food Chemical News*, Vol. 15, No. 10, May 28, 1973, p. 48.

page 172, line 26–page 173, line 2
Lucinda Franks, "FDA Approves a Challenged Dye," *The New York Times*, December 19, 1975, pp. 1, 51.

page 173, lines 3–7
James Turner, quoted by Franks, *op. cit.*, p. 51. Turner, a Washington, D.C. lawyer, author of *The Chemical Feast*, was active in the consumer movement to ban FD&C Red No. 2.

page 173, lines 7–9
Franks, *op. cit.*, p. 51.

page 173, lines 12–20
"NAS Linked to 'Special Interests,' Nader Probers Charge," *Medical Tribune*, May 23, 1973; and " 'Bias' Charges Against Food Protection Committee Surfaces Again," *Food Chemical News*, Vol. 15, No. 5, April 30, 1973, pp. 24–26.

page 173, line 21–page 174, line 31
Franks, *op. cit.* p. 51.

page 174, lines 32–33
Franks, *op. cit.*, p. 1.

page 174, line 34–page 175, line 2
"March of Dimes Urges a Ban for Now on Red No. 2 Food Dye," *The New York Times*, December 20, 1974.

page 175, lines 3–17
Lucinda Franks, "Curb on Food Dye Urged by U.S. Unit," *The New York Times*, February 3, 1975.

page 175, line 18–page 176, line 7
J. H. Edwards, M.D., "Congenital Malformation of the Central Nervous System in Scotland, 1958," *British Journal of Prevention and Social Medicine*, Vol. 12, 1958, pp. 115–30. Edwards was a member of the Department of Social Medicine, University of Birmingham, England. The quotation is from p. 128 of the article. Since then, other physicians have also suggested that food additives may be related to congenital malformations. Dr. Harold Kalter, University of Cincinnati, made this point at a meeting of the National Easter Seal Society, reported in *The Cleveland Plain Dealer*, November 21, 1972.

Chapter 11:   The Agents of Irreversible Effects: Mutagens

page 177, lines 1–5
"Do Chemicals Sow Seeds of Genetic Change?" *Medical World News*, April 26, 1968, p. 27.

page 177, lines 8–10
Science Newsletter, November 18, 1961.

page 177, line 12
"Do Chemicals Sow Seeds . . ." *op. cit.*, p. 23.

page 177, lines 15–16
Samuel S. Epstein, M.D., and Dr. Marvin S. Legator, *The Mutagenicity of Pesticides, Concepts and Evaluation* (Cambridge: Massachusetts Institute of Technology, 1971), foreword by Dr. Joshua Lederberg, p. xi.

page 177, lines 19–26
Dr. James F. Crow, "Chemical Risk to Future Generations," *Scientist and Citizen*, June–July 1968, pp. 113–17. Crow summarized the discussion of the possible dangers of chemical and physical mutagens for the human population at a conference, sponsored by the Genetics Study Section, Division of Research Grants, National Institutes of Health, at Jackson Laboratory, Bar Harbor, Maine, September 1966.

page 177, line 28–page 178, line 3
Samuel S. Epstein and Marvin S. Legator, *The Mutagenicity of Pesticides . . . op. cit.,* p. 3.

page 178, lines 8–10
W. Gary Flamm, Ph.D., testimony at the Ribicoff Hearings: "Chemicals and the Future of Man," *op. cit.,* April 6, 1971, p. 29.

page 178, lines 13–15
Senator Abraham S. Ribicoff, opening statement, *Ibid.,* p. 2.

page 178, lines 17–19
Dr. Linus Pauling, *Antivivisectionist,* October 1972, p. 117.

page 178, line 22
Dr. Albert Szent-Györgyi, *The Living State* (New York: Academic Press, 1972), p. 37.

page 178, lines 25–35
Professor Hermann J. Muller, address at The Great Issues of Conscience in Modern Medicine, Dartmouth Convocation, Hanover, New Hampshire, September 9, 1960.

page 178, lines 38–39
The Holy Bible, St. James version.

page 178, line 41–page 179, line 2
Howard J. Sanders, "The Road to Genetic Disaster?" *Chemical and Engineering News,* May 19, 1969, p. 61.

page 179, lines 8–25
Report of the Secretary's Commission . . . Environmental Health, op. cit., p. 568.

page 179, line 34–page 180, line 6
Samuel S. Epstein and Marvin S. Legator, *The Mutagenicity . . . op. cit.,* foreword by Joshua Lederberg, p. xv.

page 180, lines 7–22
Arthur R. Tamplin and John W. Gofman, *"Population Control" through Nuclear Pollution* (Chicago: Nelson–Hall, 1970), pp. 212–13.

page 180, line 23–page 182, line 30
Report of the Secretary's Commission . . . *Environmental Health, op. cit.,* pp. 569–72; and "Mutagenic Effects of Environmental Contaminants," workshop sponsored by John E. Fogarty International Center for Advanced Study in the Health Sciences and National Institute of Environmental Health Sciences, *Publication 72-65* (National Institutes of Health, Bethesda, March 1971), pp. 4–6.

page 182, lines 32–34
FDA Advisory Committee on Protocols for Safety Evaluation . . . *op. cit.; Report to the Surgeon General, USPHS Ad Hoc Committee on the Evaluation of Low Levels* . . . *op. cit.;* and *Report of the Secretary's Commission* . . . *Environmental Health, op. cit.*

page 183, lines 3–5
Ibid.

page 183, lines 6–14
Howard J. Sanders, "Chemical Mutagens . . ." *op. cit.,* p. 57.

page 183, line 15–page 184, line 20
The Testing of Chemicals . . . *op. cit.,* pp. 71–94.

page 184, line 21–page 185, line 11
Marvin S. Legator, "Chemical Mutagenesis Comes of Age, Environmental Implications," paper for the 7th Wilhelmine E. Key lecture, annual meeting, American Institute of Biological Sciences, Indiana University, Bloomington, August 1970.

page 185, lines 12–20
Samuel S. Epstein and Marvin S. Legator, *The Mutagenicity* . . . *op. cit.,* foreword by Joshua Lederberg, p. xii.

page 185, lines 21–33
FDA Advisory Committee on Protocols for Safety Evaluation . . . *op. cit.,* p. 287.

page 186, lines 1–20
Ribicoff Hearings: "Chemicals and the Future of Man," *op. cit.* Exhibit 3, pp. 69–74, Table 3, "Food and Feed Additives and Naturally Occurring Mutagens (and Related Degradation Products)," p. 71; Ribicoff Hearings: *Ibid.,* Exhibit 15, pp. 257–66; H. V. Malling, "Chemical Mutagens as a Possible Genetic Hazard in Human Populations," p. 261.

page 186, lines 21–23
Ibid; also L. E. Andrew, "The Mutagenic Activity of Caffeine in Drosophila," *American Naturalist,* Volume 43, 1959, p. 221.

page 186, lines 24–27
W. Ostertag, "Kaffeine und Theophyll mutagenese bei Zell und Leukozyten-Kulturen des Menschen," *Mutation Research,* Vol. 3, 1966, pp. 249–67.

page 186, lines 27–31
K. Shimada and Y. Takagi, "The Effect of Caffeine on the Repair of Ultraviolet Damaged DNA in Bacteria," *Biochemistry and Biophysics,* Vol. 145, 1967, p. 763.

page 186, lines 32–34
H. V. Malling, "Chemical Mutagens . . . op. cit., p. 261.

page 186, lines 34–35
D. M. Shankel, "Mutational Synergism of Ultraviolet Light and Caffeine in Escherichia coli," Journal of Bacteriology, Vol. 84, 1962, p. 410.

page 186, lines 35–36
A. M. Rauth, "Effect of Ultraviolet Light on the Colony Forming Ability of Synchronized L. Cells when Plated in Medium Containing Caffeine," Biophysical Society Abstracts, 1965, p. 170; also A. M. Rauth, "The Nature of Caffeine Sensitized Damage in Mouse L. Cells," Ibid., 1966, p. 116.

page 187, line 1
W. Kuhlmann, H. G. Fromme, E. M. Heege, and W. Ostertag, "The Mutagenic Action of Caffeine in Higher Organisms," Cancer Research, Vol. 28, 1968, p. 2375.

page 187, lines 2–3
G. Röhrdorn, "Mutagenic Effects of Long-time Treatment of Inbred and Hybrid Mice with Low Caffeine Doses," Proceedings of International Congress of Genetics, Tokyo, Vol. 1, August 1968, p. 103.

page 187, line 4
B. A. Kihlman and A. Levan, "The Cytological Effect of Caffeine," Hereditas, Vol. 35, 1949, pp. 109–11.

page 187, lines 5–7
Howard J. Sanders, "Chemical Mutagens . . ." op. cit., June 2, 1969, p. 61.

page 187, lines 7–10
Ibid., p. 61. Dr. Marvin S. Legator and his coworkers at the FDA reported that caffeine in concentrations of more than 200 micrograms per milliliter inhibited DNA polymerase.

page 187, lines 10–11
Ibid., p. 61. Dr. Samuel S. Epstein, at Children's Cancer Research Foundation, investigated whether or not caffeine interfered with repair of DNA damaged by X-ray or various alkylating agents, both established mutagenic agents. After studying several hundred mice, Epstein found no evidence that caffeine interfered with DNA repair in mice.

page 187, line 12–page 188, line 2
" 'Bias' Charges Against Food Protection Committee Surface Again," Food Chemical News, Vol. 15, No. 6, April 30, 1973, p. 25.

page 188, lines 3–5
Ribicoff Hearings: "Chemicals and the Future of Man," op. cit., Exhibit 3, p. 71; chick embryo studies of Dr. Jacqueline Verrett, FDA, see Hearings before the Intergovernmental Relations Subcommittee: "Cyclamate Sweeteners," June 10, 1970, op. cit., p. 89.

page 188, lines 6–13
Samuel E. Epstein and Marvin Legator, *The Mutagenicity* . . . *op. cit.*, foreword by Joshua Lederberg, p. xi.

page 188, lines 14–16
K. W. Petersen, M. S. Legator, and F. H. J. Figge, "Dominant-lethal Effects of Cyclohexylamine in C57 B1/Fe Mice," *Mutation Research*, Vol. 14, 1972, p. 126; Legator and colleagues found that cyclohexylamine caused chromosome breakage in the germinal cells of male rats. A low dosage of only 1 milligram of cyclohexylamine per kilogram of body weight, given daily for five days, induced a significant threefold increase in single chromosome breakage in the animals' germinal cells. Also, the amount of chromosome breakage increased linearly with increasing dosage of cyclohexylamine. Other FDA tests indicated that this cyclamate breakdown product induced chromosome breakage in cultured kidney cells of the rat kangaroo. See Howard J. Sanders, "Chemical Mutagens . . ." *op. cit.*, June 2, 1969, p. 62.

page 188, lines 17–20
Robert Shapiro, Ph.D., "Reactions of Uracil and Cytosine Derivatives with Sodium Bisulfite" (letter to editor), *Journal of the American Chemical Society*, January 28, 1970, pp. 422–24.

page 188, lines 20–22
Ribicoff Hearings: "Chemicals and the Future of Man," *op. cit.*, Exhibit 3, *Idem.*, p. 71; *Idem.*, Lawrence Fishbein, p. 34.

page 188, line 23–page 189, line 14
Thomas E. Furia, ed., "The Use of Sequestrants in Food Systems," *Handbook of Food Additives* (Cleveland: The Chemical Rubber Co., 1968), pp. 297–312.

page 189, lines 15–19
Lawrence Fishbein, W. G. Flamm, and Hans L. Falk, *Chemical Mutagens, Environmental Effects on Biological Systems* (New York: Academic Press, 1970), pp. 249–51.

page 189, lines 20–21
Charlotte Auerbach and J. M. Robson, "Production of Mutations by Allylisothiocyanate," *Nature*, Vol. 154, 1944, p. 81.

page 189, lines 30–31
H. P. Rusch, Dorothy Bosch, and R. K. Boutwell, "The Influence of Irritants on Mitotic Activity and Tumor Formation in Mouse Epidermis," *Acta Unio Internationale contra Cancra*, Vol. 11, 1955, pp. 699–703.

page 189, line 31–page 190, line 2
Lawrence Fishbein, W. G. Flamm, and Hans L. Falk, *Chemical Mutagens, Environmental Effects* . . . *op. cit.*, pp. 251–52.

page 190, lines 3–12
Howard J. Sanders, "Chemical Mutagens . . ." June 2, 1969, *op. cit.*, pp. 62–63. In addition to nitrites combining with other constituents to form nitrosamines, the insecticide carbaryl, also reacts with nitrous acid to form a highly mutagenic

N-nitroso derivative, another nitrosamine. See R. K. Elespuru and William Lijinsky, "The Formation of Carcinogenic Nitroso Compounds . . ." *Food and Cosmetics Toxicology*, October 1973, *op. cit.*, p. 807.

page 190, lines 13–35
Lawrence Fishbein, W. G. Flamm, and Hans L. Falk, *Chemical Mutagens, Environmental Effects* . . . *op. cit.*, pp. 198–203.

page 190, line 36–page 191, line 14
Ibid., pp. 253–55.

page 191, lines 17–25
Professor Ryozo Tanaka, Department of Hygiene and Public Health, Iwate, Japan, 1964 studies, cited by Karl Sax and Halley J. Sax, "Possible Mutagenic Hazards of some Food Additives, Beverages and Insecticides," *The Japanese Journal of Genetics*, Vol. 43, No. 2, May 1968, pp. 89–94.

page 191, lines 26–28
Studies conducted by Standard Research Institute and Bionetics Medical Laboratory were reported in "Sodium Saccharin Possible Mutagenicity Noted," *Food Chemical News*, Vol. 15, No. 10, May 28, 1973, p. 39.

page 191, lines 29–35
Karl Sax and Halley J. Sax, "Possible Mutagenic Hazards . . . "*op. cit.*

page 192, lines 1–18
"Radiation Preservation of Foods," *FDA Fact Sheet*, 1970; and *Federal Register*, October 17, 1968, 33 F.R. 15416, 121.3003 Low-dose gamma radiation for the treatment of food.

page 192, lines 19–22
Beatrice Trum Hunter, *Consumer Beware! Your Food and What's Been Done to It* (New York: Simon and Schuster, 1971). See "Processing by Ionizing Energy," pp. 71–78, for a detailed account.

page 192, line 31–page 193, line 2
"Dangers Are Cited in Irradiated Food," *The New York Times*, January 15, 1960.

page 193, lines 3–5
Franklin Bicknell, *Chemicals in Food* . . . *op. cit.*, p. 55.

page 193, lines 5–6
R. S. Hannon, *Scientific and Technological Problems Involved in Using Ionizing Radiations for the Preservation of Food* (London: HMSA, 1955), p. 1*ff*.

page 193, lines 13–15
"USDA Withdraws Permission for Radiation Treatment of Bacon," USDA release, July 2, 1968.

page 193, lines 18–22
R. D. Holsten, M. Sugii, and F. C. Steward, "Direct and Indirect Effect of

Radiation on Plant Cells: Their Relation to Growth and Growth Induction," *Nature*, Vol. 208, November 27, 1965, pp. 850–56.

page 193, line 33–page 194, line 7
"Irradiated Sugar Can Harm Human Cells," *Science Journal*, Vol. 2, No. 12, December 1966, p. 4.

page 194, lines 8–11
Robert C. Cowen, "Have a Six-Month-Old Irradiated Onion for Lunch Tomorrow," *The Christian Science Monitor*, September 22, 1971.

page 194, lines 13–19
Jimmy F. Kemp, "Radiation Retards Spoilage," *The Record* (Bergen County, New Jersey), November 29, 1972, p. B-10.

page 194, lines 20–23
Joint FAO/WHO Committee on the Technical Basis for Legislation on Irradiated Food: *WHO Technical Report Series 316* (Geneva: WHO, United Nations, 1966).

page 194, line 31–page 195, line 3
Cecil Jacobson's work cited by John G. Fuller, *200,000,000 Guinea Pigs . . . op. cit.*, p. 170.

page 195, lines 4–7
Samuel S. Epstein and Marvin S. Legator, *The Mutagenicity . . . op. cit.*, p. 54.

page 195, lines 9–25
Marvin S. Legator, "Chemical Mutagenesis . . ." *op. cit.*

page 195, lines 26–33
Lawrence Flamm, testimony at the Ribicoff Hearings: "Chemicals and the Future of Man," *op. cit.*, p. 29.

page 195, lines 33–34
FDA Advisory Committee on Protocols for Safety Evaluation . . . op. cit., p. 269.

page 196, lines 1–5
Report of the Secretary's Commission . . . Environmental Health, op. cit., p. 568.

Chapter 12:   The Regulators and the Regulated

page 197, lines 1–9
Harvey W. Wiley, M.D., quoted from his 1930 autobiography in Morton Mintz, *By Prescription Only* (Boston: Houghton Mifflin, 1967), 2nd ed., p. 132. Wiley, the first Chief of the Bureau of Chemistry, USDA (later to become FDA under HEW), was the father of the first Pure Food and Drug Law in 1906. He fought, unsuccessfully, to keep additives such as flour bleaches, glucose, saccharin, sodium nitrate, sodium

nitrite, and sulfur dioxide out of the nation's food supply. Wiley resigned from the office when he became convinced that he, as a private citizen, could be more effective in working to obtain adequate consumer protection from harmful food additives.

page 197, lines 11–15
Dr. Paul B. Dunbar, statement at the Delaney Hearings: "Chemicals in Food Products," 1950, *op. cit.,* p. 36. Dunbar had originally been engaged in food and drug law enforcement work in 1907 as a chemist, under Wiley. He worked for the agency for over 43 years. While Dunbar was Commissioner of the FDA, the agency was under the Federal Security Agency.

page 197, lines 17–19
George P. Larrick, *Food Drug and Cosmetic Law Journal,* Vol. 12, No. 6, June 1957. Larrick came up through the ranks of the FDA and regarded the agency's work as regulatory rather than scientific. The proliferation of numerous food additives in the nation's food supply occurred during the long years of Larrick's administration. Subsequent to his retirement, all FDA commissioners have been chosen from physicians outside of the agency. Food industry spokesmen have criticized this policy. The shift in emphasis was voiced by Charles C. Edwards, in addressing the Consumer Federation in January 1971, when he was commissioner of FDA: "Everybody seems to know that we are a regulatory agency concerned with consumer protection. *Not* everybody is aware that we are also a *scientific* agency."

page 197, lines 21–22
James L. Goddard, M.D., address to the Food Protection Committee, NAS–NRC, December 1966.

page 197, lines 24–26
Herbert L. Ley, M.D., *The New York Times,* December 30, 1969, quoted in an interview on his last day as commissioner of the FDA. Ley was being "replaced" as commissioner. He had been a casualty in the continuous bungling by the FDA and HEW of the cyclamate issue.

page 197, line 28–page 198, line 4
Charles C. Edwards, M.D., interview with United Press International, *The Evening News* (Newark, New Jersey), January 24, 1970.

page 198, lines 6–12
Alexander M. Schmidt, M.D., quoted in "Point of View," *Food and Drug Packaging,* Vol. 30, No. 3, February 14, 1974, p. 28. "Whether the manner in which Schmidt's appointment was handled was a conscientious effort to diminish the importance of the office of FDA Commissioner or was simply a case of ineptness, the net result initially has to be a lowering of prestige for the office," noted *Food Chemical News,* when Schmidt was sworn into office quietly and privately. The trade newsletter continued, "It had been believed that former Commissioner Edwards, in his new post [Assistant Secretary of HEW], would continue to direct FDA activities—with continued reliance upon FDA General Counsel Peter Barton Hutt. The handling of Schmidt's appointment confirms that belief. This leaves Schmidt in a difficult

position—since he has the responsibility for FDA at the same time he is apparently being robbed of both the authority and the prestige." See "Schmidt Appointment as Commissioner Played Down by HEW," *Food Chemical News*, Vol. 15, No. 8, July 23, 1973, pp. 49–50.

page 198, lines 14–18
Samuel S. Epstein, M.D., testimony at the Ribicoff Hearings: "Chemicals and the Future of Man," *op. cit.*, p. 23.

page 198, lines 20–26
Senator Abraham S. Ribicoff, *Ibid.*, p. 41. Ribicoff's statement was a rejoinder to Epstein's statement that the American public, rather than industry, was being asked to pay the cost of the GRAS review.

page 198, lines 28–33
"Safety First," *The Washington Post*, August 26, 1973.

page 198, lines 34–35
"FDA Begins Review of Food Additives; Nutrition Is Stressed as Well as Safety," *The Wall Street Journal*, August 10, 1970, p. 2.

page 198, line 39–page 199, line 5
Howard J. Sanders, "Food Additive Makers Face Intensified Attack," *Chemical and Engineering News*, July 12, 1971, pp. 16–21. NAS–NRC's reviews included "Safety of Saccharin for Use in Foods" and "Safety and Suitability of Monosodium Glutamate for Use in Baby Foods," both issued in July 1970; and "Safety and Suitability of Salt for Use in Baby Foods" and "Safety and Suitability of Modified Starches for Use in Baby Foods," both issued in September 1970.

page 199, lines 6–20
"Food Additives Safety Faces Scrutiny," *Chemical and Engineering News*, March 9, 1970. Senator George McGovern described the GRAS list as "the never-never land of nonregulation."

page 199, line 36–page 200, line 3
Dr. Alan T. Spiher, Jr., "The GRAS List Review," reprint from *FDA Papers*, December 1970–January 1971.

page 200, lines 4–6
The Food, Drug and Cosmetic Act, Section 2015.

page 200, line 8–page 201, line 15
James S. Turner, *The Chemical Feast* (New York: Grossman, 1970), pp. 154–55. Although Turner said that about 350 experts had replied, Dr. Spiher, "The GRAS List Review," *op. cit.*, said about 355 replied. I have chosen Spiher's figure. The chemical company representative who questioned ammonium hydroxide's safety as a food additive was Dr. Thomas H. Jukes, who was employed by American Cyanamid Company at the time. Presently, he is Professor in Residence, Space Sciences Laboratory, University of California at Berkeley, and has become an articulate defender of food additive use.

page 201, line 16–page 202, line 3
Barbara Moulton, M.D., testimony at the Senate Hearings: "Administered Prices," June 2, 1960, *op. cit.,* pp. 12048, 12049.

page 202, lines 4–16
Ibid., p. 12050.

page 202, line 17–page 203, line 2
FDA files, Bureau of Medicine, memorandum dated March 2, 1959, cited by James S. Turner, *The Chemical Feast, op. cit.,* p. 157.

page 203, lines 3–13
FDA files, Division of Pharmacology and Food, memorandum dated September 2, 1959, cited by James S. Turner, *The Chemical Feast, op. cit.,* p. 154.

page 204, lines 1–4
FDA files, memorandum from HEW Assistant General Counsel William Goodrich to FDA Assistant Commissioner Kenneth W. Kirk, January 1961, cited by James S. Turner, *The Chemical Feast, op. cit.,* p. 158.

page 204, lines 7–14
Food Processing, March 1961.

page 204, lines 22–26
James S. Turner, *The Chemical Feast, op. cit.,* p. 159.

page 205, line 32–page 206, line 21
Alan T. Spiher, "The GRAS List Review," *op. cit.;* and *Survey of Substances Generally Recognized as Safe,* NAS–NRC. Although FDA has always pleaded insufficient funding for adequate testing, Dr. Moulton testified: "No amount of increased budget will compensate for the gaps in the law, nor will any conceivable appropriations of millions of additional dollars do the job unless it is administered by individuals capable of understanding the real public health significance of the problems with which they must deal, willingness to look at scientific fact and [be] able to understand and evaluate them, and interested more in the public welfare than in the financial gains of the industries which they regulate." See Senate Hearings: "Administered Prices," *op. cit.,* p. 12024. When FDA Commissioner Ley was relieved of his office, he remarked: "Merely putting more money into the agency will not change it. A more highly motivated staff and better administration of it also is needed." See *The New York Times,* December 31, 1969; and Congressman L. H. Fountain's sharp criticism: ". . . money appropriated for FDA in 1945 amounted to approximately $3 million; in 1968, $66 million. Numbers of employees in 1945, approximately 850; in 1968, 5,100 persons. Population of the country in 1945, approximately 150 million; in 1968, over 200 million. Seizures of foods in 1945, 2,504; in 1968, 384. . . . Injunctions for violative foods in 1945, 26; in 1968, three. . . . Prosecutions for violative foods, in 1945, 278; in 1968, 70." See *Congressional Hearings,* "Cyclamate Sweeteners," June 10, 1970, *op. cit.,* p. 2.

page 206, lines 22–36
Samuel S. Epstein, M.D., testimony at the Ribicoff Hearings, "Chemicals and the Future of Man," April 6, 1971, *op. cit.,* pp. 22, 41.

page 207, lines 1–2
Alan T. Spiher, "The GRAS List Review," *op. cit.* Practically all flavoring ingredients and a few substances used in close conjunction with flavoring ingredients were excluded from the NAS–NRC survey. They were covered in a separate survey conducted by FEMA, in collaboration with the National Association of Chewing Gum Manufacturers and the National Confectioners Association. Their joint data were to be tabulated in the final overall NAS–NRC report to the FDA.

page 207, lines 3–4
Food and Drug Packaging, December 5, 1974, p. 12.

page 207, lines 8–12
Robert Bird, professional staff member of the Subcommittee of Executive Reorganization and Government Research, "Chemicals and the Future of Man," cited by John Fuller, *200,000,000 Guinea Pigs, op. cit.,* p. 301. In "Food Additive Rules Remain Subjective," Jonathan Spivak remarked, "After lengthy study, these non-governmental scientists [NAS–NRC] usually render an exhaustive, but ambiguous report, passing the buck right back to FDA." See *The Wall Street Journal,* August 25, 1970, p. 14. In 1974 the United States House of Representative's Committee on Government Operations investigated FDA's increasing reliance on advisory review committees. In recent years, FDA has allotted a significant portion of its total budget for these advisory review committees. The congressmen questioned the validity of these committees to share with the agency the responsibilities for decision making, especially in sensitive areas concerning health and life. Investigations revealed that some of these committees, termed "shadow government," were excessive in numbers, improperly constituted, wasteful, and illegal. See *Use of Advisory Committees by the Food and Drug Administrations. Hearings,* Committee on Government Operations, House of Representatives, 93rd Congress, 2nd Session (Washington, D.C.: United States Printing Office, 1974).

page 207, lines 13–23
Robert Gillette, "Academy Food Committees: New Criticism of Industry Ties," *Science*, Vol. 77, September 29, 1972, p 1173. The Food Protection Committee functions under the Food and Nutrition Board, NAS–NRC. For sources of its financial funding see the statement contained in its "Publications" listing for January 1975.

page 207, line 24–page 208, line 13
Ibid., pp. 1172–74.

page 208, line 14–page 209, line 3
FDA files, memorandum from Dr. John J. Schrogie, Bureau of Medicine, and Dr. Herman F. Kraybill, Bureau of Science, to Commissioner Herbert L. Ley, December 12, 1968, cited by James S. Turner, *The Chemical Feast, op. cit.,* p. 15. The long-awaited NAS review on saccharin, released in January 1975, found the evidence for carcinogenicity of this additive "inconclusive." The committee recommended further tests for long-term feeding, which are apt to be time consuming. Meanwhile, FDA allowed saccharin to be used under an "interim" food additive regulation, a delaying device.

page 209, line 4–page 210, line 7
"NAS Linked to 'Special Interests,' Nader Probers Charge," *Medical Tribune*, May 23, 1973; and " 'Bias' Charges Against Food Protection Committee Surfaces Again," *Food Chemical News*, Vol. 15, No. 5, April 30, 1973, pp. 24–26. In 1974, Dr. James B. Sullivan, a scientist, participated in a workshop sponsored by NAS to study oceanic oil pollution. Sullivan concluded that some members of the committee, in drafting the report of findings, censored and suppressed warnings that oil-contaminated seafood may promote cancer, birth defects, and present other human health hazards. Convinced that NAS's attitude was irresponsible, Sullivan leaked the confidential document to the press. Without any specific accusations, mention was made that scientists from two leading oil companies helped to prepare the draft report. See Richard J. Seltzer, "Scientist Leaks Confidential NAS Document," *Chemical and Engineering News*, June 10, 1974, p. 16.

page 210, lines 8–15
Robert Gillette, "Academy Food Committees . . ." *op. cit.*, p. 1172.

page 210, lines 16–26
12th Report by the Committee on Government Operations: "Regulations of Diethylstilbestrol . . ." December 10, 1973, *op. cit.*, pp. 12, 32.

page 210, line 27–page 211, line 15
Robert Gillette, "Academy Food Committees . . ." *op. cit.*, p. 1175.

page 211, lines 24–30
Harold M. Schmeck, Jr., "Public May Help Review of Foods, FDA Asks Participation in Its Wide Safety Study," *The New York Times*, July 26, 1973, p. 17.

page 211, lines 31–34
Ibid.

page 212, line 11–page 213, line 3
George Faunce, Jr., testimony at the Delaney Hearings: "Chemicals in Food," 1958, *op. cit.*, p. 250.

page 213, lines 4–12
Charles Wesley Dunn, *Idem*, p. 69.

page 213, lines 13–23
Lawrence A. Coleman, *Idem*, p. 117. In more recent times, a candid statement was made: "Additives are not added by industry just for their functional properties (effectiveness) but are used for profits." said Dr. J. David Baldock, assistant professor of food science and technology, in "How Risky Are Most Food Additives?" address at a conference for food editors, Donaldson Brown Center for Continuing Education, Virginia Polytechnic Institute and State University, Blacksburg, Virginia, April 1973. Baldock also discussed a response "that comes forth from the food industry [which is] as misleading as that of the anti-additive group. This is mostly an industrial response showing something of this fashion: Natural foods are chemicals. People are chemicals. Natural foods and people are good. Therefore, food chemicals are good." Baldock termed this view unrealistic and misleading. He also criticized an "anti-additive" view.

page 213, lines 26–29
William E. Smith, M.D., letter to Congressman Delaney, January 28, 1957, *op. cit.*

page 213, line 30–page 214, line 7
Samuel S. Epstein, M.D., prepared statement for the Ribicoff Hearings: "Chemicals and the Future of Man," *op. cit.,* p. 55.

page 214, lines 7–9
Ibid., p. 17.

page 214, line 10–page 215, line 27
Jane E. Brody, "Another Coloring Additive for Frankfurters Is Proposed by U.S." *The New York Times,* November 2, 1971; and Burt Schorr, "Opponents of Another Hot Dog Additive Appear to Make Headway at Farm Agency," *The Wall Street Journal,* March 6, 1972.

page 216, lines 4–22
"New Additive Cleared for Cooked Sausages Despite Opposition Within Agriculture Unit," *The Wall Street Journal,* August 14, 1972.

page 216, lines 23–30
"Florida Scientist Questions Safety of SAPP," *Food Chemical News,* Vol. 15, No. 10, May 28, 1973, pp. 18–20; and correspondence with Dr. Haven C. Sweet, July 10, 1973.

page 216, lines 30–35
Specifications for the Identity and Purity of Food Additives and Their Toxicological Evaluation: Emulsifiers, Stabilizers, Bleaching and Maturing Agents, *7th Report of the Joint FAO/WHO Expert Committee on Food Additives* (Geneva: WHO, 1964), pp. 32–38; and Dr. G. J. van Esch, H. H. Vink, S. J. Wit, and H. van Genderen, "Die Physiologische Wirkung von Polyphosphaten," *Arzneimittel-Forschung,* Vol. 7, 1957, pp. 172–175 [English summary, p. 175].

page 216, line 36–page 217, line 18
"Florida Scientist Questions Safety of SAPP," *Food Chemical News, op. cit.*

page 217, lines 17–25
Cited by J. M. Coon, M.D., "Food Toxicology: Safety of Food Additives," *Modern Medicine,* November 30, 1970, p. 108. Coon has supported this viewpoint on numerous occasions.

page 217, line 30–page 218, line 3
William E. Smith, M.D., letter to Congressman Delaney, January 28, 1957, *op. cit.*

page 218, lines 4–12
Wilhelm C. Hueper, M.D., "Potential Role of Nonnutritive Food Additives . . ." *op. cit.,* p. 233.

page 220, lines 6–17
"Color, Provitamin A Enhanced in Citrus Fruit," report at 167th national meeting, American Chemical Society, Los Angeles, April 1974, reported in *Chemical and Engineering News,* April 15, 1974, pp. 19–20.

page 220, line 23–page 221, line 5
Press release, David S. Wachsman Associates, Inc., September 1972 (for their client).

page 221, lines 6–16
Gilbert H. Brockmeyer, "The Story of Natural Ice Cream, 1973 (promotional flier).

page 222, lines 1–3
Dr. W. D. Bigelow, "Experiments Looking to Substitutes for Sulfur Dioxides in Drying Fruits," 1907. Bigelow had worked with Harvey W. Wiley in the early days of the FDA. His report was submitted but denied publication by USDA. This report and its suppression was reported by Wiley in *The History of a Crime Against the Food Law* (Washington, D.C.: Harvey W. Wiley, M.D. [self-published], 1929), pp. 80–81.

page 223, lines 19–33
"Lawmakers Urge Food Labels to Warn Consumers of Ingredient Changes," U.S. Congressman Benjamin S. Rosenthal, news release, February 13, 1974.

page 224, lines 11–21
American Potato Journal, Vol. 47, p. 256, cited in "The Great Potato Debate," *Medical World News*, February 16, 1973, p. 39.

page 225, lines 4–8
The New York Post, July 16, 1969.

page 225, lines 9–17
Report on the Panel of Chemicals and Health, President's Science Advisory Committee, September 1973, *op. cit.*, p. 73.

page 225, lines 18–26
George T. Stewart, "Nutrition and the Food Technologist" (editorial), *Food Technology*, Vol. 18, No. 9, October 1964.

Principal Sources

Books

Franklin Bicknell, M.D. *Chemicals in Food and in Farm Produce: Their Harmful Effects.* London: Faber and Faber, 1960.

Samuel S. Epstein and Richard D. Grundy, eds. *Consumer Health and Product Hazards/Cosmetics and Drugs, Pesticides, Food Additives,* Vol. 2 of *The Legislation of Product Safety.* Cambridge, Mass.: Massachusetts Institute of Technology, 1974.

Thomas E. Furia, ed. *Handbook of Food Additives.* Cleveland, Ohio: The Chemical Rubber Co., 1968.

Ross Hume Hall. *Food for Nought: The Decline in Nutrition.* New York: Harper & Row, 1974.

Wilhelm C. Hueper, M.D., and W. D. Conway. *Chemical Carcinogenesis and Cancers.* Chicago: Charles Thomas, 1964.

Theron G. Randolph, M.D. *Human Ecology and Susceptibility to the Chemical Environment.* Chicago: Charles Thomas, 1962.

James S. Turner. *The Chemical Feast.* New York: Grossman, 1970.

Jacqueline Verrett, Ph.D., and Jean Carper. *Eating May Be Hazardous to Your Health, the Case Against Food Additives.* New York: Simon and Schuster, 1974.

Hearings

Chemicals and the Future of Man. Subcommittee on Executive Reorganization and Government Research, Committee on Government Operations, U.S. Senate, 92d Congress, 1st session, April 1971 (Senator Abraham S. Ribicoff, Chairman).

Color Additives. Committee on Interstate and Foreign Commerce, U.S. House of Representatives, 86th Congress, 2d session, January, February, March, April, May 1960 (Congressman Oren Harris, Chairman).

Cyclamates. Subcommittee of Committee on Government Operations, U.S. House of Representatives, 91st Congress, 2d session, June 1970 (Congressman L. H. Fountain, Chairman); Subcommittee No. 2, Committee on the Judiciary, U.S. House of Representatives, 92d Congress, 1st session, September–October 1971 (Congressman Harold D. Donahue, Chairman); 36th Report by the Committee on Government Operations, 91st Congress, 2d session, 1970, U.S. House Report No. 91–1585.

Diethylstilbestrol. Subcommittee on Health, Committee on Labor and Public Welfare, U.S. Senate, 92d Congress, 2d session, July 1972 (Senator Edward M. Kennedy, Chairman); Subcommittee of the Committee on Government Operations, U.S. House of Representatives, 92d Congress, 1st session, November 1971 (part 1), December 1971 (part 2), 92d Congress, 2d session (part 3), August 1972 (Congressman L. H. Fountain, Chairman); 12th Report by the Committee on Government Operations, 93d Congress, 1st session, 1973, U.S. House Report No. 93–708.

Food Additives. House Select Committee to Investigate the Use of Chemicals in Food Products, U.S. House of Representatives, 81st Congress, 2d session, September, November, December 1950; 82d Congress, 1st session, April, May, June 1951 (part 1); October, November 1951 (part 2); 82d Congress, 2d session, January, February, March 1952 (part 3) (Congressman James J. Delaney, Chairman); 85th Congress, July, August 1957, April 1958 (Congressman John Bell Williams, Chairman).

Food Additives and Medicated Animal Feeds. Subcommittee of the Committee on Government Operations, U.S. House of Representatives, 92d Congress, 1st session, March 1971 (Congressman L. H. Fountain, Chairman).

Food and Drug Administration: Administered Prices. Subcommittee on Antitrust and Monopoly, Committee of the Judiciary, U.S. Senate, 86th Congress, 2d session, May, June 1960 (part 22) (Senator Estes Kefauver, Chairman).

Nitrites and Nitrates. 19th Report by the Committee on Government Operations, 92d Congress, 2d session, 1972, U.S. House Report No. 92–1338.

Nutrition and Human Needs. Select Committee on Nutrition and Human Needs, U.S. Senate, 92d Congress, 1972, parts 4A, B, and C: *Food Additives* (Senator George S. McGovern, Chairman).

Governmental Reports

Chemicals and Health. Report of the Panel on Chemicals and Health of the President's Science Advisory Committee, September 1973, Science and Technology Policy Office, National Science Foundation, 1973.

Evaluation of Environmental Carcinogens. Report to the Surgeon General, USPHS, Ad Hoc Committee on the Evaluation of Low Levels of Environmental Chemical Carcinogens. National Cancer Institute, April 22, 1970.

Food and Drug Administration Advisory Committee on Protocols for Safety Evaluations. Panel on Reproduction Report on Reproduction Studies in the Safety Evaluation of Food Additives and Pesticide Residues, December 1, 1969.

Report of the Secretary's Commission on Pesticides and Their Relationship to Environmental Health, Parts 1 and 2. U.S. Department of Health, Education and Welfare, December 1969 (Emil M. Mrak, Chairman).

The Testing of Chemicals for Carcinogenicity, Mutagenicity, Teratogenicity. Health and Welfare, Ottawa, Canada, September 1973.

National Academy of Sciences—National Research Council Publications

Accumulation of Nitrate. Committee on Nitrate Accumulation, Agricultural Board, Division of Biology and Agriculture, 1972.

Food Colors. Committee on Food Protection, Food and Nutrition Board, Division of Biology and Agriculture, 1971.

Guidelines for Estimating Toxicologically Insignificant Levels of Chemicals in Food. Food Protection Committee, Food and Nutrition Board, 1969.

Principles and Procedures for Evaluating the Safety of Food Additives. Food Protection Committee, Food and Nutrition Board, 1959.

Problems in the Evaluation of Carcinogenic Hazards from Use of Food Additives. Food Protection Committee, Food and Nutrition Board, December 1959.

Safety of Saccharin and Sodium Saccharin in the Human Diet. Subcommittee on Nonnutritive Sweeteners, Committee on Food Protection, Food and Nutrition Board, National Research Council, 1974.

The Safety of Artificial Sweeteners for Use in Foods. A Report by the Food Protection Committee of the Food and Nutrition Board, August 1955, reprinted May 1959.

The Use of Chemicals in Food Production, Processing, Storage, and Distribution. Committee on Food Protection, Food and Nutrition Board, Division of Biology and Agriculture, 1973.

Joint FAO/WHO Expert Committee on Food Additives

"Evaluation of the Carcinogenic Hazards of Food Additives." FAO Nutrition Meetings Report Series No. 29, *WHO Technical Report Series 220,* 1961.

"Evaluation of the Toxicity of a Number of Anti-microbials and Antioxidants." FAO Nutrition Meetings Report Series No. 31, *WHO Technical Report Series 228,* 1962.

"Procedures for the Testing of Intentional Food Additives to Establish Their Safety for Use." FAO Nutrition Meeting Report Series No. 17, *WHO Technical Report Series 144,* 1958.

"Specifications for Identity and Purity of Food Additives: Food Colors." Vol. 11, 1963.

"Specifications for the Identity and Purity of Food Additives and Their Toxicological Evaluation: Emulsifiers, Stabilizers, Bleaching and Maturing Agents." FAO Nutrition Meetings Report Series No. 35, *WHO Technical Report Series 281,* 1964.

"Specifications for the Identity and Purity of Food Additives and Their Toxicological Evaluation: Some Anti-microbials, Antioxidants, Emulsifiers, Stabilizers, Flour-Treatment Agents, Acids, and Bases." FAO Nutrition Meetings Report Series No. 40, WHO Technical Report Series No. 40, *WHO Technical Report Series No. 339,* 1966.

"Specifications for the Identity and Purity of Food Additives and Their Toxicological Evaluation: Some Emulsifiers and Stabilizers and Certain Other Substances." FAO Nutrition Meetings Report Series No. 43, *WHO Technical Report Series No. 373,* 1967.

"Specifications for the Identity and Purity of Food Additives and Their Toxicological Evaluation: Some Food Colors, Emulsifiers, Stabilizers, Anti-Caking Agents, and Certain Other Substances." FAO Nutrition Meetings Report Series No. 46, *WHO Technical Report Series No. 445,* 1970a.

"Specifications for the Identity and Purity of Some Food Colors, Emulsifiers, Stabilizers, Anti-Caking Agents and Certain Other Substances." FAO Nutrition Meetings Report Series No. 46B, *WHO Food Add/70.37,* 1970c.

"Specifications for Identity and Purity and Toxicological Evaluation of Some Anti-microbials and Antioxidants." FAO Nutrition Meetings Report Series No. 38, *WHO Technical Report Series No. 309,* 1965.

"Specifications for Identity and Purity and Toxicological Evaluation of Some Food Colors." FAO Nutrition Meetings Report Series No. 38B, *WHO/Food Additives/66.25,* 1966.

"Toxicological Evaluation of Some Anti-microbials, Antioxidants, Emulsifiers, Stabilizers, Flour-Treatment Agents, Acids and Bases." *FAO Nutrition Meetings Report Series No. 40 A, B, C,* 1967.

"Toxicological Evaluation of Some Flavoring Substances and Non-Nutritive Sweetening Agents." *FAO Nutrition Meetings Report Series No. 44A,* 1967.

"Toxicological Evaluation of Some Food Colors, Emulsifiers, Stabilizers, Anti-Caking Agents and Certain Other Substances." FAO Nutrition Meetings Report Series No. 46A, *WHO Food Add/70.36,* 1970b.

Periodicals

Chemical and Engineering News. Washington, D.C.: American Chemical Society. "Food Additives" (part 1) October 10, 1966, (part 2) October 17, 1966; "Chemical Mutagens, the Road to Genetic Disaster?" (part 1) May 19, 1969, (part 2) June 2, 1969; "Food Processing: Growth in New Directions," August 23, 1971.

Food Chemical News. Washington, D.C.: Food Chemical News, Inc.

Food and Cosmetics Toxicology. Oxford, England: Pergamon Press.

Articles

Tom Alexander. "The Hysteria About Food Additives." *Fortune,* March 1972, pp. 63–65; 137–41.

Julius M. Coon, M.D. "Food Toxicology: Safety of Food Additives." *Modern Medicine,* November 30, 1970, pp. 103–08.

———. "Protecting Our Internal Environment." *Nutrition Today,* Summer 1970, pp. 14–16, 28–29.

———. "Toxicology of Natural Food Chemicals: A Perspective." *Toxicants Occurring Naturally in Food,* Washington, D.C.: National Academy of Sciences, 1973 (2nd ed.), pp. 573–91.

Leo Friedman, Ph.D. "Safety of Food Additives." *FDA Papers,* March 1970 [reprint].

G. O. Kermode. "Food Additives." *Scientific American*, March 1972, pp. 15–21.

H. F. Kraybill, Ph.D. "Part 2, Carcinogenesis Associated with Foods, Food Additives, Food Degradation Products, and Related Dietary Factors." *Clinical Pharmacology and Therapeutics*, Vol. 4, No. 1, January–February 1963, pp. 73–87.

Richard L. Hall, Ph.D. "Food Additives." *Nutrition Today*, July–August 1973, pp. 20–28.

Wilhelm C. Hueper, M.D. "Carcinogens in the Human Environment." *Archives of Pathology*, Vol. 71, (part 1) March 1961, pp. 237–67; (part 2) April 1961, pp. 355–80.

———. "Potential Role of Non-Nutritive Food Additives and Contaminants as Environmental Carcinogens." *Acta Unio International contra Cancrum*, Vol. 13, 1957, pp. 220–52.

Stephen D. Lockey, Sr., M.D. "Allergic Reactions Due to FD&C Yellow No. 5, Tartrazine, an Aniline Dye Used as a Coloring and Identifying Agent in Various Steroids." *Annals of Allergy*, Vol. 17, September–October 1959, pp. 719–21.

———. "Reactions to Hidden Agents in Foods, Beverages and Drugs." *Annals of Allergy*, Vol. 29, September 1971, pp. 461–66.

Index